Hitler's Secret Pirate Fleet

HITLER'S SECRET PIRATE FLEET

THE DEADLIEST SHIPS OF WORLD WAR II

James P. Duffy

Westport, Connecticut
London

Library of Congress Cataloging-in-Publication Data

Duffy, James P., 1941–
    Hitler's secret pirate fleet : the deadliest ships of World War II / James P. Duffy.
      p. cm.
    Includes bibliographical references and index.
    ISBN 0–275–96685–2 (alk. paper)
      1. World War, 1939–1945—Naval operations, German.   2. Cruisers
(Warships)—Germany. I. Title.
    D771.D84   2001
    940.54′5943—dc21   00–049162

British Library Cataloguing in Publication Data is available.

Library of Congress Catalog Card Number: 00–049162
ISBN: 0–275–96685–2

First published in 2001

Praeger Publishers, 88 Post Road West, Westport, CT 06881
An imprint of Greenwood Publishing Group, Inc.
www.praeger.com

Printed in the United States of America

∞™

The paper used in this book complies with the
Permanent Paper Standard issued by the National
Information Standards Organization (Z39.48–1984).

10 9 8 7 6 5 4 3 2 1

For
Kathy, Alexandra,
and Olivia

Germany's deadliest sea raider . . . was Japanese, another day she might be Dutch, Norwegian, or even British.

Louis L. Snyder
Historical Guide to World War II

CONTENTS _____

A photo essay follows Chapter Four.

ACKNOWLEDGMENTS _____

No book like this one can be written without the help of others. In the case of this book, I want to thank my wife Kathy for all the time she spent and effort she expended in reading and rereading the manuscript and making suggestions and asking challenging questions. For their assistance in contributing invaluable material to the research for this book, I want to express my gratitude to Charles Spiegel, Ricky Law, and David Westwood. Also to Dennis Shorthouse of a wonderful little shop in Hopewell, New Jersey, called On Military Matters. A very special thank you goes to Karen Rochford for a great job in preparing the maps used in the book. Finally, but certainly not least, I must extend my gratitude to my editor, Heather Ruland Staines, whose patience concerning a long overdue manuscript is without equal.

INTRODUCTION ─────────────────

Attacking and sinking, or taking as prizes, cargo ships of enemy nations is a practice as old as naval warfare itself. During the American Civil War, Confederate commerce raiders sank so many Union merchant ships that the American Merchant Marine never fully recovered from its losses. During the First World War, Imperial Germany put several raiders to sea in an effort to disrupt the shipping routes on which Great Britain relied. The first of these were primarily warships. Costly to operate and difficult to hide from the Royal Navy, they met with limited success. Most were either sunk or bottled up and made impotent by British warships. These were followed by raiders disguised as cargo vessels. Their success rate was much greater than their predecessors, and most returned home safely after their cruises. Then the face of naval warfare changed with the introduction of submarines. Suddenly ships carrying valuable cargos could be sunk by an enemy that could not be seen.

With the approach of World War II, Admiral Erich Raeder, Commander-in-Chief of the German Navy, hoped to be able to build a world-class navy around a fleet of battleships and aircraft carriers. With the limited resources available to him, his desired navy never materialized; instead he had to rely on a small number of battleships, cruisers, and destroyers to fight against what was the largest and most powerful navy in the world, Great Britain's Royal Navy. Limited access to the world's oceans was another problem for Germany, one that was made more difficult by Britain's ability to put dozens of ships on blockade duty. Unable to challenge the supremacy of the Royal Navy, Raeder depended on two types of vessels that offered the best success to cripple the British lifelines across the seas, U-boats and disguised surface raiders. The latter, known officially as Auxiliary Cruisers, went to sea camouflaged as cargo ships. Hidden behind their fake structures and plywood hull sections was an array of weapons capable of challenging most enemy ships, with the exception of larger warships.

Like pirates and privateers of old, these ships could sail around the world almost at will, taking on the guise of a peaceful cargo ship of almost any nation. Originally built for merchant service, they appeared to an enemy or a neutral as what they had once been. It was only when the German naval ensign, with its large swastika, was raised and the guns were exposed that their true identity was revealed. By then it was too late. They carried a large assortment of flags that matched the disguises they were able to create by raising or lowering masts and funnels, and altering their profiles with dummy bows and structures. To further confuse identification, the raiders were regularly repainted different colors while at sea, utilizing a unique ability to pump their fuel from front to back and side to side, exposing portions of their hull high above the waterline.

Like the pirates of the sailing ship days, they usually preferred to capture an enemy vessel and either return it and its cargo to a home port, or confiscate valuable cargoes, such as food and fuel they could use, before sending their victims to the bottom of the sea. Unlike many of those pirates, they usually attempted to capture an enemy ship with the minimum cost of life.

Crews taken from victim ships were generally well treated under the unwritten code of the sea. Among the thousands of crew members and passengers taken as prisoners by the raiders, few report being badly treated by the German sailors. For the most part they ate the same food as the Germans, and were usually allowed periods each day to go on deck and exercise and get fresh air. Raider doctors looked after the sick and injured among the prisoners with the same care and concern they did their own crews. When taken aboard a raider, prisoners were searched for weapons. Any items taken from them were listed on a receipt and usually returned before they departed. Cases of thievery by German sailors, though rare, were treated harshly by the raider captains when discovered.

By far the worst thing that could happen to a man, woman, or child captured by one of these raiders, other than the raider being attacked by a British warship, was to be turned over to Germany's allies, the Japanese. Although the raider captains were not especially enthusiastic about this, they were routinely ordered to turn prisoners over to Japanese authorities in Pacific and Indian Ocean ports, or put them aboard supply ships heading to Japan. In truth there was often not much else they could do with what was sometimes hundreds of prisoners who were not only overcrowding the ship but quickly reducing its food and water supply. In one case a large number of prisoners were put ashore on a tropical island, given weapons to defend themselves, food and water for an extended time, and several small boats with which to reach nearby occupied islands.

The nine disguised commerce raiders whose cruises are described in this book sank or captured nearly 140 ships totaling close to one million tons. They accomplished this during a period of less than three years. But their true value was not only in the ships they sank, but in the disruption they caused the Royal Navy by sending false signals of raider activity that forced the British to spend invaluable time and fuel chasing down ghosts across all the seas of the world. In addition, they could seed the entrances to enemy ports with hundreds of mines right before the enemy's eyes as they appeared to be friendly freighters passing by on their way to some other destination.

These raiders stayed at sea for prolonged times, feeding off of enemy freighters and tankers, and German supply ships steaming out of Japanese, French, and Italian African ports. They in turn often supported the U-boat fleets by refueling submarines and restocking their larders to extend their cruises. It was not unusual for a raider disguised as a peaceful freighter to rendezvous with a U-boat in an isolated location of the Atlantic Ocean to pump fuel into her tanks and transfer torpedoes to her.

Raider captains were handpicked for their strong leadership and daring nature. Their crews were so highly regarded by the German Navy that when word was received about the sinking of one of them, and the survival of most of the crew, six German U-boats and five Italian submarines abandoned all other operations to rescue the crew and bring them home.

Because of the very nature of commerce raiding, many people during the war, and for some time after, believed that these ships were commanded by bloodthirsty killers who made the old-time pirates look like boy scouts. Rumors were widespread that German raider crews used lifeboats filled with survivors for target practice, and reveled in killing helpless people in small craft at sea. It appears that these stories, none of which was based on fact, started when two life boats were picked up in the Indian Ocean from a ship that was known to have been sunk by a raider. The boats were riddled with bullet holes, and there was a quantity of dried blood in one of them. In truth, the raiders shot up lifeboats and other larger craft after everyone was taken off. In addition to serving as target practice for light gun crews, the primary objective was to wipe out all evidence of what had happened in order to add to the confusion caused by a ship's disappearance. It was thought to be better if the enemy did not learn of the fate of a ship but was left to wonder.

According to one officer aboard the raider *Atlantis*, the two lifeboats that seem to be at the root of the rumor were left floating by sheer accident. The bullet holes were made long after the people in them had been taken aboard the raider, and the blood was from an injured merchant seaman whose wounds were treated by one of the doctors assigned to the *Atlantis*.

Several raiders made extensive use of additional weapons with which they had been equipped. These included lightweight seaplanes that could extend the vision of a ship many miles. Unfortunately these planes generally proved too fragile for regular landings in the ocean and were often lost. Small armed motorboats sometimes helped a raider "surround" an enemy ship and convince its captain to surrender.

Life aboard a raider at sea for many months could be boring for seamen, but it was never without its tension. One never knew what to expect when a lookout reported sighting smoke on the horizon. Was it an unarmed or lightly armed freighter, or was it a British warship bearing down on the raider preparing to fire into her from a distance that would render the raider's guns useless? On several occasions it was the latter, which usually meant destruction for the raider and her crew.

The nine raiders are offered here in chronological order, based on the date each first sailed.

1

ATLANTIS

"UNDER TEN FLAGS"

The Germans had given the rendezvous location the code name Lily 10. It was 350 miles northwest of Ascension Island in the South Atlantic, one of those normally calm portions of the sea where a surface vessel could refuel a submarine in relative safety. In the predawn hours of November 22, 1941, a cargo vessel waited for just such a meeting.

Heading toward the rendezvous was the German submarine U-126. Her commander, Lieutenant Ernst Bauer, had requested and received permission to return to Europe in order to have engine repairs done that could only be accomplished at a shore facility. Bauer's U-boat had sunk three vessels off Cape Town in the previous month, and was part of a wave of submarines that Admiral Donitz had hoped would improve his underwater raiders' recently poor record in the South Atlantic. Under normal circumstances, U-126 would receive the fuel she required for her trip home from the supply ship *Kota Pinang*. Unfortunately she had been sunk on October 4 by two British cruisers alerted to her mission as a submarine supply vessel by intercepted and decoded German messages.

Also heading in the general direction of Lily 10 was the British London-class heavy cruiser *Devonshire*. The *Devonshire*, commanded by Captain R. D. Oliver, along with the heavy cruiser *Dorsetshire* and the light cruiser *Dunedin*, had been sent into the South Atlantic to search for German submarines and their supply ships. A prime objective of their searches were the areas where the waters were known to be normally relatively calm, such as Lily 10.

KMS *Atlantis*: March 31, 1940–November 22, 1941

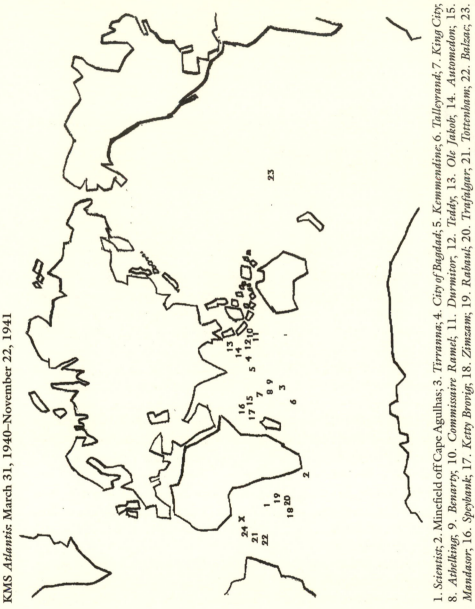

1. *Scientist*; 2. Minefield off Cape Agulhas; 3. *Tirranna*; 4. *City of Bagdad*; 5. *Kemmendine*; 6. *Talleyrand*; 7. *King City*; 8. *Athelking*, 9. *Benarty*; 10. *Commissaire Ramel*; 11. *Durmitor*; 12. *Teddy*; 13. *Ole Jakob*; 14. *Automedon*; 15. *Mandasor*; 16. *Speybank*; 17. *Ketty Brovig*; 18. *Zimzam*; 19. *Rabaul*; 20. *Trafalgar*; 21. *Tottenham*; 22. *Balzac*; 23. *Silvaplana*; 24. Sunk by HMS *Devonshire*; X. Location of HMS *Devonshire*. Courtesy of K. Rochford.

The cargo vessel waiting at Lily 10 for the U-126 was actually Germany's premier disguised commerce raider, the Auxiliary Cruiser *Atlantis*. She had been at sea since March 11, 1940. In that time, the *Atlantis* had sunk or taken as prizes twenty-two Allied ships. The British Admiralty knew her as Raider C, and there was little the Royal Navy wanted more than to send her to the bottom of the ocean. To the great joy of the men who served aboard her, the *Atlantis* was traveling home to Europe.

Earlier in the month, the *Atlantis* had rendezvoused and refueled the U-68. The meeting had gone well, and although the raider's skipper, Captain Bernhard Rogge, was uneasy about this kind of duty, he had agreed to the request that he perform the same service for U-126. Sitting in the open sea with lines and an umbilical cord connecting your vessel to another is an extremely vulnerable position for any ship of war, and not one favored by its captain. To make matters worse, two days before the scheduled meeting with the submarine, the raider's reconnaissance seaplane had crashed into the ocean while attempting to land. The crew and the aircraft had been rescued, but the plane was too badly damaged for a speedy repair. Two additional craft were in crates in the *Atlantis*'s hold, but there wasn't enough time to bring them on deck and assemble one of the replacements. This was a bad omen that many of the crew would later recall.

Just after dawn the long low gray U-boat with smiling, waving bearded men crowded into her conning tower came into sight. The sea was calm with gentle swells, and the sky was dull and slightly overcast. It seemed to be a good day for two warships to conduct their business without incident.

The raider sent her large motorboat out to meet the sub and bring her captain and several officers back before the ships were tied together. For Ernst Bauer, setting foot aboard a surface vessel had several welcome benefits. He could enjoy a meal in a comparatively luxurious dining room prepared by a cook with relatively abundant supplies, and best of all, he could wash away the grit and grime in that rarest of all pleasures for a submariner, a hot bath. For Captain Rogge it was also an opportunity to question Bauer, who had left Europe in late September, and receive uncensored news of the war back home.

As breakfast was being served, the raider's Chief Engineer Kielhorn approached Rogge with some bad news. According to Kielhorn, a piston in the ship's port engine had to be replaced as soon as possible. The Chief Engineer wanted to take advantage of the fact that the raider was standing idle to do this job. Rogge agreed, but admonished his officer to accomplish the repair as quickly as possible. The vulnerabilities of the *Atlantis* were mounting. Tied up to a submarine, her port engine out of service, and her Arado aircraft unable to fly and watch for enemy ships was not where Rogge wanted to be.

3

The Walrus seaplane with which the British cruiser *Devonshire* was equipped had no problem at all being launched from her catapult. She rose with the dawn and began her usual search pattern of the ocean that remained beyond the sight of the warship's lookouts. The *Devonshire* had been launched in 1927 and represented many advances in naval technology. She boasted three funnels and a top speed of thirty-two knots. Her main armament consisted of eight 8-inch guns, four 4-inch guns, and a wide array of antiaircraft guns. On the morning of November 22, with some helpful hints from German naval radio messages intercepted by the Royal Navy code breakers, she was an aggressive hunter in search of prey.

As the handful of men in the *Atlantis*'s officers' dining room ate breakfast and talked about the war, the Walrus passed far overhead, beyond the hearing of the men on watch. She did not come in for a closer look, but returned to the *Devonshire* to report the sighting of a cargo ship evidently drifting. Curious and a bit wary, Captain Oliver set his course toward the unsuspecting *Atlantis* and increased speed to 25 knots. He would send the Walrus up again for a closer inspection once the unknown ship was in sight.

At about 8:10, the cruiser's lookouts spotted the *Atlantis*, and the ship slowed to a stop. Within minutes the German lookouts saw the long-hulled three-funneled ship in the far distance and sent up the alarm. It was soon obvious to all that this was a British cruiser, and she was keeping her distance before determining her next action.

Captain Rogge called down to Chief Engineer Kielhorn to get that port engine running right away. The lines were cast off from the sub and the fuel line shut, capped, and disconnected from the U-boat. The only boat in the water at the time was the *Atlantis*'s motorboat, but she was standing beside the sub, so Lieutenant Bauer was unable to get back to his ship. He paced back and forth on the *Atlantis*'s deck cursing his bad luck as his young First Lieutenant quickly took the sub down.

Rogge calmly watched what he now saw was a "County" class Royal Navy cruiser as she launched her seaplane. He ordered the crew to battle stations, but warned that no weapon should be uncovered. Greatly outgunned by a warship that could sink his ship without coming within range of his own guns, Rogge knew that his only hope of surviving this encounter was to fool the British as to his identity so that they would either leave or come within range for a closer look.

The Walrus circled overhead, looking down on what appeared to be a simple cargo ship, except for the fuel line and large pool of oil alongside. We cannot be sure if the pilot or his observer actually caught sight of the U-boat itself before it disappeared beneath the waves, but he definitely saw the huge bubble rise in its place. There was no mistaking that a submarine had been alongside the ship and that it had quickly submerged. Using his signal light, he sent a message back to the *Devonshire*, the "SSS" code that he had spotted a submarine. The message was seen by one of the raider's lookouts who informed Rogge.

The port engine was started, and the raider turned away and began to move in a south-southwest direction, away from the cruiser. Overhead, the Walrus continued to circle. Several of the raider's crew stepped into full view of the aircraft and waved in as friendly a manner as they could. Everyone had the same hope their captain did, that they could fool the British into thinking that they were a friendly cargo ship, and nothing more.

Although not quite sure what the unknown vessel was, Captain Oliver began to suspect that it might be one of the notorious disguised commerce raiders the Germans had been using with so much success. Perhaps he was recalling that in the previous year two British Armed Merchant Cruisers had been badly mauled by one of these raiders, and in the past April a third, the *Voltaire*, had been sunk by one. Determined that this vessel was not going to escape, he was also determined to remain just within range of his 8-inch guns, surmising that if this was a raider, she would have nothing bigger than 5.9-inch guns. He was correct.

When the suspect cargo ship began to move away with a large motorboat trailing along her side, he ordered two warning shots fired over her. That brought the *Atlantis* to a stop. Rogge remained convinced that his only hope was to somehow trick the cruiser's captain into coming within range of the raider's smaller guns, or giving the U-boat the opportunity to get her within its torpedo sights.

Below, the U-126's First Officer interpreted the two explosions as bombs dropped on him by the British aircraft he had glimpsed before diving. He ordered the submarine to dive farther down for its protection. The U-boat was out of the action.

Rogge ordered a flag signal sent aloft indicating that he was stopped. He then instructed the radio operator to begin broadcasting an alarm claiming that he was aboard the Dutch cargo ship *Polyphemus* and that she was under attack by an unidentified surface vessel. Meanwhile, the German signalman requested that the unknown ship's question be repeated several times, as his captain ordered, then replied that his ship was the *Polyphemus*. They would do everything they could to buy time with the hope that the British ship would come closer, or the submarine could launch a successful attack.

Captain Oliver wasn't fooled by the alarm broadcast by the ship, or the reply to his demand for her identity. By now he was certain he had cornered a German raider, but to reaffirm, he sent a request to the Admiralty seeking the present location of the *Polyphemus*. He was also concerned that the ship now under his guns might contain any number of British prisoners. There was also that U-boat the Walrus had claimed to have seen. If it was out there near the ship, it might be preparing to launch an attack against the Devonshire. He would have to take evasive action while he awaited a reply from the Admiralty. As a result, the cruiser steamed back and forth on an erratic course to make a potential torpedo attack more difficult, while remaining between 16,000 and 18,000 yards distant from the ship that claimed to be the *Polyphemus*.

From the cruiser came a signal demanding the ship's identity. The raider returned a jumbled message that required a request from the warship for clarification. Both captains were playing a waiting game, using the message flags as a slow and sometimes unclear way of sending messages. Rogge was waiting with the hope that the cruiser would come within range, and Oliver was waiting for confirmation of the *Polyphemus's* location.

Meanwhile, the Walrus seaplane continued circling overhead. According to reports, the pilot and his observer possessed a photograph that had been secretly taken of the complete profile of the *Atlantis* by a *Life* magazine photographer who had been a passenger on board a ship sunk earlier in the year by the raider. The photo had been published in the magazine for all the world to see. By studying the photograph and the ship below them, the crew of the seaplane became convinced that the vessel they were circling was not the *Polyphemus* at all, but the German raider known as Raider C.

At about 9:30 the cruiser received a message from Freetown indicating that the real *Polyphemus*, which had recently sailed from a Spanish port, was confirmed to be at a different position. The game was over. From a range of 16,500 yards, the mighty cruiser opened fire with several salvos from her 8-inch guns. The first salvo fell short of the raider, and the second passed overhead, but with the third the British gunners had their range. The aircraft hanger holding the damaged Arado was hit and burst into flames, and part of the ship's electrical system was destroyed.

Rogge ordered the helm to turn hard to starboard and instructed the engine room to quickly make as much smoke as possible to reduce the British accuracy. He was helpless to defend himself as long as the cruiser stayed out of range, so all he could do was create as difficult a target as possible. Rogge was now caught in every raider captain's nightmare, being shelled by an enemy ship he could not reach with his own guns.

For a few minutes the smoke helped. Rogge stopped his vessel inside the smoke screen while the cruiser's gunners fired overhead, to prevent an attempted escape. Rogge knew that escape was impossible. His only thought now, with most of the electrical and communications systems put out of commission by additional salvos, was to save as many of his crew as possible. The order went out to quickly abandon the ship. Secret documents had to be destroyed so that they did not fall into enemy hands, and charges had to be placed by the scuttling team. When all had been accomplished and the captain was sure that every live member of the crew was off the vessel, he left himself in the company of Chief Coxswain Pigors.

Having found the range again as the smoke cleared, the *Devonshire*'s gunners pumped salvo after salvo into the *Atlantis* as she burned and slowly sank into the water. Finally, at 10:00 Germany's most successful disguised commerce raider, flying no national flag or naval ensign, disappeared forever. The men in the lifeboats and rafts and the more than 100 clinging to bits of wreckage in the water gave her a farewell cheer. Many could not believe that their luck, which had been so good for so long, had suddenly turned so bad. In a stroke of irony, Germany's first and most successful disguised commerce raider was sunk without firing a shot in her own defense.

All faces suddenly looked up as the Walrus seaplane made a final pass over the scene to ensure that the ship was gone. They then looked toward the horizon for a final glimpse of the instrument of their destruction, the British heavy cruiser, but she was nowhere to be found.

Once convinced of the enemy's destruction, Captain Oliver's primary concern was the U-boat. He expected that the submarine would come to the rescue of the German sailors from the raider, but thought it prudent to leave the scene as quickly as possible to avoid a battle with the submerged enemy.

The *Atlantis* was built in 1937 for the Hansa Line. As the express freighter *Goldenfels* she plied a route between Germany and Seattle, Washington. The 7,862-ton vessel was nearly 500 feet long and over 60 feet wide. She had barely discharged her last civilian cargo in Bremen in September 1939 when she was taken over by crews of men assigned to convert her to a disguised commerce raider. There were no set plans for this conversion, for each ship had to be handled differently because they were mostly different types of vessels. Captain Bernhard Rogge (he received that promotion in November, while the ship was being converted) was a man of great energy and wonderful connections. He used both to their fullest value in managing to handpick the officers and crew who would man his ship, and in influencing some of the design and work.

Rogge rejected many of the men originally sent to him for assignment. He refused to accept malingerers, men with little or no skills, and men who had been troublesome in other assignments. He knew that his ship would be at sea for at least one year, and in that time there would be a great many opportunities for malcontents to create problems for the captain and the rest of the crew. He demanded, and received, the right to review every man's record before accepting him. When it came to officers, he used his influence and the power of his personality to have men with whom he sailed and in whose ability he had confidence, assigned to his ship. In the end, all the effort paid off.

Over the next fourteen weeks the peacetime cargo ship was converted into a deadly warship, a warship whose weapons were ingeniously hidden behind a complex system of movable walls and opening hull sections. To all outward appearances she was still a cargo ship built to transport goods from one port to another, but in reality she had become a hunter and killer intended to roam the world's seas in search of enemy ships. Skillfully hidden below her upper decks and behind hull sections that could be opened in seconds were six 5.9-inch guns. Below the waterline were four 21-inch torpedo tubes, two on each side of the ship. Arrayed in concealed locations throughout, but able to be exposed and prepared for action in seconds, were an assortment of rapid fire weapons including a 75-mm gun, two twin 37-mm guns, and four 20-mm guns. Stowed away were torpedoes and ninety-two mines for deposit in enemy shipping lanes. In order to give the raider eyes that could see over the horizon, two seaplanes were put on board in Hold 2, which had been altered to act as an aircraft hanger. They were Heinkel He 114Bs. One was disassembled and stored in crates, while the other was fully assembled. It could be lifted from the hold by a crane and placed into the water in a matter of minutes.

The raider's flying officer, the man expected to fly most if not all the reconnaissance missions, was Richard Bulla. He didn't like the somewhat fragile Heinkels, and requested that they be replaced by the somewhat sturdier Arado AR 196A-1, but he was told that none were available. Taking off and landing in ocean swells was a tricky business, and Bulla, as would later be proven correct, did not believe that the He 114Bs were up to the task.

The original plan was for the *Atlantis* to sail in February, during the equinox when the long dark nights would help to cover her passage, but difficulties with ice slowed her progress. On March 31, 1940, she sailed through the Kiel Canal on her way to the North Sea. Ahead of her was the old World War I battleship *Hessen*, which served as an icebreaker. Behind her were two more raiders, the *Orion* and the *Widder*.

Once free of the ice and with her orders to proceed into the Atlantic Ocean, the *Atlantis*, disguised as a Norwegian freighter, sailed north through the North Sea close to the coast of Norway. During the first day in the open sea, she was escorted by two torpedo boats and several aircraft. During the night, she altered her disguise so that by dawn she had changed into the Russian auxiliary ship *Kim*. A U-boat remained with her for a while, but it too withdrew and returned to its base. The *Atlantis* was now alone in a North Sea known to have a large number of British warships, including heavy cruisers, on patrol.

Over the next few days Rogge altered her appearance by raising and lowering the masts and the one actual working funnel. The second funnel, which was for disguise purposes only, was stowed away. The weather during the next weeks was terrible, which was good for a ship trying to make its way through enemy waters undetected. Overcast skies during the day reduced visibility that was already at a minimum due to heavy rain and long periods of fog.

The *Atlantis* passed through the edge of the Arctic Circle north of Iceland and headed south along the fog bound coast of Greenland toward the Atlantic. The journey was made without serious incident, because every effort was made to avoid contact with other ships. From the frigid windswept waters of the Arctic region, the raider headed south toward the equator. The trans-Atlantic shipping lanes were full of ships passing both east and west, and Rogge had all he could do to continuously alter course to avoid all contacts. The air-waves were alive with transmissions giving the positions of dozens of ships. If his orders had permitted it, Rogge could have picked off numerous victims in the region, but his orders were to head south and await further instructions without making any contact with enemy ships. Naval headquarters did not want to reveal the presence of its first Auxiliary Cruiser in the Atlantic until it was ready.

Finally, on April 17 the raider received the long-awaited orders. She was to proceed into the South Atlantic and attack shipping in the Cape Town-Freetown route. The intentions were obvious to Rogge. With the *Atlantis* suddenly appearing in the South Atlantic, and the *Orion* just as suddenly making an appearance in the North Atlantic, the Royal Navy might be forced to withdraw some of its warships from the North Sea where they were harassing German forces following the German invasion of Norway. Those ships would be needed to protect Great Britain's lifeline to North America. *Atlantis* headed south at full speed.

Because of the unlikelihood of finding a Russian ship in the South Atlantic, the *Atlantis*'s disguise was altered. She was now the Japanese freighter *Kasii Maru*. To effect this disguise, the paint that had been applied to the raider's hull after her conversion had to be removed. As it turned out, much of it had been dislodged during the storms of the arctic region. Based on the information in Lloyd's Register of Shipping, at least one copy of which was included in the items carried by each raider, the hull was painted black, the masts and venti-lators were painted yellow, the interior of the ventilators were colored red, and the single funnel was repainted in black with a red top and a large "K" in white. The "K" stood for the Kokusai Steamship Company, owner of the authentic *Kasii Maru*. A complete inspection of Lloyd's found that twenty-six vessels had a resemblance strong enough to the *Atlantis* that they might be used as disguises. A few nation's ships were excluded. In addition to Allied vessels that would have been given secret codes for their identities by the British Admi-ralty, these included the Greeks whose vessels were too conspicuous because of their coloring, and the Americans, about whose call signals very little was known at this time.

Once in their operational area, the crew of the *Atlantis* waited anxiously for their first encounter. It appeared to be about to happen on Thursday, May 3, when the masthead lookout reported smoke approaching in the distance. The crew was quickly sent to battle stations, and several men who were to be actors in an imaginary play donned costumes that were intended to fool the ship. A handful of men who had the darkest skin and might pass for Japanese from a distance remained in full view on deck. They wore white headbands, as was the practice on Japanese cargo vessels, and wore their shirts outside their trousers, also a Japanese custom. To add to this disguise, an officer put on a dress and pushed a baby carriage around on the deck as if she was taking her infant for a stroll. All Rogge required was a brief hesitation on the part of an enemy captain, just enough time to give the raider the advantage of surprise.

As the vessel passed at a distance of seven miles, Rogge could see that it was a large passenger liner named the *City of Exeter*. He judged by the number of lifeboats hanging at her sides that she probably carried about 200 passengers. She was also armed with one 4.5-inch gun and several small antiaircraft guns. He decided to turn away slowly and let her pass, to the disappointment of many of the crew. The liner was moving swiftly and would have plenty of time to send out an alarm if the raider turned toward her, and then there was the question of taking perhaps as many as 400 people, passengers and crew, aboard as prisoners. It just wasn't worth the trouble.

Aboard the *City of Exeter*, several officers watched the Japanese ship through glasses. They weren't quite sure what to make of her, and later, when they were far enough away to feel safe, they sent a message out describing what they termed a "suspicious ship."

The following day the *Atlantis* found and took her first victim. She appeared on the horizon a few minutes before 2:00 P.M. on a course that would come close to the *Atlantis*. For the next half hour, most of the crew remained hidden at their battle stations while only a handful of people were visible to anyone watching from the approaching ship. Rogge set the stage again: two men on the bridge who would appear to be Japanese merchant officers, and several passengers strolling around the deck, including a woman with a baby carriage and a gentleman in a suit. Minute by minute the ship, now clearly identified as a British cargo vessel with a gun mounted on her stern, approached.

The two ships gradually drew closer together, and yet each appeared to be ignoring the other. The tension reached a peak on the *Atlantis* as the men waited for the order to drop their disguise and expose their weapons. When it finally did come, it took them only seconds to convert their peaceful Japanese freighter into a German warship. The German ensign was rapidly raised as were the signal flags. Two messages were sent to the passing ship through the flags. The first was to stop, and the second was a warning not to use their wireless radio. In addition, a warning shot was fired over the vessel. Then a strange thing happened, the ship did not respond in any way. It was as if she would continue to ignore the presence of the raider. The men aboard the *Atlantis* looked in disbelief at the ship that acted as if they weren't there. More than a few mouths dropped open in surprise.

On board the 6,199-ton British freighter *Scientist*, the boom of the gun awakened Captain Windsor from his midday nap. The officer of the watch had kept an eye on the passing Japanese freighter, but even later admitted that he had never been suspicious of her intentions. When Captain Windsor realized that his vessel was being stopped by a German ship, he immediately rounded up all the secret documents his ship carried, such as code books, and secured them in a heavy metal box made for just such a purpose and threw it overboard. It quickly sank into the sea. He then ordered a return signal hoisted on the *Scientist*'s mast that was a simple acknowledgment that the raider's signal had been seen and understood. But, to the surprise of the Germans, he did not stop.

Baffled by the enemy's action, or lack of action, Rogge ordered one of the starboard 5.9-inch guns to fire two additional warning shots. They did, and a few seconds later two large pillars of white water erupted in the ocean ahead of the *Scientist*.

The *Scientist*'s answering flag message merely moved up slightly in further acknowledgment, but she continued on her course and speed. Aboard the freighter, Captain Windsor had decided to make a run for it. The *Scientist* suddenly blew off steam, something it would do if it was preparing to stop. Smiles began to appear on the faces of the *Atlantis*'s crew at the sight of their first enemy ship stopping as commanded. But then another surprise came, the freighter suddenly turned away from the raider and moved out at top speed. The word came from Leading Seamen Helmke, known by the raider's crew by his nickname, the Frog. The freighter was sending out an alarm that she had been ordered to stop by an unidentified merchantman. Helmke, as he was trained to do, immediately began broadcasting gibberish in an effort to jam the freighter's call for help.

By now the *Atlantis* was badly situated for firing, and Rogge had to bring her around and pursue the enemy. He ordered the starboard guns to fire into the departing ship, which they did with great accuracy. The first salvo struck the *Scientist*'s stern and started several fires. When she did not stop, a second salvo hit her below the bridge and more fires started along with a grey colored smoke that poured from the shell holes.

Rogge ceased fire to watch for a reaction. When word came from Helmke that the freighter was continuing to broadcast an alarm, Rogge told his gunnery officer, Lieutenant Kasch, to fire at will. The next few salvos missed the *Scientist* entirely due to a sudden problem with the range-finding equipment, but one lucky shot brought the freighter's radio aerial crashing down on the radio shack's roof. A few more direct hits and Captain Windsor ordered his ship to a stop and told his crew to abandon the ship.

When Rogge saw the boats being lowered and the men scrambling over the sides, he ordered a cease-fire. He also ordered his motorboat to be lowered and search and demolition parties to prepare to board the *Scientist*. Rogge had hoped to take his first victim as a prize and send her home, but it was obvious, standing on the bridge of the *Atlantis*, that she was being consumed by flames. Although the fire did not disturb the chromium in several of her holds, the jute in a rear hold was burning beyond anyone's ability to suppress it.

The boarding party, lead by Adjutant Ulrich Mohr, motored to the freighter as the *Scientist*'s crew, most of whom were in lifeboats, headed toward the raider. The Germans were heavily armed with submachine guns, pistols, and carbines. They never knew what to expect when they were boarding an enemy vessel they had attacked, so they were always prepared for the worst. Mohr and his men climbed the *Scientist*'s Jacob's ladder and were met by the only two men remaining on the vessel, Captain Windsor and First Officer Watson. The two British merchant officers gave them a correct but icy greeting. After a brief questioning, Mohr left them in the charge of two armed sailors and went in search of any documents or items he could save that might be of use to the *Atlantis*. The demolition crew set their charges deep inside the ship. No one went close to hold five, in which the jute had been stored. By now the entire hold was one glowing mass of fire that could only be extinguished by filling the hold with seawater.

Mohr emptied the contents of the radio shack's wastepaper basket into his bag, and swept up a pair of binoculars, a chronometer, signal flags, and other items he thought might be useful. The demolition crew set their charges and opened the *Scientist*'s seacocks to fill her hull with water in order to speed up her sinking. Lines from the charges were run on deck and then dropped over the side to the motorboat. The Germans, along with Windsor and Watson, climbed down into the boat and moved away from the doomed ship. They motored among the lifeboats, gathering up their lines and then towed them toward the *Atlantis*. Once far enough away, the fuses were lit. In seconds the charges blew, but the ship merely slipped down a little into the water and listed slightly.

Watching from the bridge, Rogge instructed his gunnery officer to prepare to pump some shells into her at the waterline once Mohr's men and the crew of the *Scientist* were on board. Although the gunners were successful in their target practice, the ship refused to go down. She was now beginning to burn so brightly that she must have been visible from a long distance, so Rogge decided to use one of his valuable torpedoes to finish her off. He had been reluctant to do so, since he could never be sure when he would receive another supply. He could not leave the vessel floating with the hope that she would sink eventually. The last thing any raider captain wanted was for an enemy warship to come on a vessel he had attacked still on the surface. Its location could then be used to surmise the location of the raider. It was much better if the vessel just vanished and no one missed her until after she was overdue in port. In the case of the *Scientist*, she was scheduled to arrive at her next port of call, Sierra Leone, on May 10. All things considered, the authorities would not begin worrying about her for at least two more days. By then the raider would be long gone and

> On the very day the *Scientist* was due in port, May 10, 1940, 136 German Army divisions invaded Holland, Belgium, and Luxembourg.

there would be no trace of the action left behind to give anyone a clue as to what transpired. It was often the case that ship owners, and the families of their crews, knew nothing of their fates until after the war.

That night the *Atlantis* discharged her full load of mines. Every man aboard the raider was glad to see them go, for there was always the worry that any enemy ship might fire a lucky shell through the hull and hit them, blowing the raider to bits. The mines were seeded in the waters off Cape Agulhas, at the southern tip of Africa. They were so close to the shore that the men on deck could see the headlights of cars passing along the shore road. It was not the best night for such a secretive operation, because the sky was clear and the bright moon reflected off every movement in the water, but the job got done.

In order to fool anyone who might spot them, Rogge first sailed east beyond the Cape and then turned back around to give the impression that his Japanese ship was sailing to West Africa from somewhere in the Indian Ocean. The entire operation went off without a hitch. The *Atlantis* then turned back and headed into the Indian Ocean to search for prey.

Eight days later the raider intercepted a radio message announcing that the lighthouse at Cape Agulhas had reported an explosion just offshore. There was no accompanying report of a sunken or damaged ship, so Rogge had no way of telling if the effort had been successful. It in fact did not succeed, because that first explosion, probably caused by the mine breaking loose from its mooring, warned the South African authorities who in response sent minesweepers out. Of the ninety-two mines seeded, eighty-one were picked up, one exploded, and the remainder probably drifted off to explode harmlessly miles away. The effort was wasted; it sank no enemy ships, and had only a minor impact on enemy shipping schedules.

On May 22, the *Atlantis* intercepted a message of even greater importance. This one was a warning from the Royal Navy that a suspected German raider had been spotted disguised as a Japanese freighter. Someone had finally taken heed of the suspicions of the captain of the *City of Exeter*. The following day the raider was repainted and altered to resemble the Dutch steamer *Abbekerk*. The rising sun flag was replaced by the flag of the Netherlands, a country that was now occupied by the German armed forces.

In another strange quirk of fate, the Norwegian freighter *Tirranna* was chased and eventually overtaken by the *Atlantis* on June 10, 1940, the day following the capitulation of the Norwegian armed forces and government to the invading German troops. After removing food supplies, including thousands of cans of peaches, the *Tirranna* was eventually sent home to Germany under a prize crew of Germans and Norwegians. In the meantime, she was sent south to standby and wait for orders from Rogge.

When a San Francisco radio broadcast announced the sinking of the *Abbekerk*, the raider was forced to once again change its disguise. Now sailing under the Norwegian flag, she was now the *Tariffa*.

Life on board a raider generally consisted of long periods of monotony with men driven to terrible boredom by routine daily chores and long hours of off duty time. Movies were shown, occasionally the crew engaged in sketches to entertain each other, or they simply lounged around waiting for something to happen. These times were only rarely broken by the sudden activity generated by shouts from lookouts that masts or smoke had been seen on the horizon. Days and weeks could go by without another vessel being sighted, then suddenly one would come into view and everything would explode in a flurry of action as guns were prepared and tension mounted.

On June 22, France signed the terms of surrender laid down by Hitler. The humiliation of the event was underscored by the fact that the ceremony took place in the same railroad car in which the Germans surrendered following World War I. Hitler had the car taken from its museum just for the occasion.

During the month of July, the *Atlantis* sank two ships, both British freighters. The 7,506-ton *City of Bagdad*, a sister ship of the *City of Exeter*, met her fate on July 11. Her large smoke cloud, indicating that she was burning a low grade of coal, was first spotted in the very early morning mist, but there was a period of time during each morning that was reserved for distress signals. These might be from ships encountering an enemy, or simply ships or survivors of ships that had met the fate of thousands of other vessels over the years that had fallen victim to the vagaries of the sea. During this period each morning, all shore stations and ships at sea listened to the frequency selected for this purpose. It was a time during which all radio signals ceased, and all ears listened for a possible call for help. None came on this morning.

Rogge did not want to arouse suspicion on the approaching ship during this time when most of the world was listening, so he kept his distance from the freighter. Several officers recognized her as a German-made ship of the Hansa Line, and indeed she had been until she was transferred to the British as part of Germany's reparations payment following World War I.

Once normal radio transmissions were resumed, the *Atlantis* increased her speed to catch up with the freighter that had passed some 7,000 yards across her bow. In at least one sense, it was a replay of what had occurred with the taking of the *Scientist*; the captain was asleep and the officer on watch had decided that the sight of a Dutch freighter in these waters did not warrant awakening him. It was not until the *Atlantis* had dropped all disguise, run up the German ensign, and fired two warning shots that Captain Armstrong White was aware that he and his ship were in trouble.

White quickly surmised that he was under attack, and ordered his radio operator to send out the proper signal. He then began rounding up all important or secret documents to prepare to throw them overboard. On the *Atlantis*, Leading Seaman Helmke listened carefully to see if the freighter started to broadcast. Evidently no one on board had taken notice of the signal flags ordering her to stop and not to use her wireless, because she continued to move and she suddenly began broadcasting. "QQQQ, shelled by a ra . . . " was all she could get clear before Helmke starting jamming the airwaves with his more powerful radio.

Rogge ordered more shelling, and the freighter's radio cabin was demolished and her main mast brought down. Captain White ordered the ship halted and sent the order to abandon the ship. The *Atlantis* ceased firing, and signaled the crew to stay aboard. The crew, probably influenced by propaganda about mistreatment by the Germans, dropped all pretense to civility and created a panic attempting to get off the ship.

Suddenly another message reached *Atlantis*. It was the American ship *Eastern Guide*. She had picked up the freighter's partial distress signal before the jamming and asked, "Who shelled by . . . ?" Helmke responded that there was nothing to worry about, but the American radio operator evidently recognized that the second signal was from a different radio. He told Helmke to stop transmitting and once again asked the question. Then for some unexplained reason a shore station interrupted and instructed the *Eastern Guide* to cease transmitting. The radio fell silent.

Adjutant Mohr and his boarding party and demolition team set out for the freighter now stopped dead in the water. While Mohr immediately proceeded to the Captain's quarters to confiscate what valuable documents he could find, the crew was pulled from the sea and their boats and forced to return to the ship. The Germans had learned by their brief experience that they would quickly run out of supplies for prisoners if each one came aboard with just what he was wearing. The crew of the *City of Bagdad* was instructed to get their personal items, including clothing, and prepare to be transported to the raider. They did so under the watchful eyes of Mohr's well-armed boarding party.

Mohr found Captain White in his cabin attempting to destroy documents. The Captain had been forced to stop this work earlier in an effort to control the panic of his crew. He was once again stopped, this time by a polite German naval officer speaking English with an American accent. Needless to say he was shocked by Mohr's sudden presence in his cabin. Mohr politely informed White that he was under arrest and asked that he join his officers and crew on the deck. The Adjutant then gathered up so many documents that he could barely believe his luck. Among them were copies of merchant fleet codes and Admiralty routing instructions.

Two days after capturing and sinking the *City of Bagdad*, the raider came on a passenger liner carrying 147 people. Rogge attempted to capture the vessel without damaging her because he thought that she would be a good home for the more than 200 prisoners he had on his overcrowded raider. Unfortunately a misguided sailor on board the 7,770-ton *Kemmendine* took it on himself to defend his ship and fired a shot at the raider from the ship's antiquated 3-inch gun. There was also some confusion concerning whether the liner had radioed or not—she hadn't, the signals picked up by the *Atlantis*'s radio room had come from their own ship—so Rogge was forced to fire on her. All this happened after the liner had signaled that she was stopping as ordered. As luck would have it, the *Kemmendine* caught fire, and after all the crew members and passengers were taken aboard the raider, she was sunk. No lives were lost.

Angered that he had been forced to fire on a ship carrying a large number of women and children, Rogge held a court of inquiry concerning the firing of the *Kemmendine*'s stern gun. The court was composed of several German officers and Captain Reid of the *Kemmendine*. The offending sailor turned out to be a London window washer pressed into service for the war. He had not heard the Captain's order to abandon the gun because of the noise from a broken steam pipe, and acted in good faith partially based on his inexperience. No charges were brought against him.

On July 29, the *Atlantis* rendezvoused with the *Tirranna*, which had been lying low to the south waiting instructions. Rogge intended to put his prisoners aboard the prize ship, give her enough fuel oil to reach Europe, and send her on her way.

Four days later, on August 2, while the two vessels were side by side with lines and an oil hawser connecting them, another ship suddenly came into view. The ship was coming directly for them, so the crew rapidly separated the raider from her prize and Rogge got up speed as quickly as possible.

Aboard the 6,732-ton Norwegian freighter *Talleyrand*, the officer on watch had seen the two cargo ships standing next to each other and assumed that one must have had some trouble, perhaps an engine breakdown, and the other was lending a hand. He recognized the profile of one of them as the *Talleyrand*'s sister ship the *Tirranna*, and decided to see if he could help. He was not aware that the *Tirranna* was now in German hands.

When the *Atlantis* and the *Talleyrand* approached each other and the former dropped her disguise and raised the German ensign, a brief gun battle ensued. The Norwegian freighter carried a single old gun on her stern and was no match for the raider. Within minutes she had signaled that she was stopping. The crew was moved to the *Tirranna*, where there were some joyous reunions among not only old friends, but also between two brothers who had not seen each other in several years, and between a father and son. The *Talleyrand* was stripped of everything that could be used aboard the *Atlantis*, including fuel, foodstuffs, and a motorboat, and sunk. On August 5, the *Tirranna* sailed toward the Atlantic with eighteen men from the raider and the entire party of prisoners.

The *Atlantis* continued prowling her portion of the Indian Ocean. Two more raiders had joined her, the *Pinguin* along the African Coast, and the *Orion*, which was operating closer to Australia. This was not to Captain Rogge's liking. He felt three were too many and would result in additional Royal Navy hunting patrols, and might even result in two raiders accidentally coming across each other and engaging in a potentially deadly gunfight before they identified each other.

On the same day that *Tirranna* left for Europe, the first operational plans for the invasion of the Soviet Union were submitted to the German Chief of Staff, General Halder.

The British freighter *King City* was under charter to the British Admiralty when she sailed from Wales with more than 7,000 tons of coal. Her destination was Singapore. Off the coast of Madagascar she began to have trouble with an engine ventilator. It was shortly after midnight on August 25 when she stopped to attempt to make repairs. It was at this time that the raider sighted her, standing still in the water. It was too dark to clearly identify her, so among those watching from the *Atlantis*, there were guesses that she was a cargo ship, a British destroyer, or even a small aircraft carrier judging by her flat appearance, or she might be an Armed Merchant Cruiser about to draw an unsuspecting German raider into a trap.

Suddenly she started to move, but after a short time stopped again. Rogge and his officers did not know what to make of her actions. An increasing number of them became fearful that they were being lead into a trap.

What the Germans could not know was that the *King City* had repaired the ventilator and resumed her cruise, but stopped again because it failed again. They were busy trying to make repairs as dawn began to slip over the eastern horizon. One of the merchant ship's officers finally saw the raider and ran for a light to signal what he believed was another merchant ship, when Rogge, fearful of being trapped by a more powerful ship, opened fire. It was only a matter of minutes before he realized his mistake and ceased the gunfire. Six members of the *King City*'s crew died, while the remaining thirty-nine fled from the ship that had burst into flames.

During September 1940, the *Atlantis* sank three more ships. Two were British, the 9,557-ton tanker *Athelking*, and the 5,800-ton freighter *Benarty*. The third was the French passenger-cargo ship *Commissaire Ramel*. At 10,061 tons, the latter was the largest ship sunk by the raider. The *Athelking* had refused orders to stop and attempted to escape from the raider. It took ninety-one shells from the *Atlantis* to bring her to a halt. By that time her captain was dead, and she had been too badly damaged to survive herself. The *Benarty* was attacked by the seaplane as she tried to flee after hearing the alarm signals sent by the *Athelking*. The *Commissaire Ramel* had managed to get off a series of radio alerts before she was shelled into silence, so Rogge decided to leave the general vicinity and head northeast.

On September 9, a Royal Navy crew took possession of the first of fifty destroyers the United States had traded in return for bases in the West Indies and Bermuda. It was a major step toward providing active aid to the British war effort.

The month ended with sad news that left a pall over the ship. The *Tirranna* had managed to make it all the way back to France, and was actually waiting offshore for a minesweeper escort to bring her in when she was struck by three torpedoes fired from the British submarine *Tuna*. One member of the German crew and sixty prisoners, including women and children, perished when the ship sank in a matter of minutes. Also lost to the war effort were the numerous documents and military mail that had been taken from captured ships, and the first mail the crew of the *Atlantis* had been able to send home.

October offered up only one prize, but it was one Rogge was glad to have. After nearly a month of drifting and slow steaming in order to conserve fuel, the *Atlantis* finally saw the signs of another ship on October 22. She was still disguised as the Norwegian freighter *Tariffa* and keeping a watchful eye on the Sunda Strait. A waterway that runs between Sumatra and Java, the Sunda Strait was a busy commercial shipping route because it connects the Java Sea with the Indian Ocean. Rogge was especially interested in the routes taken by ships entering the Indian Ocean through the Strait. An attempt to use the seaplane to expand his vision beyond what the lookouts atop the mast could see proved disastrous when the craft, which was much too fragile for the mission it had been assigned, crashed while attempting a landing. The crew was rescued, but the plane was beyond repair.

The only vessel to be sighted that month finally came into view on the morning of October 22. At first it was taken to be Dutch, perhaps a passenger ship, which would serve Rogge's purpose if it could be captured without causing serious damage to it. The last thing he wanted was added prisoners. It turned out to be an old coal burner flying the flag of neutral Yugoslavia.

The *Durmitor* was 5,632 tons of tired old ship in 1940. Originally built for the bustling pre-World War I British tramp steamer routes in 1912, the *Plutarch* was already well worn by the time the Yugoslavs purchased her in 1922 and renamed her. She burned an excessive amount of coal and appeared, when she came into full view, as if she hadn't been cleaned in decades. Her holds carried more than 8,000 tons of unprocessed salt that was being transported from Spain to Japan, two more neutral nations. By the rules of war, Rogge should have let this ship pass by unimpeded because she was owned by a neutral nation and carrying goods between two other neutrals.

With more than 250 prisoners to feed and care for, Rogge was anxious to find a reason to take the old coal burner as a prize and send the prisoners to the nearest Axis port, which was in Italian Somali land. In his desperation to ease the living conditions for all aboard his raider, Rogge found two violations of the internationally recognized Prize Regulations. The first was that the *Durmitor* had sent out two quick SOS signals when first ordered to stop and not transmit. They were actually harmless because they gave no position in which a potential rescuer could locate the vessel. According to the German skipper, this was a violation of Article 39, section 3, and Article 40, section 1: "Assistance given to the enemy by wireless despite orders to remain silent." An inspection of the ship's records discovered that before loading the salt in Torrevieja, she had carried coal from Cardiff, Wales, to British controlled Oran. This, Rogge claimed, was in violation of Article 23, section 3, and Article 28, section 2: "Carrying contraband via enemy ports." It was a stretch of sorts, but it gave Rogge a vessel with which to transport his prisoners to a friendly port.

Four days later the prisoners were transferred to the *Durmitor*. Rogge spoke to them first, warning that anyone resisting the German prize crew put aboard her would be dealt with severely. He met with the merchant captain prisoners and obtained their pledge to keep order among the prisoners and not engage in any sabotage or attempt to mutiny. Living conditions were horrible aboard the Yugoslav ship, which was crawling with rats and other vermin. Not built for passengers, most of the prisoners had to sit and sleep on the huge piles of salt in the holds. The raider provided enough food for the journey, and barely enough water, because Rogge's own supplies were running low. The supply of coal was supposed to be enough to reach Japan, so it was estimated that it would also be enough to reach Somali land, which should have taken about nineteen days. A young sub-lieutenant named Dehnel was put in command.

He was given a prize crew of twelve men to keep order and make sure the vessel did not fall into enemy hands.

Dehnel proved to be a resourceful man in many ways. To help keep the peace, he used imaginary communications with the *Atlantis* to give the impression to the prisoners that the raider was close enough to the *Durmitor* to be able to rush to its aid on short notice. The prisoners were kept in the forward part of the ship, and behind a ball of barbed wire. Then there were the two machine guns mounted on the bridge and pointing toward the bow. It was not an easy task to sail a ship when you were outnumbered by nearly 300 to 13.

For those who made this journey, the name of the vessel was changed to the *Hell Ship*. It was soon discovered that a huge empty space existed in the coal bunkers, meaning that there was not as much fuel as originally believed. Dehnel tried to compensate for this by shutting the boilers down at night and using the hatch-cover tarps as sails. He did this at night because he feared that an Allied warship sighting a steamer under homemade sails might require further inspection. During the long hot and humid days, the ship moved at a snail's pace of 5 knots, in part to conserve fuel and because her hull was so fouled she could hardly make any more speed than that. Adding to the difficulties, the slow speed meant that the voyage would be longer than expected, which in turn meant that the already rationed food and water supply would have to be rationed even further.

By the time the prison ship reached the African coast, everything on board that could burn had been torn from its place, hacked up and thrown into the furnaces. Nerves were frazzled, and fights had broken out among some of the prisoners. The merchant captains had kept their word to Rogge, doing all in their power to prevent chaos from breaking out and providing assistance to Dehnel in carrying out his thankless task.

After twenty-nine days, Dehnel arrived in Somali land. His orders were to put in at Mogadishu, but on approaching the port he learned that the Royal Navy was shelling it, so he went further north. Arriving at a small port, he sought the help of a pilot, but none was forthcoming, so he was forced to ground the ship. Adding insults to injury, Italian troops arrived and arrested the whole group, including the German sailors and the neutral Yugoslavs. After being paraded before gawking crowds of Somalis as evidence of Italian military might, Dehnel was able to set matters straight with the ranking authorities. He and his prize crew rejoined the *Atlantis* four months later.

Meanwhile, the *Atlantis* had steamed toward the Bay of Bengal in search of busier shipping lanes. The move proved productive. On November 9, 10, and 11, three vessels were taken. The first of these was the 6,750-ton Norwegian tanker *Teddy*, which was taken exactly the way Rogge preferred, without firing a shot.

Shortly before midnight on November 8, while sailing on the Colombo-Singapore route off the east coast of Ceylon, the raider's lookouts sighted a smoke cloud barely visible against the night sky. The *Atlantis* was running to the east of the target, so her presence would not be as visible to those aboard the *Teddy*. She had the additional advantage of having a rain squall behind her, making her even more invisible. Over the next few hours the raider gradually closed on the tanker, until she was about 500 yards away, at which time her huge spotlight was turned on and trained on the *Teddy*'s bridge, effectively blinding the helmsman and the officers on duty.

Once she had the attention of those aboard the tanker, the raider used her signal lamp to order her to stop and not to transmit. She then asked her identity. "Teddy, Oslo. What do you want?" came the reply. The Norwegians were told that their ship would be searched and were reminded not to use their radio. They responded with a simple "Okay." They then asked the identity of the vessel stopping them. Rogge signaled back that his ship was the British Armed Merchant Cruiser *Antenor*. He knew that the *Antenor*'s profile was somewhat similar to that of the *Atlantis*, and this might help to maintain the subterfuge until his boarding party arrived on the *Teddy*. It worked. The *Teddy* gave the international signal that she was stopping, three long blasts from her whistle, and slowed to a stop.

Needless to say, the Norwegians were surprised when the boarding party that arrived consisted of German, not British, sailors. The tanker was found to be loaded with 10,000 tons of fuel oil, and 500 tons of diesel fuel. The former was of no use to Rogge, but the latter could be used to supply the *Atlantis*'s diesel engines for about two months. The crew was transferred off the tanker and replaced by a German prize crew. She was then sent about 500 miles to the south, out of danger of discovery by British or Australian patrols, to wait for a future rendezvous with the *Atlantis*. Having no use for the oil, Rogge thought he might send her to Japan where the German authorities could trade her cargo to the Japanese for supplies for use by the raiders after he had pumped out the diesel fuel.

On the tenth, the Heinkel seaplane, which had been patched up following her last mishap, was sent aloft to search for another target. Flying Officer Bulla, anxious to prove the usefulness of his mission, was determined to find something worthwhile. He did. It was a tanker that appeared to be fully loaded. It was to the north of the raider's position and was sailing on an easterly course. Rogge plotted his course and brought the raider to full speed, hoping to catch the tanker during the dark hours after sundown.

Once again Rogge hoped to take this ship without firing at her. Tankers were an especially valuable prize to raiders operating virtually isolated in the seas, especially if one was found with a large quantity of the type of fuel used by the raider. Another reason for the Captain's desire to capture her without firing on her was the risk such action entailed to the lives of the crew. He wanted to kill as few of these seamen as possible; after all, they were not members of warships' crews whose very mission was to engage in combat, but merchant sailors who plied the seas for a living. Then there was the spectacle caused by a tanker loaded with thousands of tons of flammable liquid. The flames and the smoke would be seen for miles and might attract an enemy patrol vessel to the scene before the raider could make its departure.

This time the *Atlantis* did not have a rain squall in which to hide as she approached the tanker. As a result, someone aboard the 8,306-ton Norwegian tanker *Ole Jakob* spotted the raider at about the same time the raider's lookouts saw her. Almost immediately the tanker began sending a distress call that she was being followed by an unknown ship, and giving her position.

The *Atlantis* continued to rapidly close with the *Ole Jakob*, signaling to her that she was the AMC *Antenor*. The tanker asked why she was being followed, to which Rogge replied that he wished to search her. The Norwegians responded, "OK, stopping." But the radio operator continued to send his alert, adding that his ship was being stopped by this unknown vessel. She finally stopped when the *Atlantis* lowered her cutter and the Norwegians could see that it was commanded by a man wearing a Royal Navy uniform. It was, of course, Mohr, wearing the coat of a British officer over his own German uniform. Hidden under a tarp in the cutter were then ten heavily armed men of the boarding party. Despite the suspicions of the *Ole Jakob*'s officers, the subterfuge worked again and the tanker was taken in a matter of minutes.

As soon as he was aboard the tanker, Mohr was glad there had been no gunfire, for the entire ship was engulfed in the fumes of high octane aviation fuel. She was carrying 10,000 tons intended for British forces in Egypt. She would have made quite a blast and a fire that would have been visible for many miles. Mohr used the tanker's transmitter to signal a cancellation of the alert she had sent earlier, and to which several other ships had responded. A small prize crew replaced the Norwegians, and the tanker was sent to a rendezvous position not far from that of the *Teddy*.

The third ship taken that month was another story. The 7,528-ton freighter *Automedon*, of the British owned Blue Funnel Line, was carrying a mixed load of military goods to the Far East, including vehicles, aircraft, machinery, and medicines. On the morning following the capture of the *Ole Jakob*, the *Automedon* was sighted approaching on a course that would bring both ships into close proximity of each other. Rogge thought his best action was to do nothing to alarm the freighter, so he simply continued on his way as if these were two ships about to peacefully pass each other.

When the *Automedon* was less than 5,000 yards away, the *Atlantis* dropped all disguises, ran up her ensign, and exposed her guns. The freighter immediately responded by transmitting an alarm. All she was able to get clear was the alarm and her name before the Germans successfully jammed her transmissions. Rogge ordered a salvo fired. The gunners let loose at a range of 2,000 yards with shells from four salvos that slammed into the freighter's bridge and her midsection. A fifth salvo was fired when a man was seen running toward the freighter's stern gun. He never reached it. The ship quickly came to a stop.

When Mohr and his boarding party arrived on the *Automedon*, they were met by the First Mate, because all the officers, including the Captain, had been on the bridge and had been killed instantly. Mohr later described the condition of the ship as the worst he had seen. The shelling, at so close a range, had destroyed virtually every structure above the hull. Nothing was left undamaged. Six wounded men were quickly transferred to the raider for medical attention, and the rest transported shortly after.

The freighter's cargo, though valuable to the British forces in Singapore, was of little value to a raider at sea, so there was no thought of attempting to recover it. Mohr made a thorough search for items of interest and turned up fifteen bags of mail labeled "SECRET." The greatest prize was in a small green bag kept on the bridge and equipped with holes to allow water in should the Captain throw it overboard in an emergency. Inside was an envelope addressed to the Commander-in-Chief of British forces in the Far East, and marked clearly that it was to be opened by him personally. Inside the envelope were documents prepared by the Planning Division of the British War Cabinet. Among them were evaluations of the strength and status of British land forces and naval forces in the area, and a detailed report on the defenses of Singapore. There was also information concerning the role to be played by Australian and New Zealand forces in the event Japan joined the conflict on the Axis side. Though of little use to Germany, the documents would prove invaluable to Japan if she entered the war. Captain Rogge was extremely pleased with what had been found aboard the old freighter.

The *Automedon* was towed a few miles away and sunk. The diesel fuel in the *Teddy* was pumped out, and she was sunk in a fiery explosion that consumed the 10,000 tons of oil that was worthless to the *Atlantis*. The British documents were put aboard the *Ole Jakob*, which was sent to the German authorities in Japan. Rogge hoped that the aviation fuel she carried would prove extremely valuable to the Japanese, as would the documents. In Japan they were traded for much needed fuel for the raiders working the Pacific and Indian Oceans, and other items, such as a seaplane for the *Orion*.

Rogge was correct about the documents. After Japan had entered the war and Singapore had fallen to the Imperial Army, Captain Rogge was presented with a samurai sword with the compliments of the Emperor of Japan, obviously for the information he had provided concerning Singapore and the British forces. Only two other Germans were awarded a samurai sword during the war, Hermann Goring and Field Marshal Erwin Rommel.

With two prizes sunk, and the third sent to Japan with 154 prisoners on board, the *Atlantis* was once again alone.

One problem about being alone was the constant worry about supplies, especially fresh water. The *Atlantis* was equipped with a distilling plant, but it ran on coal, and the raider had none to spare. The coal was used as ballast to help maintain the vessel's stability. To reduce this supply endangered the ship, especially in rough seas. As November closed, the *Atlantis* was beginning to run dangerously low on water. After examining his options, Rogge decided to seek a supply of fresh water in one of the most desolate places in the world, Kerguelen Island, which was first discovered by French explorer Yves-Joseph de Kerguelen, in 1772, who mistook the 100-mile-long volcanic island in the south Indian Ocean for the Antarctic continent and named it South France. When he realized his error, he changed the name to the more descriptive Isle of Desolation. It was later renamed after Kerguelen. Before the war, it had been used as a base station by the Norwegian whaling fleets. It was now abandoned and would be used periodically by a number of German raiders as a safe port with its numerous deep water bays in which to hide from prying eyes.

In late November the *Atlantis* headed south, planning to leave the hot, humid weather behind. On December 1, a signal was intercepted from the raider *Pinguin* that she was sending a captured Norwegian tanker, the *Storstad*, to Germany with several hundred prisoners and 10,000 tons of diesel oil. Normally reluctant to use his radio for fear that the enemy would hear his transmission and surmise his location, Rogge broke his silence and requested that headquarters have the tanker meet him at location Tulip so that he could refuel. The request was approved, and seven days later, the *Atlantis*, the *Pinguin*, and the *Storstad* rendezvoused. For the officers and crew it was a joyous occasion. When the *Pinguin*'s commander came aboard, he was the first German naval officer to set foot on the raider who was not a member of the crew since she had begun her voyage some 300 days earlier.

In November, the German U-boat force operating in the Atlantic was joined by twenty-six Italian submarines. On the twelfth of the month, Hitler issued an order that in spite of ongoing talks with the Soviets, invasion planning was to continue.

With the mission accomplished, the *Atlantis* resumed her voyage to Kerguelen Island. While there, she grounded on a large chunk of coral that ripped a hole in her outer hull that required extensive repairs. Fresh glacial water was abundant on the island. Collecting the raider's fire hoses and oil lines, a makeshift pipeline was assembled from a waterfall to the *Atlantis*. One thousand gallons of the clean, clear, fresh water were pumped from a waterfall through the 1,200-foot long line. The war was forgotten briefly while the crew celebrated Christmas so far from home and far from civilization, but returned on January 11, 1941, when the *Atlantis*, disguised as the Norwegian freighter *Tamesis*, left its sanctuary and resumed its search for enemy ships.

On January 6, President Roosevelt made clear to the nation that he wanted the United States to be the "arsenal of democracy." It was another step down the long road to entering the war against Germany.

The 5,144-ton British freighter *Mandasor* sailed from Calcutta on January 13 with a cargo of mostly pig iron and tea destined for Great Britain. She was heading for the African coast, which she would hug until she could round the Cape into the Atlantic. This was a longer route than the more direct one of going straight across the Indian Ocean, but it offered the protection of avoiding an area in which at least one German raider was known to be operating, and had the additional benefit of potential air cover from land bases.

On January 23 the *Atlantis* and the *Mandasor* passed each other on opposing courses at a distance of more than 10 miles. It was an extremely hot day when Captain Hill was informed of the passing ship. Following strict Admiralty orders, he turned his freighter hard to starboard, away from the other ship. As if also following the same instructions, the other vessel turned hard to port. As far as Captain Hill was concerned, they were both obeying the same orders given to Allied merchant captains when sighting another ship. Hill turned back to port and continued on, keeping a watchful eye on the unknown ship, which did the same.

On board the *Atlantis*, Captain Rogge waited until he knew that it was a British freighter with at least two guns on board. Once it was over the horizon, then he reversed course and began to trail the *Mandasor*. He wanted to wait until dark to sneak up on her, thus giving her less time to call for help, which, being so close to the Seychelles, might be in the form of British bombers. The plan failed. During the night the raider lost track of her prey. By dawn Rogge decided to use his seaplane to silence and stop the freighter. Flying Officer Bulla was sent aloft with instructions to locate the ship and pull her radio aerial down and drop his limited supply of bombs as close to the bridge as possible.

Shortly after 8:00, Bulla found his target and launched an attack. On his first pass he succeeded in ripping away the aerial and dropping several bombs amidships. Someone aboard the freighter returned fire with a machine gun, so Bulla made another pass, this time with his cannons and machine guns blasting away. A few minutes later the raider came over the horizon moving toward the freighter at full speed. Hill's radio man had assembled another aerial and began broadcasting the ship's name and position and the fact she had been bombed and was under attack by a raider. Despite efforts to jam the alarm, the radio operator on board the freighter kept sending. When the raider closed to within 8,500 yards, Rogge fired salvo after salvo at the vessel until it finally fell quiet. All but six members of the freighter's crew were rescued.

The incident ended on an unfortunate note for the *Atlantis*. As Bulla attempted to land his aircraft, one of its floats snapped off and the entire plane turned over and sank. The crew was pulled from the water by the raider's cutter.

Concerned over the responses of several shore stations to the *Mandasor*'s calls for help, Rogge decided to leave the area and head for the routes taken by tankers entering and exiting the Persian Gulf. His prudence paid off, for one heavy cruiser and several light cruisers were sent to search for the vessel that had attacked the *Mandasor*.

During the night of January 31, outside the Gulf, the lookouts reported seeing a smoke trail on the darkened horizon. The *Atlantis* approached at full speed, and once within range, fired several salvos over the unknown vessel and turned her blinding spotlights on her. She was the 5,154-ton British freighter *Speybank*. She gave up without any difficulty. Rogge decided to make this one a prize and use her as a support ship. There were three factors behind his decision. First, she was undamaged. Second, there were at least seven other "banks" of identical construction, so she could change her identity by simply changing her name. Third, she carried a cargo of manganese, teak, ilemite, and monazite, all valuable to Germany's economy. The *Speybank* was sent off to the south for a future rendezvous with a German prize crew in charge of her.

The following day a ship of the Blue Funnel Line was seen about 16 miles away. The lookouts aboard the liner *Troilus* caught sight of the raider at about the same time and quickly sent word to Captain Braddon. The liner began evasive maneuvering and commenced sending an alarm of a suspicious ship. The alarm was sent nine times in the clear without the Germans being able to jam it. Rogge soon realized that he had very little chance of catching her, and feared that her alarms would bring a rapid response, so he turned and fled at full speed. Once again luck was with the German commander, for not far away was the British fleet carrier *Formidable* and the cruiser *Hawkins*, both of which did respond. When they met the *Troilus*, the suspicious ship was long gone.

On February 2, the day following the close encounter with the *Troilus*, a Norwegian tanker was taken with only one shot fired and no injuries. She proved to be another valuable prize, considering that she carried more than 6,000 tons of various types of oil and 4,000 tons of diesel fuel. The 7,031-ton *Ketty Brovig* was an old sea dog, having been built in 1918. Despite some difficulties in getting her steam up, she would make a serviceable fuel supply vessel, at least until her cargo ran out, so Rogge put a prize crew aboard her and sent her off with instructions for a future rendezvous.

The *Atlantis* met at the agreed position with the *Speybank* on February 8. Two days later they were joined by the *Tannenfels*, a German supply ship that had escaped from an Italian Somalian port just before a Royal Navy fleet arrived. She was accompanied by an Italian submarine, which Rogge refueled before it went its own way. On board the *Tannenfels* were Sub-Lieutenant Dehnel and the members of the *Durmitor* prize crew. The following day the *Ketty Brovig* arrived as planned, and Rogge now commanded a minifleet of German ships in the Indian Ocean.

Together the convoy sailed south, far enough out into the Indian Ocean to be relatively safe from British patrols, where they met with the Pocket Battleship *Admiral Scheer*. The *Scheer* took on a supply of fuel from the *Ketty Brovig*, and after exchanging magazines, news, and some foodstuffs, she steamed away in one direction, the *Atlantis* in another. The *Speybank* went with the raider to act as an extra pair of eyes, but over the next few weeks all they found were some Vichy-French submarines in company with a supply ship, and a Japanese cargo vessel. The prisoners on board the raider were transferred to the *Tannenfels*, and she was ordered to steam to France, arriving at Bordeaux on April 19.

A planned second meeting between the battleship and the cruiser did not materialize when the *Scheer* was forced to flee the Indian Ocean when it was learned that she was being pursued by a British fleet that included an aircraft carrier and five cruisers. Instead of the battleship, the rendezvous was made by a prize the *Scheer* had captured, the tanker *British Advocate*.

Rogge decided that he had too many ships in his convoy to continue going unnoticed, so the *British Advocate* was sent to France on February 27. She arrived at Bordeaux ten days after the *Tannenfels*.

The next month was spent searching the Indian Ocean for ships that were no longer there. Vessels sailing between Australia and Great Britain were now using the Panama Canal to avoid the raiders in the Indian Ocean. Cargo vessels were sailing closer to shore, where they could take advantage of British air cover. Merchant captains were starting to obey Admiralty orders concerning avoiding contact with all ships while at sea, and immediately signaling when approached by an unknown ship. The *Speybank* was sent to Bordeaux, and the *Ketty Brovig*, which had been sent to meet another German supply ship, was reported sunk. The *Atlantis* was once again alone. In the beginning of April she headed back to the South Atlantic.

After meetings with several supply ships, the *Atlantis* lookouts spotted a large ship in the distance in the predawn hours of April 17. It had four distinctive masts that Captain Rogge recognized as belonging to the ships of the British Bibby Line, ships used in the last war to transport troops for the British

Army. The ship was sailing on a haphazard zigzag course and was completely blacked out, two sure signs that she belonged to a belligerent nation. No longer able to afford the luxury of slipping up on a ship, or firing a warning shot across her bow, because merchant captains had been warned to signal if approached despite the danger to their ships and crew, Rogge simply opened fire on her. The second salvo destroyed the ship's radio room, and the part of the electrical system that powered the signal lamp on the bridge. This prevented the Scotsman in charge of the vessel, Captain William Gray Smith, from signaling that he was stopping. Finally he was able to locate a flashlight, and the firing ceased. By then it was clear that the vessel was beginning to take on water and was going to go down.

It was then that the Germans realized that they had not been firing at a British ship. What had once been the Bibby liner *Leicestershire* was now the Egyptian cargo and passenger ship *Zimzam*. In addition to the mostly Egyptian crew of 128, the ship was carrying 202 passengers, 150 of whom were missionaries or members of missionary families, including 77 women and 31 children. The passengers included many Americans, some of whom were volunteers with the American Ambulance Corps. Other nationalities represented were Italians, Canadians, South Africans, Norwegians, and Greeks. Among the Americans was Charles J. V. Murphy, editor of *Fortune* magazine, and *Life* magazine photographer David E. Sherman. The latter managed to hide a roll of film that included photos of the raider inside a tube of toothpaste and publish them after he was turned over to American representatives as a neutral civilian. His photos were published in *Life*, and were used by the crew of the Walrus seaplane that later circled over the raider as the British warship *Devonshire* bore down on her.

The Germans rushed to rescue the people from the sinking ship, but their efforts were hampered by many members of the crew who had ignored their duty to the passengers and had lowered boats into the water and abandoned the ship. There were several instances of the raider's crew having to threaten *Zimzam* crewmen with their weapons in order to keep them from attempting to climb aboard the *Atlantis*'s boats that were intended for the passengers. Everyone was rescued from the *Zimzam*. The raider's doctors worked on the wounded, but three died of their injuries.

Captain Rogge quickly realized that with so many Americans aboard, the pro-war press in the United States could turn the sinking of the *Zimzam* into another *Lusitania* incident. On May 7, 1915, a German submarine sank the British liner *Lusitania* within sight of the Irish coast with a single torpedo. What was at the time the world's largest ship sank in less than eighteen minutes following a second and much larger blast probably caused by the cargo of munitions the liner was carrying. Among the 1,959 passengers and crew were 159

Americans, of which 39 were among the 759 survivors. Although the sinking did not bring America into the war, it helped to arouse American public opinion against Germany. Rogge certainly did not want to be the captain of the raider responsible for the *Lusitania* incident of this war. As a result, he made an extra effort to accommodate his prisoners, especially the Americans, as best as he could.

As the *Zimzam* gradually slipped below the surface, German crewmen made relay runs back and forth from the *Atlantis*, bringing back clothing and other personal articles they could gather up from the cabins on the upper decks. In this way, the prisoners were able, for the most part, to be clothed properly because many had fled the ship in their nightclothes.

The following day the German supply ship *Dresden* arrived for a rendezvous with the *Atlantis*, and the passengers and their belongings were transferred to her. Rogge sought permission from the German naval authorities to arrange a transfer of the prisoners, especially the women and children and the neutrals, most notably the Americans, to either the first passing neutral ship or he would drop them at a neutral port. His request was denied. The *Dresden* eventually ran the British blockade of Europe and landed the prisoners in France.

Rogge was correct about the publicity accorded the sinking of the *Zimzam*. It was used by pro-war forces in the United States as an example of German disregard for international law, yet few of these writers noted that the ship was carrying American-made trucks intended for the British army, or the fact that a neutral vessel is required to sail with its lights on at night, and the *Zimzam* was crossing the Atlantic with her lights extinguished under orders from the British Admiralty. The sinking was a mistake based on the fact that Rogge was not aware that the vessel had been transferred to Egyptian ownership just before the war began. Had the vessel been sailing with its lights on and the Egyptian flag clearly visible, it is doubtful Rogge would have even approached it. Then, there is the question of Egypt's neutrality, considering that British forces were using the nation as a staging area for combat against German and Italian forces.

During the following month, May 1941, the *Atlantis* sank two British freighters, and two more in June. On May 14 it was the *Rabaul*, sailing from Great Britain to Cape Town with a load of coal, and ten days later it was the *Trafalgar*, also with a cargo of coal. On June 17, the *Tottenham* was sunk along with her cargo of military aircraft and spare parts. The final ship that month was the *Balzac*, which was transporting more than 5,000 tons of rice from

On May 9, U-110 was forced to surface as a result of a depth charge attack. Royal Navy forces boarded the sub before her enigma machine could be thrown overboard and took charge of it and much other valuable enigma related items.

Rangoon to England. After a protracted chase, she was sent to the bottom of the Atlantic on June 22.

Plans for the raider to return home were scrapped by two incidents in which she played no role. The first was the sinking of the pride of the Royal Navy, the battleship HMS *Hood* by the German battleship *Bismarck* on May 24 with the loss of 1,413 men. This blow to British pride brought every warship the British could find into the Atlantic to search for the offender. The subsequent sinking of the *Bismarck* three days later left the Atlantic bristling with British warships in search of the weather ships and supply ships that normally accompany a battleship to sea. In the next few weeks nine German supply ships were either captured or sunk. Some of these were intended for use by the *Bismarck*, but others were assigned to refuel and resupply the raiders. As a result, the *Atlantis* was ordered back into the Indian Ocean and made directly for the Pacific. By that time things would be expected to calm down in the Atlantic, and the raider could round the Cape and return to the South Atlantic and head home. She was being sent on a cruise completely around the world to take her out of harm's way. Rogge was informed that he would meet a German tanker out of Yokohama in the Society Islands in September from which he would be fueled for the final leg of his cruise.

For the next ten weeks, Germany's most successful commerce raider sailed across the Indian Ocean, keeping far to the south, outside of shipping lanes. She passed far to the south of Australia and far out into the Pacific before turning north, thus giving a wide berth to New Zealand. Invisibility was the key to reaching her destination.

On September 10, 1941, while passing half way between New Zealand and the Society Islands, the *Atlantis* came on her twenty-second and final victim. It had been eighty days since they had seen their last enemy vessel, but the lookouts made no mistake about the ship that suddenly appeared out of a squall two hours after sunset when they said she was a Norwegian freighter. The *Silvaplana*, a 4,793-ton motorcraft was carrying a cargo of rubber, tin, copper, coffee, and spices. It was a valuable cargo for a nation at war. She also carried fifty wooden cases filled with hand carved figures from Bali, some of which the raider's crew thought were bad omens. Despite the fact that the *Silvaplana* had managed to get off a signal that she was being approached by a suspicious ship, the Norwegian was taken without damage. A prize crew was put aboard her, and a future rendezvous with the *Atlantis* was planned. Rogge then continued on for his meeting with the tanker sailing down from Japan.

The *Munsterland* was at the assigned position when the *Atlantis* arrived, and so was the raider *Komet*, which had sailed across the top of Russia and into the Pacific in a record-breaking cruise that put her in the war without the Allies knowing anything about her. Accompanying the *Komet* was the Dutch freighter *Kota Nopan*, which she had taken as a prize. Ammunition, fuel, and food supplies were divided between the raiders and the prize, which was heading back to Europe along with prisoners taken by the *Komet* and some of those from the *Atlantis*. Four German ships at one location wasn't something to inspire the ship's skippers to feel comfortable about, so they soon dispersed. The *Atlantis* met once more with *Silvaplana*, then sent her prize on to France.

After brief stops at Vana Vana, where several hundred fresh coconuts were obtained in trade for a supply of flour, and an inspection of the famed but unpopulated Pitcairn Island, the *Atlantis* headed south for her trip around the Cape and back into the South Atlantic. After eighteen months at sea, the raider was heading home. What Captain Rogge and his crew did not know was that before reaching their destination, they were first going to encounter the British heavy cruiser HMS *Devonshire*, which would prove fatal to their ship.

The encounter had taken place at Lily 10, and the *Devonshire* and her seaplane were now gone, as was the *Atlantis*. All that remained were the boats and rafts carrying the crew and some few prisoners that had been on board. A new danger suddenly erupted in the form of hungry sharks, and a few men were taken by them before they were finally driven off.

With the enemy gone, the U-boat resurfaced and the wounded were put aboard her. Much to his disgust, the sub commander agreed that there was nothing to be done but turn his warship into a towboat, because the 300-plus men from the raider could not be accommodated in or on the small submarine. They decided that their best hope for survival and not becoming prisoners of war was to head for Brazil, where there was a large German community that might be able to help them. It was a plan born of desperation, for the South American coast was more than 900 miles away, and because the submarine would be towing a long line of boats, it would have to move very slowly. In spite of this, it seemed to be their only hope. Each man said his own personal prayer that an enemy ship or aircraft did not approach them, for they all understood what would happen if the U-boat was suddenly forced to dive. It would be the end for them all.

A signal was sent home explaining their plight and requesting help. They waited for a reply.

For three days they traveled west, toward Brazil, the surfaced German submarine trailed by a line of wooden and steel boats jammed with the survivors of the *Atlantis*. Boats made to carry twenty men were crammed with fifty. Clinging precariously to the sub's deck were fifty-two men wearing life jackets. They had been told to jump overboard and swim as fast as they could away from the sub if they heard the dive alarm. This would help them avoid being sucked down by the sub if she dived.

During the day the tropical sun beat down on the men who had no protection from it, and at night they shivered in the exposed cold. Periodically the lines would break, and the entire caravan would halt until the exhausted men in the boat that had broken loose could manage to row themselves back to the broken line and repair it. On the wooden boats the strain of the towing pulled some of the planking apart, and the men were forced to take turns bailing just to keep their boat afloat. Then word arrived that a supply ship and several U-boats were being sent to rescue them.

Help arrived on the third day in the form of the supply ship *Python*. The crew and the single prisoner from the *Atlantis* were taken aboard, and with some foresight, the boats the submarine had been towing were lifted aboard, repaired, and restocked with supplies. While the crew of the *Atlantis* was made comfortable and injuries were looked after, the *Python* refueled and replenished the U-126. The submarine had used most of its food supply feeding the extra men on board and in tow. The U-boat then continued its voyage home.

The *Python* also had to resume its business in spite of all the extra seamen it now had on board. The supply ship's primary function was to provide the U-boats operating in the area with fuel and supplies, and orders soon arrived sending the *Python* southwest for a rendezvous with several submarines.

Arriving at the prescribed location, the *Python* was joined by U-68 on the evening of November 30. The following morning they were joined by a second U-boat, UA. All that day, the three ships rolled in the gentle swell of the quiet ocean while the refueling and restocking of supplies took place. For the first time in more than twenty months the crew of the *Atlantis* had nothing to do except help with the watch. The *Python*'s crew was expert at their duty, and they required no help from the raider sailors.

As the work of resupply went on, the lookouts aboard the *Python* kept a sharp eye on the horizon in all directions. Suddenly at 3:30 in the afternoon the shout was heard that a three funneled ship was approaching at high speed from a distance of about 19 miles. The alarm was sounded, and the work was broken off. The fuel lines were quickly disconnected, and the two submarines started their engines and began to move away. Three funnels and high speed could only mean a warship.

Bearing down on the *Python* and her submarines was the British cruiser *Dorsetshire*, sister to the *Devonshire*. Her Walrus aircraft had sighted the supply ship and suspected that it was standing still, which could mean she was busy refueling a submarine. If this were the case, the cruiser would have to maintain a safe distance and use antisubmarine maneuvers to protect against an attack. Of course, thought Captain Alger on the bridge of the cruiser, there was always the possibility that it was an allied or neutral cargo ship that had stopped to pick up survivors of a U-boat attack. He raced down on his quarry at nearly thirty knots, zigzagging to avoid torpedoes, real or imagined.

The *Python* carried no armaments for her own defense. Supply ship captains were under orders to sink their vessels if approached by warships to avoid them falling into enemy hands. The *Python*'s captain thought he might be able to run, placing the two U-boats between himself and the British cruiser, so he quickly ordered the engines fired and called for speed. Meanwhile, U-68, which had been loading torpedoes when the cruiser was spotted, had difficulty diving and fell into an almost straight dive that the crew managed to correct only with great difficulty. This put her out of action for several critical minutes. UA was in much better shape, and actually fired five torpedoes at the *Dorsetshire*, but the cruiser's speed and maneuvering were effective and she was unscathed.

Captain Alger was concerned about the possibility of British prisoners being aboard the ship he suspected was a German supply vessel, so he fired several of his 8-inch shells over her as a warning. It seemed to work, for the ship, which had suddenly begun blowing smoke, just as suddenly stopped.

Aboard the *Python* the men of the *Atlantis* rounded up all the food, water, and other supplies they knew from experience they would need for themselves and the *Python*'s crew. The boats were lowered, and the *Python* was scuttled. Rogge watched once again as a German ship went down from her own charges. Satisfied that the enemy ship was sinking, and that her crew would be picked up by the submarines the Walrus had reported were alongside her, the *Dorsetshire* turned and left the scene just as the *Devonshire* had done. Before she was out of sight, her Walrus made one more low pass over the scene to photograph the men in the water and in the lifeboats.

With the cruiser gone, the two U-boats surfaced. They found 414 men in lifeboats or clinging to small rafts waiting for them. As senior man on the scene, Captain Rogge took charge. He divided the crews of the *Atlantis* and the *Python* into two groups of about 207 men each. Each group was assigned to one of the submarines. About 100 men were placed aboard each sub, some below and others in rubber boats on the deck. Each sub took five boats in tow with the remaining men distributed among them. Ahead was a 5,000-mile voyage to German occupied territory. It was obvious to all, including the naval staff when they received word of the *Python*'s sinking, that the men could not survive such a trip. Two U-boats were diverted from their patrols to help, and four Italian submarines rushed out to lend a hand. In this way, all the men eventually found cover from the elements and survived the trip home. By December 29, all eight submarines had arrived in France, and the crews of the *Atlantis* and the *Python* were finally safe.

Rogge had become a national hero and received several awards. The crew of the *Atlantis* was welcomed home to Germany with cheers and feasts. Only one man regretted arriving in Europe, the lone prisoner who was on the *Atlantis* when she went down, volunteer ambulance driver Frank Vicovari. He had not been transferred off the raider because he had one leg in traction and the other in a cast, so he had no choice but to join the crew of the *Atlantis* in its adventure. Unfortunately, America had entered the war following the Japanese attack on Pearl Harbor on December 7, and Vicovari's status was changed from that of a neutral detainee to a prisoner of war.

Captain Rogge was promoted to Rear Admiral, and then to Vice Admiral before the war ended. At one point he commanded a task force that bombarded Russian positions near Danzig, but otherwise he saw little action. He retired to civilian life after Germany's surrender, but was recalled to duty in 1957. As a Rear Admiral in the reconstructed Bundesmarine, he commanded NATO naval forces in Schleswig Holstein until his final retirement in 1962.

The rescue of the *Atlantis*'s crew, along with the crew from the *Python*, was hailed by friend and foe alike as a spectacular event without parallel. If nothing else, it helped enhance the reputation of Germany's most successful disguised commerce raider of World War II.

2

ORION _____

THE BLACK RAIDER

If there was ever a warship ill suited to her mission, it was the Auxiliary Cruiser *Orion*. She had formerly been the 7,021-ton single screw steamship *Kurmark* of the Hamburg-Amerika Line. Built by Blohm and Voss in 1930, she was driven by engines that had previously served as half the power plant of the passenger liner *New York*. In order to keep up with the larger and faster passenger ships being built in Britain and France, the *New York* was lengthened and provided with more powerful engines. Half of the old engines were refitted and installed in the *Kurmark*. Those engines were a constant source of problems for the *Orion* during her entire cruise. Even working to capacity, she could make no more than 14 knots.

The *Orion* set out on April 6, 1940, disguised as the Dutch steamship *Beemsterdijk* of the Holland-America Line. In preparation, her hull was painted black with a yellow band. While the painting proceeded, a work party dismantled the vessel's second smoke stack and stowed it in Hold 1. For the last few months the second stack almost constantly emitted smoke as part of the ship's disguise. Inside the huge, hollow, fabricated stack, Leading Seaman Paul Schmidt, a fisherman from Rugen Island, had the comfortable assignment of burning oil-soaked cotton and other refuse to simulate engine exhaust. Schmidt spent long leisurely hours stoking the small forge fire and relaxing. He could even smoke on duty, and was convinced he had the best duty of the 377 man crew.

Concealed behind false structures and inside prefabricated, easily removed hull sections were the armament typical of these warships. The *Orion*'s in-

KMS *Orion*: April 6, 1940–August 23, 1941

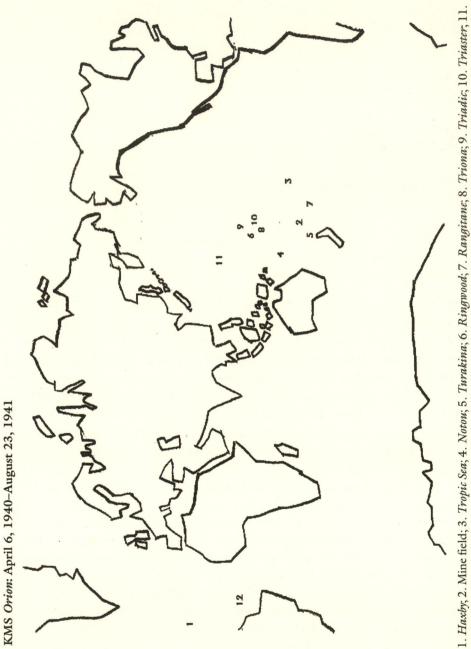

1. *Haxby*; 2. Mine field; 3. *Tropic Sea*; 4. *Notou*; 5. *Turakina*; 6. *Ringwood*; 7. *Rangitane*; 8. *Triona*; 9. *Triadic*; 10. *Triaster*; 11. Maug Island; 12. *Chaucer*. Courtesy of K. Rochford.

cluded six 5.9-inch guns, one twin 37-mm, one 75-mm, and four 20-mm anti-aircraft guns, an assortment of smaller weapons, and six torpedo tubes. Also included in the weaponry were 228 mines, and an Arado AR 196A-1 floatplane. Her operational area was the eastern portion of the Indian Ocean, where she was to lay her mines across some of the world's busiest sea-lanes.

The crew's creature comforts were not an issue during the *Orion*'s transformation into a ship of war. As a result, life aboard the black vessel was substantially less enjoyable than on other raiders. Port holes were nonexistent in the holds where the crew's living quarters were located, as was any other form of effective ventilation. Below the steel decks, the living spaces were permeated by "odors of cooking, the sweat of a hundred men, tobacco smoke of every known quality." Added to this was the stench produced by those men who, unused to the rough seas, fell to seasickness.

The *Orion* was commanded by thirty-nine-year-old Captain Kurt Weyher. A short, wiry, energetic man, Weyher was the son of an educator. He joined the Imperial Navy in 1918, and was the youngest naval cadet at the time World War I ended. In the chaos and civil disorder that followed the collapse of the Kaiser's government, Weyher joined the right-wing Free Korps, but by 1922 was back in the navy as an ensign.

The *Orion* was the second disguised raider to put to sea. Conditions for her escape into the open sea were not favorable. Her passage was through the North Sea at the same time that the German navy's Operation Norway, the invasion of that country by German forces, was to take place. A planned U-boat escort was cancelled at the last minute because the boat was needed to support ships involved in the Norwegian invasion, and the Luftwaffe reported that heavy rains and winds prevented the scheduled help of air reconnaissance. The raider was on her own in the middle of what was quickly shaping up as a major sea battle zone.

On April 7, 1940, the entire German surface fleet, divided into six groups, sailed from home ports. Most headed toward Norway carrying combat troops or escorting troop ships. The British were slow to realize what was happening, but, during the next few days the North Sea began to teem with British warships of every size and description.

As both the German and British navies geared up for the impending fight along the Norwegian coast, the airwaves were filled with harrowing messages of nearby enemy aircraft and warships. There was little Weyher could do but slowly make his way north and hope the large Dutch flag painted on his vessel guaranteed her safety. Despite the presence of numerous British cruisers and destroyers, several of which came within hailing distance of the raider, the passage was made without incident. Not one British warship challenged the Dutch freighter. This was likely due to their preoccupation with the imminent

German invasion of Norway and the actions of German warships along the Norwegian coast.

North of the war zone, the *Orion*'s career as a raider came close to ending before it had even begun. At 4:00 P.M. on April 8 the ship's alarm went off following the cry of "Destroyers ahead!" Weyher was in the chart room when the alarm was given and immediately rushed to the wheelhouse. He was shocked to see what lay dead ahead of him. About 10 miles off lay a large ship that he could not identify. It may or may not have been a warship, he couldn't tell. But the more immediate problem was the four Royal Navy destroyers that were positioned around her. Reacting quickly to the new danger, Weyher ordered the raider to turn hard to starboard. He hoped to lose his ship from sight inside a thickening rain squall that might give him enough protection to avoid the destroyers until dark.

As the quartermaster called out each ten degrees of the turn, all eyes in the wheelhouse were on the destroyer. All hands were at battle stations, but the camouflage hiding the guns was held in place pending a final decision about the need to fight. The last thing Weyher wanted was to be forced to fight four destroyers. His unarmored vessel was no match for a single destroyer, much less four. With the amount of fuel, mines, and torpedoes stored throughout the ship, one well-placed shell from a destroyer could blow the *Orion* and her crew to kingdom come.

The men held their collective breaths as they attempted to avoid detection. Then suddenly one of the destroyers turned toward her and increased speed. A second followed close behind. The seconds crept by as the two ships approached. The gunnery officer kept in touch with his crews, giving them the ever closing range and changing gun elevations.

The only crewmen not at battle stations were a handful who were detailed to support the ship's disguise. They were dressed as civilian sailors, and stationed themselves either along the port wing of the bridge or on the deck where they could be clearly seen by the approaching British sailors. Added touches included having the cook, in his white apron, looking out from the galley to see the warships, and another man who walked to the edge of the deck and emptied a bucket of kitchen waste over the side. Surely nothing could look less suspicious than a tired old freighter making her way peacefully through a rain squall. It worked. Both destroyers came close enough to read the name of the ship and to get a good look at her. Satisfied that she was what she claimed, the Dutch freighter *Beemsterdijk*, they turned and resumed whatever duty they had been engaged in prior to their investigation.

The final hurdle to be faced by the *Orion* before reaching the open sea was the tight cordon the Royal Navy maintained between northern Norway and Iceland. Fortunately, this blockade had been thinned out by the transfer of several ships down the Norwegian coast where they were needed in the fight against the German invasion fleet. The *Orion* made the Arctic Circle without further contact with an enemy ship.

Once off the coast of Greenland, Weyher decided to change the ship's identity. Dutch ships this far north were extremely rare, and he wanted to be as inconspicuous as possible. Added to this was the fact that the radio room had picked up a message intended for the real *Beemsterdijk*, which indicated that she was somewhere in the West Indies. Weyher feared that the message might also have been intercepted by the Royal Navy and cross referenced with the reports of several destroyers that they had seen the same vessel in the North Sea.

During the bitter cold night of April 9, the *Beemsterdijk* vanished from the Greenland coast to be replaced by the *Soviet*, a Russian repair ship out of Odessa. Although included in international ship registries, the *Soviet*'s physical description was not available anywhere. This gave the Germans some latitude with their disguise. The yellow strip around the hull was painted over to match the rest of the black. The funnel was also painted black and a red band was added into which was painted the star and hammer and sickle of the Soviet Union.

On April 9, the German army invaded Denmark under the command of General Kaupitsch. They captured Copenhagen in less than twelve hours. In Norway, German seaborne landings began near Oslo, Bergen, Trondheim, Kristiansand, Stavanger, and Narvik.

By the evening of April 11, the raider neared the open ocean. The bitterly cold weather prevailed. Despite the terrible odors accumulating in the unventilated holds, the crew kept all exterior doors and hatches closed tightly. Added to their existing discomfort, the ship's steam heating system had to be shut down because it created a drain on the fuel supply. The precious fuel was needed to feed the engines which consumed the oil at an incredible rate. Most of the crew found it impossible to sleep in the cold. They battled to keep their bodies warm enough to sleep by layering every article of clothing the navy had issued them, and then wrapped themselves securely in their blankets. Outside, the hurricane force winds and the driving rain reduced visibility to less than 100 yards. The number of lookouts was reduced to the bare minimum seven men, and the length of their watches was drastically slashed to prevent them from freezing to death.

Meanwhile the ship lumbered along, gradually making its way south toward less frigid climes. Struggling against the combination of her own inadequate power plant and the fierce winds, the ship could manage to advance no more than 36 miles in a twenty-four-hour period. The only advantage the weather offered was the unlikelihood that an enemy warship would spot her and attack while she was so vulnerable. Unlike most of the other raiders, the *Orion*'s weapons were all topside. Having their crews exposed to the cold and the winds made operating the guns extremely difficult.

April 14, as the raider headed toward the Grand Banks off Newfoundland, offered the crew their first opportunity to strip off the extra clothing. Although the temperature was still low, the warm sunshine that accompanied the day was a welcomed relief. It also gave them a chance to survey and repair the damage the storms had caused, especially to the extensive canvas sections that hid the ship's guns.

They were now beyond the area in which a Soviet auxiliary ship might reasonably be found, so the *Orion* was given a new look and a new name the following day. The masts were lowered, and the funnel raised to a new height. Construction crews altered the appearance of the superstructure using wood planks and sections of canvas. Additional paint changes were made as the ship was able to cruise at her maximum of 12 knots. Dabs of rust coloring were applied where they would ordinarily be found on a Greek tramp steamer, and a new name was painted on the hull. The *Orion* was now the *Rocos*, out of Argostoli, and owned by the Ionian Steamship Company.

Still headed south, toward her ultimate destination in the Indian Ocean, the *Orion* was crossing the routes normally taken by British convoys when she received a message from the Naval Warfare Command. The raider was advised to take whatever means possible to convince the Royal Navy that a German pocket battleship was operating in the North Atlantic. Unable to alter her appearance so drastically to convince an observer that she was considerably larger and more heavily armed and armored than she actually was, Weyher had a plan. He decided the best way to accomplish his mission was to sink an enemy ship and send out his own call for help, identifying his assailant as a warship. The signal to be used by a merchant vessel under attack by a regular warship, which the British would likely interpret as being one of the pocket battleships, was the alert RRR, followed by the victim's identification and location. To make this deception appear as real as possible, the *Orion* had to quickly locate and sink an enemy ship. So far, although they had picked up quite a bit of neutral shipping radio traffic and had sighted several ships sailing with their lights on, no enemy ship had yet been seen. An enemy-owned vessel would maintain radio silence except in an emergency, such as coming under attack, and would run without lights to reduce the possibility of being seen by U-boats or German surface craft.

The greatest opportunity for the *Orion* to find a likely victim was the nearby intersection of two heavily traveled shipping lanes. One was the route between New York and Gibraltar. The second was the even more traveled route between the English Channel and the Panama Canal. On April 18, the *Orion* arrived at the point where the two shipping lanes intersected. She crossed back and forth across both lanes, first the New York–Gibraltar then the Channel-

Canal lane, but failed to sight a potential enemy ship. Several vessels were seen along the second lane, but they ran with their lights on, indicating that they were neutral.

Finally, about one hour before noon on April 22, a ship was sighted approaching from the opposite direction. All hands rushed to their battle stations, and the lookouts tensely watched the oncoming vessel. When the watch officer on the bridge announced that he believed the ship's funnel was red, a sigh of disappointment arose from the crew. If he was correct, it meant that the ship was Soviet, and thus belonged to a friendly neutral nation. It soon became apparent that he was wrong. The funnel, Weyher and the others on the bridge saw, was actually blue, but had been painted with so much red lead antirust paint that it at first appeared red. As she drew closer, the stranger was seen to be a passenger ship and had several guns mounted and manned on her decks. Obviously, she was an enemy ship.

On April 21, German forces captured the Norwegian city of Lillehammer. The following day they attacked the British 148th Brigade north of the city and began the process of driving the British into retreat.

As the two ships passed each other at a distance of 4,000 meters, Weyher had to make a quick decision about engaging the ship. He decided not to do so. The vessel was obviously faster than the *Orion*, and was armed heavily enough to put up a good fight. Under such circumstance, she would be able to send a message to the Royal Navy clearly indicating that she was under attack by an Auxiliary Cruiser. This would not help Captain Weyher carry out his orders to deceive the enemy into thinking that he was a battleship. He allowed the enemy ship to pass while maintaining his disguise as a Greek freighter.

Two days later as dawn slowly drew a thin line on the eastern horizon, one of the lookouts saw what he believed to be a shadow in the almost total darkness. The officer of the watch left the chartroom and joined the lookout on the port wing of the bridge. He too saw the shadow if only fleetingly. Captain Weyher, who had fallen asleep in one of the bridge's chairs, soon joined the two men. The last of the night's cool breeze gently swept over them as they stared expectantly into the darkness. The unknown ship was traveling with its lights out, an indication that she belonged to a belligerent nation, so Weyher was fairly confident that she was an enemy. The big question in his mind was what was. She could be an unarmed or lightly-armed freighter, or she could be a warship. He had little choice but to wait and see. Weyher ordered the silent alarm be issued that sent the crew to battle stations. Several guns were quietly uncovered, and the canvas covers prepared to drop over the Greek markings. The German naval ensign was prepared to be run up. International law required that the attacking vessel identify itself as a ship of war and the nation it represented prior to firing a shot. Weyher was always scrupulous about obeying this law.

Weyher maneuvered the *Orion* in order to keep her to the west of the unknown vessel. This kept his ship on the dark western horizon and hidden in the darkness as long as possible. Except for the churning of the waters behind both vessels, a tense quiet hovered over the scene as the ships drew closer together. As the dawn sun inched its way across the gently moving water, the vessel's hull began to take shape and she could be seen to be a freighter. The Germans used their binoculars both to identify the other ship's nationality and to watch for movement. There was no movement aboard the freighter, leading Weyher to assume that the crew was probably still in their bunks, and the men on watch may have fallen asleep.

In the *Orion*'s radio room, the operators listened for signs that the freighter might suddenly begin broadcasting an SOS. The freighter's radio was as silent as her decks.

The sun was quickly casting light on the ships. Because the freighter was to the *Orion*'s east, she soon became little more than a silhouette with the sun behind her. The *Orion*, on the other hand, was gradually being exposed by the sunlight. Anyone watching from the freighter could see that she was an armed ship prepared to fight.

Weyher decided to change their positions and put the *Orion* into the sun. He also told the engine room to fabricate a boiler failure by blowing heavy black smoke out of the stack. The response was immediate as the engine room crew choked off the boilers' air intake. This sent unfired oil into the funnel, causing the thick black smoke a boiler failure would produce.

The minutes crawled as the *Orion* came around the freighter, and still nothing aboard the vessel stirred. It was then that Weyher caught sight of the two guns mounted on the freighter's stern. This was all the evidence he needed to identify the ship as an enemy vessel. Neutrals did not mount weapons on their freighters. "Hoist signals," the raider Captain ordered. The Greek markings were quickly covered over, and the German ensign raised. A small gun mounted on the forecastle fired a warning shot over the freighter while hundreds of eyes on the raider watched to see what action the enemy would take.

Within seconds the ship, which turned out to be the 5,207-ton British freighter *Haxby* traveling from Glasgow, Scotland, to Corpus Christi, Texas, to pick up scrap metal for British steel mills, turned away and increased speed. She also began broadcasting an alert. Her signal was monitored and part of it was allowed to go through unhampered. For some reason, the *Haxby*'s radio operator broadcast an SOS that identified his assailant as a warship. Instead of the QQ. used to identify an Auxiliary Cruiser, he used the letters signifying a standard warship, which could very well be a pocket battleship. The remainder of his message, the part including the name and position of his ship, was scrambled by the interference of the *Orion*'s radio room.

The order to fire was given, and the *Orion*'s guns sent salvo after salvo into the freighter. One of the first shells landed near the two stern guns of the *Haxby*, effectively putting them out of action before they could be used. Unable to offer any means of defense, the freighter's captain, Cornelius Arundel, followed the Admiralty's orders to keep broadcasting and attempt to escape. In less than six minutes from the firing of the first salvo of shells, the freighter ceased broadcasting, and figures could be seen on her decks attempting to lower her boats. One of their boats had been destroyed in the shelling, a second sank as soon as it was lowered into the water.

Captain Weyher ordered the firing stopped and sent three boats to rescue as many survivors as possible. Of the crew of forty, twenty-four, including Captain Arundel, were rescued.

The *Haxby* burned in several locations, but refused to sink. Evidently, the shells that pierced her hull became imbedded in the sand she carried for ballast and exploded with little effect. The sand then apparently filled the openings and acted as a patch over the shell holes. This resulted in the burning vessel producing a large plume of black smoke that drifted high into the air and could probably be seen for 20 or 30 miles. Fearing that a British warship might see the smoke and decide to investigate, Weyher took the step all raider captains hated—he used one of his valuable torpedoes to sink an already dying ship. The torpedo explosion cut the *Haxby* in half, and she quickly went to the bottom with her cargo of sand.

Eleven of the crew from the stricken freighter were sent to the sick bay, where the *Orion*'s two doctors looked after their wounds. The remainder were sent to the prisoner quarters three levels down from the deck.

As the *Orion* prepared to get under way and continue her journey south, she sent several partially garbled messages purporting to be under attack by a pocket battleship. With that done, Captain Weyher believed that he had accomplished his mission. Unknown to him was the fact that not one of the messages from the *Orion* or the *Haxby* was received by any station anywhere in the world. The deception aimed at convincing the Admiralty that a German battleship was at large in the North Atlantic, leading them to withdraw warships from the Norwegian coast in response, did not work.

The *Orion* now headed for the Pacific Ocean via the Cape. Once around the other side of South America, she was to cross the Pacific and lay mines in the waters around New Zealand. Captain Weyher and every sailor aboard the raider looked forward to getting those mines off their ship. No one ever forgot that their ship was only a pseudowarship. Her hull was not the extra strong shell of a warship designed to offer protection from enemy torpedoes, but the thin shell of a commercial vessel. A lucky shot from an enemy ship or submarine could pierce the hull and impact into the mines. The result could be a blast that would blow the *Orion* into thousands of pieces. Few if any would be lucky enough to survive such an explosion.

Before leaving the South Atlantic, the *Orion* had to replenish her supply of fuel. She had been burning it much too quickly by running at or near top speed. The reason for leaving the South Atlantic was that the raider *Atlantis* had been operating in the area, and Weyher feared encountering one of the numerous British warships searching for her. At her maximum speed of 13½ knots, the raider consumed fifty tons of oil daily. This could be reduced to twenty tons if she slowed to 10 knots, but that meant that she would be in these dangerous waters even longer. Weyher was anxious to exit the South Atlantic as soon as possible.

On May 10, German forces launched a unified attack against France, Belgium, and Holland. By the end of the day, the Germans had struck deep into Belgium and Holland and appeared to be about to succeed in their plan to draw the best British and French forces north to those countries, enabling additional German units to attack their flank.

Several coded messages were sent to SKL, German Naval Warfare Command, to arrange a rendezvous with a tanker. After two days the message was answered, and the *Orion* was given a set of coordinates at which to meet the tanker *Winnetou*. The instructions indicated that the *Winnetou* would be at a location code-named "Max," which was about 600 miles north of South Georgia, from May 12 through May 20.

Arriving at the designated location on May 12, the *Winnetou* was nowhere to be found. The following day the Arado seaplane was launched with great difficulty. This craft, which carried a pilot and an observer, was better suited for calm waters. It took about one hour to get the plane aloft in the Atlantic swells. In less than an hour she spotted the tanker and signaled her the direction to sail to meet the *Orion*. The crew members of the tanker must have been shocked to see an airplane bearing the iron cross flying overhead so deep into the South Atlantic.

The *Winnetou* was in sorry shape. In her earlier life, she had been a Royal Navy tanker during World War I. Her appearance showed clearly that she had not been home for four years. Her funnel belched a foul-smelling black smoke that made her visible for miles. When the war began, she had been at Aruba. She had attempted, but failed, to run the British naval blockade in order to return to Germany. The navy decided she was better able to serve the war effort by serving the fuel needs of the raiders at sea. She had remained at the Canary Islands until ordered to meet the *Orion*. Her long wait at the Canaries resulted in a thick growth of barnacles on her hull that reduced her maximum speed to 7 knots. She barely crawled across the Atlantic toward her meeting with the raider.

It took the efforts of nearly 200 men to pass a line between the two ships and begin the process of pumping oil into the *Orion*'s tanks. Several times, as the winds increased and the seas continued rising, the line twisted and kinked so badly that the flow of oil stopped. After nearly 2,000 tons of fuel had passed from the *Winnetou* to the *Orion*, the connection was broken and the ships parted. When the seas calmed the following afternoon, Captain Weyher and Captain Steinkrauss of the *Winnetou* met aboard the *Orion* and agreed on a second meeting in the South Pacific near the Tubuai Islands.

The *Orion* steamed away first, heading toward the Cape and her voyage through the Drake Passage. The tanker quickly disappeared behind her as the raider steamed south and west. The notorious winds of the Passage were not too active, so apart from the freezing Antarctic temperatures, the trip was not as hazardous as it might have been. Once in the Pacific the *Orion* was forced to buck powerful head winds that slowed her speed dramatically. On at least one occasion she was forced to stop and allow the winds to roar around her. Captain Weyher was especially concerned about the buffeting the ship was taking because the mines in the holds more than once threatened to break loose and bounce around the ship's interior.

As she struggled across the South Pacific, the *Orion* had to deal with chronic engine failures. Her crew struggled also, against the isolation in which they lived, so far from home, and extended periods of looking at nothing but the sea. Because there was no planned entertainment, some of the men made attempts to occupy their time, but boredom was generally the rule of the day. Cramped quarters, poor food poorly prepared by amateur chefs, and the ever present danger of the load of mines made life aboard the ship barely livable. During the voyage, the ship's markings and identity were altered so that she took on the appearance of a nameless ship of the Dutch-Africa Line.

On June 12, 1940, the *Orion* arrived at her destination, Hauraki Gulf near the entrance to the New Zealand city of Auckland. Her orders were to lay her mines across the various shipping lanes leading in and out of the city's large harbor.

The German skipper was surprised when he learned that he could track what air defensive measures the New Zealand government was taking by simply listening to the local radio station's news broadcast. Each day the broadcast included the weather forecast, the movement of shipping, and the schedule for the Air Force's reconnaissance flights. The country was acting as if they never expected the war to

Meanwhile, British Prime Minister Winston Churchill met with French leaders in Briare to bolster their resistance to the German advances. He failed. Two days later, Paris fell to the Germans. On June 12, the Soviet government issued an ultimatum to Lithuania for territory it claimed. Three days later, the Lithuanian cities of Vilna and Kaunas were occupied by Soviet troops.

reach them. With this knowledge, Weyher was able to alter his original instructions, which called for laying the mines inside the gulf during a period of unusually dark nights. With that period long in the past because of the time it took for the *Orion* to cross the South Pacific, he decided instead to lay several mine fields in the approaches to the gulf.

On the night of June 13, with visibility as much as 12 miles, and the shore clearly visible from aboard the German raider, all the mines were released in a series of five minefields. During this exercise the ship came well within the beam of the Cuvier lighthouse. The cone of light, so brilliantly flooded the whole port side each time it came around that the men working there involuntarily sought cover. When the light had swept past and darkness returned, tiny lights could be seen at the base of the lighthouse. These were probably the mooring lights of launches tied up there.

By 2:00 A.M., June 14, the entire load of 228 mines had been slid down the launching rails at the *Orion*'s stern, and the harbor of Auckland was successfully seeded with death. The amazing thing about this feat is that the mines were dropped within full sight of either the shore or several lighthouses that protected the entrances to the harbor. The raider zigzagged across the shipping lanes in what should have been considered a mysterious maneuver, yet no one either saw it or thought enough of it to report it to the authorities. It remains a mystery why the lighthouse keepers took no action to identify the ship and determine why it was steaming in such a manner.

The mines laid by the *Orion* eventually sank four British ships. These were the passenger liner *Niagara*, and the freighters *Puriri*, *Baltanic*, and *Port Bowen*.

Having accomplished her task, the *Orion* headed toward the Kermadec Islands, northeast of New Zealand. Two major shipping routes passed close to these islands. First was the route between Auckland and San Francisco. The second was the Sydney-Samoa-Honolulu passage. On the late afternoon of the 15th, shortly after the islands came into view, a large steamer was sighted. Unable to clearly identify her, Weyher decided to let her pass. He was still within range of the New Zealand air forces, and didn't want to risk attacking a ship that might use its radio to attract enemy aircraft to the scene.

The German army continued to sweep across France. Between June 18 and June 20, Cherbourg, Brest, Nantes, Dijon, and Lyons were taken. Allied fleets struggled to evacuate tens of thousands of soldiers from trapped enclaves along the French coast.

On June 19, radio broadcasts were picked up reporting the sinking of the passenger liner *Niagara* outside the Auckland harbor. It was the first success of the mines the *Orion* had laid. That same day a slow-moving three-masted steamer was spotted on the horizon. So as not to alert her to the potential danger she faced, the raider ran at full speed until she was well ahead of the steamer, then she slowed down to a crawl, allowing the other vessel to gradually catch up with her. The other ship did not appear to sense the danger, for she came to within 3,000 meters without taking any kind of evasive action. When the two vessels were abreast of each other, the raider fired a shot across the steamer's bow. Simultaneously, the German ensign was run up and the ship was told to stop and not to use her radio.

When the unidentified steamer failed to respond, a salvo was fired short of the vessel. This caused a loud series of explosions and a wall of white water to rise between the two ships. Finally there was a reaction. A sailor was clearly visible running along the deck toward the aft where he raised the Norwegian flag. The ship stopped, and using signal flags, identified herself as the Norwegian freighter *Tropic Sea*.

Captain Weyher was in a bit of a quandary. Since the occupation of Norway had taken place, some Norwegians were considered friendly, while others were enemies. Into which category did the *Tropic Sea* fit? He sent a prize crew aboard the steamer to answer this question. The *Tropic Sea* was found to be carrying more than 8,000 tons of Australian wheat. Her captain claimed that it was heading toward the United States and produced documents substantiating that assertion. Weyher remained suspicious, so he ordered the prize officer, Lieutenant Raschke, to make a thorough search of the vessel. The search unearthed additional documents indicating that the ship was under charter to the British Ministry of Food. The ultimate destination of the precious wheat was not the United States, but Great Britain. The *Tropic Sea* was taken as a prize.

A few days later, the *Orion*, with the *Tropic Sea* following close behind, rendezvoused with the *Winnetou* to refuel. The latter had made her long, arduously slow voyage around the Cape and into the Pacific without incident. Following a meeting between Captain Weyher and Captain Steinkrauss of the *Winnetou*, it was decided that only a thoroughly experienced sea captain like Steinkrauss would be able to sail the *Tropic Sea* back around the Cape and north to Europe. No extra fuel could be spared for the voyage, which Steinkrauss said was no problem because if he ran out of oil, he could use her sails to complete the trip. His first officer could be left in command of the tanker.

A few days later the Norwegian freighter, her name having been changed to the *Kurmark*, began her long journey toward Europe with the hope of bringing the wheat into a German-controlled port. In addition to the Norwegian crew, the survivors of the *Haxby* were placed aboard. The vessel sailed under the control of a German prize crew comprising crewmen from both the *Winnetou* and the *Orion*. In the first week of September, as she neared her destination, the *Kurmark* was stopped and challenged by the British submarine *Truant*. Reluctant to surrender his crew and his cargo to the enemy, Steinkrauss ordered the vessel scuttled. The submarine and a seaplane picked up the British crewmen from the *Haxby* and several of the Norwegians. The rest of the Norwegians along with the German sailors made it to the nearby Spanish coast where they landed their lifeboats.

When news of the rescue reached England, the London papers ran the story on their front pages. The *Daily Telegram* headline read: "Submarine Rescues Crew Captured by Nazi Raider." It was the second time the *Truant* made headlines at home. The first was as a result of action off the Norwegian coast on April 9, 1940. The *Truant* had fired three torpedoes into the German light cruiser *Karlsruhe*, damaging her so badly that her escort vessels had been forced to send her to the bottom.

On August 1, 1940 Hitler issued Directive 17 concerning the invasion of Great Britain which was planned for sometime between September 19 and 26. On August 5, the first operational plan for a German invasion of the Soviet Union was given to the German Chief of Staff, General Halder.

Meanwhile, in the South Pacific, the *Orion* traveled throughout the shipping lanes with no luck. Weeks went by slowly as the men suffered from the extreme heat. The raider traveled to the various islands of the South Pacific, crossing and recrossing numerous shipping lanes without ever sighting another ship. The most they ever saw was small coastal vessels that hugged the shorelines of the islands and were too small to risk exposing the raider's presence.

On August 8, the *Orion* sucked the remaining oil from the *Winnetou*'s tanks while floating in the Coral Sea and sent the rusted worn-out ship on its way to Japan and safety. Life aboard the raider had been reduced to "immeasurable boredom" that even the beautiful sunrises and sunsets could not offset. Hour after hour led to day after day and week after week of unrelenting boredom. Routine work aboard the ship added to the feelings of frustration. The men began to give up any hope of ever seeing action. The monotonous nature of their survival became even worse when several cases of scurvy began to appear despite efforts to avoid it. Added to this was the fact that the ship was no longer carrying the mines and had not been able to replace their weight with some kind of ballast. As a result, the *Orion* rode high in the water and was subjected to every wave and swell. She rolled back and forth constantly.

Out of desperation, Captain Weyher decided to head for Australia and approach Brisbane Harbor. He would get as close as possible, ever wary of the fact that the Australians, unlike the New Zealanders, were more war conscious and maintained regular air and sea patrols around important locations. Once again they found nothing. Weyher decided to try his luck close to the French possession of New Caledonia. Finally, at just after 10:00 A.M. on August 10, smoke was spotted on the horizon, about 24 miles away, by one of the lookouts.

The *Orion* once again ran at full speed in order to position itself far ahead of the unidentified ship, allowing it to gradually catch up. Weyher decided to wait until after 4:00 P.M. to attack. This meant that any aircraft responding to a call for help would have to do so just as darkness was settling on the ocean. When the attack was launched, the raider bore down on the ship, which was by now identified as the *Triona*, owned by the British Phosphate Commissioners. The *Triona* became suspicious of the approaching vessel, turned quickly, and was able to make itself virtually invisible by entering a rain squall. Weyher decided against pursuing her. The *Orion* had a maximum speed of only 3 knots greater than the *Triona*, and because the ships were 10 miles apart, it would take several hours to catch her. The rain would just add to the problem. In the meantime, she had sent no radio distress call. This was probably because she was only taking precautionary measures. If the approaching ship began to chase after her, she would surely have signaled for help. Now frustration was added to the boredom that consumed the lonely raider.

On August 12, the *Orion*'s radio operator picked up a message from SKL indicating that the enemy was now aware that ships from the HAPAG, especially those of the "mark" class were engaged in commerce raiding. Those ships—which included the former *Kurmark*, now the *Orion*—were to take immediate action to alter their appearance totally if they had not already done so. After the hot sun went down that evening, the crew busied themselves making the necessary changes. The fore and main top masts were shortened, the funnel was lengthened, and paint schemes were changed. When the work was completed, Captain Weyher had a motor launch lowered so that he could circle the ship from a distance and judge the effort. It passed the test.

The *Orion* returned to the waters around New Caledonia where, on August 16 she sank the New Caledonian coal ship *Notou*. She was carrying 3,900 tons of coal that was to be traded in Australia for nickel. The prisoners, taken aboard before the *Notou* was blown up, included several Frenchmen, some Kanakas, and a mixed group of islanders and Malayans from the South Pacific area. When the local radio station began attempts to contact the coal ship, Captain Weyher decided to head south toward the Tasman Sea before the Australian Air Force began looking for the *Notou*.

The same day, the Luftwaffe flew 1,715 sorties in the Battle of Britain, severely damaging several Fighter Command bases. In the United States, President Roosevelt announced that talks were taking place with the British concerning U.S. acquisition of British bases.

Four days later, while battling high seas and rain squalls about 260 miles northwest of Cape Egmont, New Zealand, a steamer was spotted heading toward Cook Strait. The raider estimated the as yet unidentified freighter's speed at about 11 knots. The only hope the raider had of encountering the ship was to attempt to cut her off from her approach to New Zealand, because her speed excluded her being caught outright. As the two vessels gradually pulled closer together, the *Orion*'s lookouts could see the large gun mounted on the other ship's stern. She was clearly an enemy vessel.

The alarm went up at about 5:30 that evening. The men had prepared for it by ensuring that they had their warmest clothes ready, for they were now entering an area subjected to the cold of Antarctica. The temperature had dropped so dramatically that the ship's heating system had been turned on. The encroaching darkness combined with the rain squalls enabled the raider to approach the freighter without the latter sighting her. That changed when the two were 14,600 meters apart.

The ship the *Orion* was bearing down on was the seventeen-year-old *Turakina*, a 9,691-ton refrigerated freighter owned by the New Zealand Shipping Company. She was carrying a partial cargo that included lead, wool, grain, and fruit. She was headed for Wellington, where the remainder of her load, frozen meat for the rationed citizens of Great Britain, was to be loaded aboard. With such a valuable cargo, the *Turakina* was scheduled to join a convoy to the Panama Canal.

The freighter's lookouts finally spotted the ship rapidly approaching them through the curtain of rain. The alarm was given. The *Turakina*'s skipper, Captain J. B. Laird, had vowed earlier to fight off any enemy vessel that tried to stop him. As it turned out, he was true to his pledge. When informed of the approaching ship, his suspicions were aroused because he had been told by Admiralty authorities that there was no other ship in the area that would be at this position simultaneously with the *Turakina*. He immediately ordered his vessel turned hard to starboard until her stern faced the unknown ship. This minimized the raider's target, and provided the *Turakina* an opportunity to run if the ship turned out to be an enemy warship.

On board the raider, Captain Weyher gave the order for his port guns to prepare to fire. The distance was still too great, and the rough seas would make accurate targeting difficult, but he wanted his gunners ready. The *Turakina* increased her speed, as did the raider—the raider gradually decreasing the space between them.

At 5,500 meters, Weyher gave the signalman instructions to use his lamp to tell the ship to stop and not use its radio. Captain Laird responded by ordering his radio officer, S. K. Jones, to alert the authorities that he was under attack. Jones set about his task with courage and determination. Laird then ordered his gun crew into action and sent Seaman S. Mander up the foremast to direct the firing of the gun.

Seeing that the enemy was not about to surrender without a fight, Weyher ordered several salvos fired from his starboard battery, which now had a clearer line of vision to the freighter than did the port guns. The first few shells missed, but the Germans quickly found their target despite the pitch and roll of their own vessel in the increasingly rough seas. The *Turakina*'s gun crew responded with rapid fire from their 105-mm stern gun.

Those first salvos from the raider that found their mark had a devastating effect on the *Turakina*. Within fifteen minutes of the start of the battle, half the crew of fifty-seven men were dead, and many others were wounded. The ship was aflame near the bow, and the bridge had been all but destroyed. Yet, Jones kept sending his QQQ alert, giving the name and position of his ship. Try as he might, the *Orion*'s radio operator could not jam the *Turakina*'s signal.

The freighter's equally courageous stern gun crew ignored the damage around them and kept up a steady barrage of fire. Unfortunately they too had to deal with the effects of the rough seas, so their shells, though coming dangerously close to the vulnerable raider, did not do serious damage to her.

Despite severe wounds to himself, Jones kept transmitting his alert for eighteen minutes, until both the New Zealand and Austrian stations responded that they had received and understood his message. The responses were also heard by the *Orion*'s wireless room. More ominous, though, were standard local radio broadcasts picked up a few minutes later from Wellington. Regular programming was interrupted by urgent appeals for crew members of the 7,030-ton light cruiser H.M.N.Z.S. *Achilles* who were on leave to return to the ship immediately. A few minutes later a similar message was heard from the radio stations in Melbourne calling all sailors back to the cruiser H.M.A.S. *Perth*. Trouble was brewing for the German raider.

Meanwhile, the battle continued until the *Turakina*'s foremast was hit by a shell. The mast came crashing down. Part of it smashed into the deck, while the remainder tumbled into the sea. Along with the mast came down the radio antenna, which halted the broadcasts, and Seaman Mander, which stopped the firing from the stern gun. The gunners no longer had a fire control spotter to help them aim their weapon.

The guns on both ships fell silent. Aboard the freighter, which was little more than a burning hulk being knocked about by the seas, Captain Laird gave the order to abandon the ship. Unfortunately, two of the lifeboats had been destroyed in the fighting, and a third sank as soon as it landed in the water.

Captain Weyher ordered his helmsman to close with the dying vessel in order to rescue its surviving crewmen. Much to his shock, when the two ships were about 3,000 meters apart, the *Turakina*'s stern gun opened fire again. Evidently the members of the gun crew who were still alive had waited until the raider had drawn close enough for them to aim without the aid of the fire control spotter. Every gun aboard the *Orion* capable of aiming at the freighter immediately returned fire, including the antiaircraft gun. Shells and tracers poured into the freighter, increasing the flames that were quickly consuming her. The *Turakina*'s stern gun once again fell silent, this time for good, and the *Orion* stopped firing.

The burning ship continued to drift. Flames leaped so high into the air that she must have looked like a beacon from miles away. With the knowledge that enemy warships would soon be searching for him, Captain Weyher ordered a torpedo fired into the hulk to sink her and extinguish her flames. The first struck the *Turakina* near her stern, but did little damage. A second hit her amidship and sent her to the bottom. It was two hours after the raider had first sighted her. Weyher put out the order to watch for survivors.

For nearly six hours the *Orion* circled the area picking up survivors. The task was made more difficult than usual by the high seas that prevented the raider from lowering boats. Instead, inflatable life rafts with long leads attached were flung into the water wherever voices were heard in the dark, and the men were pulled in usually one at a time. In all, twenty-one crewmen were rescued in this way. Among the crew members not found was Captain Laird, who it was believed died in the explosion from the second torpedo and went down with his ship.

The *Orion*'s medical staff looked after the new prisoners, many of whom had been wounded. Most of them also suffered from shock after their long stay in the cold waters. The following morning, despite the best efforts of the doctors, Seaman Mander, the man who had acted as fire control spotter for the *Turakina*'s gun, succumbed to his internal injuries. He was buried at sea with full military honors. Captain Weyher, who was a strong believer in the brotherhood of seamen, officiated at the ceremony.

While the *Orion* searched for survivors from the *Turakina*, the cruisers *Perth* and *Achilles* put to sea to search for her. Their efforts were joined by reconnaissance aircraft and several smaller warships. As the raider raced around the other side of Tasmania for the Great Australian Bight, where she expected to find active shipping, her radio operator listened to the wireless communications between Australian and New Zealand ships, planes, and land stations. Several times enemy planes came close, but the favor of a low ceiling and blinding rain squalls protected her from prying eyes. On August 22, two days after sinking the freighter, the air raid alarm was sounded. Still disguised as a Dutch freighter, the *Orion* was treated to an inspection by a Haviland bomber out looking for a German warship. Apparently satisfied that she was what she claimed, the bomber circled a few times and then continued on her way.

While luck prevented the *Orion* from being a target of enemy ships and planes, it was not with her as a hunter. Shipping throughout the entire area around Australia and New Zealand was tightly restricted in part because of the *Orion*'s attack on the *Turakina* and the success of her mines. Days went by without so much as sighting a mast or a stream of smoke. The days turned into weeks, and the old feelings of isolation and frustration returned to haunt the crew and even the prisoners. Below decks most of the day, with usually two periods when they were allowed on deck to exercise and breathe fresh air, the crew members of now dead ships made the best they could of their existence.

On September 2, desperate for something to do for the war effort, Weyher had his engineers convert several steel beer drums into counterfeit mines that were then set adrift. If the raider couldn't find an enemy ship to sink, perhaps she could throw some off course and force the New Zealanders and Australians to waste time and effort sweeping for his fake mines. Unfortunately, during the manufacturing of these decoys, which required the inclusion of a small amount of explosive to sink the "mine" when someone attempted to snag it, one accidently blew up, killing one seaman and severely wounding another.

Seven days later the *Orion* received radio instructions to proceed to the Marshall Islands, where she was to rendezvous with two supply ships. Several days later the raider was told to keep a sharp eye out while in the Marshalls because one of the supply ships that was scheduled to meet there, the tanker *Weser*, had been captured leaving a Mexican port. It was feared by the naval command that the location might have been given to the enemy by the captured master of the *Weser*. Weyher was also told he would then meet the Auxiliary Cruiser *Komet* at the Caroline Islands after provisioning from the other supply ship, the *Regensburg*.

On September 2, the United States took a step closer to entering the war with the announcement that she had traded fifty World War I vintage destroyers to Britain in return for bases in the West Indies and Bermuda. The next day the German invasion plan for England, Operation Sealion, was issued. The date for the invasion was set for September 21. The following day, the United States warned Japan against making aggressive moves in Indochina.

On the way to the Marshall Islands, the *Orion* shed her latest disguise as a British merchantman and took the identity of a Japanese freighter. The final step in the transformation was to paint the new name on the hull. Unfortunately, no one on board could decide how to spell out the name Maebsai Maru in Japanese characters. They settled for copying a set of characters from a Kodak advertisement produced in Yokohama. Captain Weyher suggested that they probably meant "exposure" or "super-sensitive."

Arriving at Ailinglapalap Atoll in the Marshalls on October 10, the *Orion* found the four-masted steamer *Regensburg* at anchor awaiting her. She was also using a Japanese identity, calling herself the *Tokyo Maru*. The raider's sailors, who had not seen land other than a few small islands for months, were entranced by the beauty that appeared before them. Gleaming white sand beaches reflected the hot sun, and beyond them were thick walls of green foliage. Small groups of native huts could be seen along the far edges of some of the beaches.

Two days later, after the *Orion* had taken on 3,000 tons of fuel and an assortment of provisions that included Japanese beer, cigarettes, and vegetables, the two left Ailinglapalap for their rendezvous with the *Komet*. The *Regensburg*, the faster of the two, steamed ahead of the *Orion*. She was prepared to signal with her flags if she saw any other ships the raider might consider a potential target.

On October 12, Operation Sealion was postponed until spring 1941. Two days later the Italian War Council finalized its decision to attack Greece without first notifying its German allies. On October 16 the United States began registration for a military draft under the terms of its Selective Service Act. On the 18th, Vichy France introduced a law barring Jews from public service and positions of authority in the media and in industry.

On October 14, 1940, nearly two months since taking her last victim, the *Orion* crept up on a Norwegian freighter in the predawn hours and took her without any trouble. Two shots across her bow brought the 7,203-ton *Ringwood* to a halt. The freighter's captain, sailing under orders from the Norwegian government in exile in London, was taking his ship in ballast to Ocean Island to pick up a cargo of phosphate intended for Bermuda or Halifax. He offered no resistance, even failing to attempt to escape in the dark, because he thought he was being approached by a British warship. He was shocked to discover that the boarding party his crew helped come aboard were German sailors. Thirty-five prisoners were added to the raider's prisoner quarters, and the *Ringwood* was sent to the bottom.

Disguised as Japanese ships, the last thing the *Orion* and the *Regensburg* wanted was an encounter with a genuine Japanese vessel. Japan was still neutral in the war, and although her neutrality was tipped in the direction of Germany, Weyher and the other German captains feared endangering the international situation if Japan discovered that the raiders were using Japanese markings to cover their activities. But that was exactly what happened as the *Orion* approached the Caroline Islands atoll of Lamotrek.

One of the *Orion*'s lookouts sighted an unidentified vessel heading toward the lagoon of the atoll. Both the *Orion* and the *Regensburg* gave chase, hoping to identify her before she entered the protected waters of the lagoon. As the unknown ship increased speed and turned into the lagoon, the rising sun of Japan could be clearly seen painted on the side of her hull. She was in fact the passenger ship *Palao Maru*. The Japanese captain must have been surprised to find two Japanese vessels already riding at anchor in the lagoon, and to see two more following closely behind him. The four were actually part of Germany's commerce raiding fleet that by a terrible coincidence had opted to disguise themselves as peaceful Japanese ships. Already in the lagoon were the tanker supply ship *Kulmerland*, using the same name as the *Regensburg* was using, the *Tokyo Maru*, and the raider *Komet*, disguised as the *Manyo Maru*. Entering the lagoon were the *Regensburg* and the *Orion*. The latter still displayed the completely imaginary name that Captain Weyher hoped appeared to be close to *Maebasi Maru*.

At 3,287 tons, the *Komet* was one of the smallest raiders. Under the guidance of Captain Robert Eyssen, she had made a name for herself before she even entered combat with an enemy ship by sailing the Northeast Passage across the top of Russia with the aid of Soviet icebreakers. (This feat is described in a later chapter.)

There was some undecipherable radio chatter between the authentic Japanese ship and the port, which the German captains assumed was about the mysterious vessels using Japanese identifications. The Germans were driven to further concern when many of the passengers aboard the *Palao Maru* busied themselves snapping photographs of the four ships. There was nothing the Germans could do about this other than ensure that their guns remained out of sight.

Shortly after the *Palao Maru* left port with its gaping picture-taking passengers, a Japanese government vessel arrived. Obviously sent to investigate the four ships in the lagoon, the twin-masted sailing ship dropped anchor alongside the *Komet*. An official wearing a uniform boarded the raider and asked its identity. Captain Eyssen explained that the ships were German cargo vessels attempting to cross the hostile Pacific and return to their home ports. They had entered the lagoon simply to exchange fuel and supplies, and would soon be gone. Eyssen claimed that they were using Japanese identification marks to protect them from British warships. This helped, because Japan was substantially less than friendly with Great Britain, which was seen as an interloper in Japan's own sphere of influence in the western Pacific. Eyssen also produced authentic Japanese documents that had cleared the two supply ships, the *Kulmerland* and the *Regensburg*, from ports in Japan where they had purchased supplies. The Japanese official never realized that he was on board a warship whose armaments had been excellently concealed. When the official next attempted to board the *Orion*, he was kept off by a combination of language problems and the absence of a gangway for his use. He finally gave up and returned to his own vessel, which soon sailed away.

On October 20, the four ships left the quiet, palm tree lined lagoon. The *Regensburg*, emptied of its entire cargo, headed back to Japan with a long shopping list for the raiders' future use. The *Orion*, the *Komet*, and the *Kulmerland* sailed together in a southeasterly direction. The three ships steamed abreast of each other with the *Kulmerland* in the center. During daylight hours they spread apart so as to cover a wide area of the ocean. In this way they could maintain visibility across an area of 80 to 100 miles. At night they drew closer together to prevent their accidental separation.

While traveling this way, Captain Weyher decided that too many Japanese passengers aboard the *Palao Maru* had photographed his ship for his own comfort, so he had her repainted. In addition, her silhouette was altered using canvas and plywood. The result was that barring a close inspection, the *Orion* no longer resembled the ship that had anchored in the Caroline Islands lagoon.

By the end of October, the *Orion* was developing almost daily engine problems. The engines drew their water from a system of evaporators that turned expelled steam into fresh water. On October 30, the worst of all problems reached a dangerous level. It was discovered that the engines were losing more water then could be replaced by the evaporators, so fresh water had to be drawn from the ship's supply of drinking and bathing water. On top of this, a small epidemic of flu broke out among the crew.

The days dragged on into weeks without a sighting. This was in part the fault of the *Orion*. Its attack on several ships in the area and the mining of New Zealand harbors had caused the British Admiralty to alter shipping habits in the South Pacific. Now all ships carrying valuable cargo were required to join convoys. Rare was the ship sailing alone in waters known to be infested with at least one German commerce raider. The only ship sighted during this time was an American vessel, the *City of Elwood*. Unfortunately it had taken the American so long to respond to a signal to identify herself that a shot had been fired across her bow before the flag painted on her side could be seen through a rainstorm.

By the end of November the Italian invasion of Greece had failed, and most Italian troops had either been killed, taken prisoner, or driven back into Albania from where the invasion had been launched. Hitler decided on his own invasion of Greece to save Italian face. He also issued Directive 18, the plans for the invasion of the Soviet Union. On November 18–19 an event occurred that had momentous impact on the German U-boat force. A U-boat approaching a convoy was detected by a British plane using a new form of radar called ASVI—Air to Surface Vessel. This is the first time this happened and gave convoy escorts additional eyes for spotting enemy submarines.

At last, on November 25, a target was sighted off the coast of Chatham Island. It wasn't much, just a 546–ton New Zealand coaster on its way to Lyttelton in South Island. It was the *Komet* that first sighted the vessel, and Captain Eyssen moved quickly to stop and capture it. Eyssen transferred the prisoners, seventeen crewmen and twelve passengers, to the *Komet*. He then divided as many of the 1,370 live sheep aboard the coaster as possible among the three German ships forming this odd minisquadron. The men on all three ships welcomed the opportunity to enjoy fresh meat, a commodity in extremely short supply. The stock that could not be removed perished with the ship when it was sent to the bottom. Spirits aboard the three ships, which had been miserably low due to various illnesses and boredom, began to pick up.

The little coaster was named the *Holmwood*. It was later claimed that her skipper did not transmit a signal that he was being approached by a suspicious vessel because he was carrying women and children as passengers and did not want to endanger their lives. Unfortunately, his failure to alert other ships and the authorities about the presence in the area of a potential enemy ship probably resulted in the *Komet*'s next success. As a result, a New Zealand commission of inquiry suggested that "unnecessary passenger traffic" be avoided by all ships.

At 3:00 A.M.on November 27 the alarm was sounded on the *Orion*. A ship had been sighted in the dense mistlike drizzle and darkness off the starboard bow. She was large and running without lights. Weyher and his officers were unable to determine whether the unknown vessel was a freighter or a warship. About all they could tell was that she was large.

The *Orion* informed the *Kulmerland* and the *Komet* of her sighting, using signal lamps. The *Kulmerland* quickly withdrew, because she was unarmed and could contribute nothing to the expected attack. The *Komet* circled out and around the target, hoping to catch her between the two raiders.

On board the darkened ship, which was the passenger liner *Rangitane*, Captain H. L. Upton was awakened and rushed to the bridge in his pajamas, taking only enough time to throw a heavy coat over himself. To his great dismay, Upton found not one but two suspicious vessels approaching his ship from either side. He immediately ordered the radio operator to begin broadcasting an alert. From the *Orion* came a morse lamp signal to stop the vessel and cease radio transmissions. The *Orion* then snapped on her powerful searchlights, but the mist was so thick that the light only succeeded in reflecting back at the raider, partially blinding her gunners.

From the other side of the passenger ship, the *Orion*'s searchlights gave the gunners aboard the *Komet* a clear silhouette of their target. At Captain Eyssen's order they opened fire. The *Orion* followed suite, but because she was blinded by her own lights, her shots were wide of the mark.

Instead of stopping his transmission, Captain Upton quickly changed it to inform the authorities that he was under attack by two warships. He attempted to turn away, but the raiders had him boxed in. His radio operator kept transmitting the distress signal until the mast carrying the radio antenna was shot away. At that point the Captain decided that he could do little else but surrender. Boarding parties from all three German vessels set out for the passenger liner in what was nothing short of a race to be the first to claim the ship as a prize. The *Komet*'s party reached the *Rangitane* first.

The 16,712-ton passenger liner was the largest vessel sunk by a disguised raider. She was on her way from Auckland to Liverpool via the Panama Canal. In addition to more than 300 passengers and crew, the big ship carried more than 124,000 cases of butter, 33,255 cases of frozen pork and mutton, as well as equally large quantities of cheese, cocoa beans, and other foodstuffs. Also, on board were forty-five bars of silver. Even more surprising to the Germans, the liner was heavily armed and armored for a passenger ship. Mounted on her stern were two guns, a 126-mm and a 76.2-mm. Several American-made light antiaircraft guns were located on the wings of her bridge, and she was equipped for launching depth charges. For defense, the bridge was armorplated, and she boasted devices to protect her hull against magnetic and contact mines. Yet, she made no attempt to defend herself against the raiders, or break out of their trap. Ironically, if she had been able to escape their cross fire, she could have easily outrun both raiders.

Unfortunately for the sailors on board the three German ships, there was only time to remove the passengers and crew before the burning liner was torpedoed by the *Komet*. Her valuable cargo went to the bottom with her. The *Rangitane*'s distress calls had been received and rebroadcast to New Zealand and Australian naval units. Radio traffic made it clear that warships and planes were rushing to the scene.

Racing from the area themselves, the Germans decided to head north for the equator. They planned to attack shipping around the island of Nauru. This isolated British possession was rich in phosphate and shipped between 700,000 and 800,000 tons of it annually. Nauru is an 8.2-square-mile, oval-shaped, raised coral island located just south of the equator. Aside from pretty beaches, its only real value was as a source for the phosphates used in manufacturing fertilizer and some animal feed supplements. This made it an important little possession for any European power. Germany had taken control of it in 1888, but lost it to the British during World War I. Now the Germans were coming back, not to possess the island, but to destroy its ability to supply the British with the badly needed phosphate. The idea was Captain Eyssen's, and as senior commander of the three ship squadron, the others agreed to his plan.

Approaching Nauru, the raiders cornered and sank the phosphate ship *Triona*, which had so successfully eluded the *Orion* in early August. The following two days, December 7 and 8, 1940, the *Orion* and the *Komet* accounted for four phosphate ships in the vicinity of Nauru. First was the Norwegian Motor Vessel *Vinni* of 5,181 tons. It was followed by three British freighters, the *Komata* of 3,900 tons, the *Triadic* of 6,378 tons, and the *Triaster* of 6,032 tons. It was a very successful forty-eight hours with the exception that Captain Eyssen's plan to land men on the island and destroy the phosphate processing plant could not be accomplished because the seas remained too high.

By now the three German ships were becoming crowded with prisoners. It was decided to land all but a handful of New Zealand and Australian military personnel who had been passengers on the *Rangitane* on the remote Emirau Island. The island was known to be inhabited by two families of English planters and a small number of workers from other islands. Viewing the island from their anchorage, the Germans surveyed a beautiful tranquil scene. The warm turquoise sea lapped onto white sand beaches broken only by a small group of bright colorful bungalows. The British planters made their way to the beach in an ancient Ford automobile to see what was going on. They must have been shocked to see a motor launch approach flying the German naval ensign and occupied by officers and men in dress white uniforms. The greetings on both sides were cordial despite the ongoing war. The planters confirmed that they had neither transportation nor radio communications with other islands in the area, and agreed that they could look after the prisoners until other help came along.

More than 500 prisoners were put ashore on December 21. They were given radios, kerosene, food, cigarettes, and even several rifles for their own protection in case unfriendly characters landed on the beach. Before departing, the Germans left a small seaworthy boat with masts and sails with the understanding that it would not be used to contact the nearest island, some seventy miles away, for at least twenty-four hours.

The minisquadron then disbanded. The *Komet* headed toward Borneo with plans to attack the oil depot at Miri. The *Kulmerland*, emptied of all her supplies, went north to Japan to replenish, and the *Orion* headed back to Lamotrek Atoll in the Caroline Islands, where she was to meet the tanker *Ole Jakob* and spend time on a badly needed overhaul of her engines.

On December 18, Hitler issued Directive 21, calling for the German army to "crush Soviet Russia in a rapid campaign." Operation Barbarossa was scheduled to begin May 15, 1941. On December 29, President Roosevelt told the American people that he wanted the United States to become the "arsenal of democracy." He also indicated that he wanted to extend full aid to Britain in her war with the Axis powers.

The *Orion* arrived back at Lamotrek Atoll on Christmas Day, 1940. Waiting for them, they found the 8,000 ton tanker *Ole Jakob*. The ship was practically brand new, having been launched in 1939; she virtually sparkled in the bright hot sunlight. Captain Weyher and the entire raider crew were surprised and cheered to find the vessel under the command of Captain Steinkrauss, whom they last saw as he sailed away toward Germany in the *Tropic Sea*. Steinkrauss explained that after returning to Germany from Spain, he was offered command of the *Ole Jakob*, which was docked in Japan. Steinkrauss traveled across Russia via the Trans-Siberian Railway, and now was back supplying the raiders.

The *Orion* and the *Ole Jakob* were soon joined by the *Regensburg*, her holds bulging with supplies including large stocks of Japanese beer in her cold storage sections. The crews of all three vessels celebrated New Year's Eve together, putting a substantial dent in the beer supply.

The reunion was dampened by the decision of the naval command to bring the *Orion* home. She was consuming oil at a pace that made her too costly to keep at sea. The worst of it was that Weyher was instructed to return to Europe by way of the Indian Ocean after his vessel had been overhauled. He was told to abandon Lamotrek Atoll, which it was suspected the British had learned was being used by the raiders. The raider was in the midst of a complete overhaul of her boilers and engine room equipment. Some of this equipment had been operating virtually nonstop for the entire 286 days the *Orion* had been at sea. The men had to stop the work and hastily reassemble the machinery so that she could get under way. While this was being done, the *Regensburg* departed with her holds emptied for the return trip to Japan and another resupply. The following day the *Ermland* arrived to take the *Orion*'s prisoners. The freighter was in deplorable condition. Her holds were encrusted in dirt and filled with roaches and other vermin. Captain Weyher had her thoroughly washed down before he transferred his prisoners to her. The next day, the *Ole Jakob* sailed away, followed the next morning by the *Orion*.

On January 9, 1941, the *Orion* and the tanker dropped anchor at the harbor of Maug Island in the Marinas. The ship, which by then had traveled well over 65,000 miles, settled into this protected harbor for completion of her refitting. The island was little more than an extinct volcano rising up out of the calm waters. The harbor, inside the crater, was almost totally hidden from passing ships.

The island was believed to be uninhabited, so the Germans were surprised to see a small jetty jutting out from the beach. At its far end was a small group of wooden buildings centered around a flagpole flying the Japanese flag. A landing party was greeted by nine Japanese and forty Filipinos busily constructing a weather station. The Germans asked for, and received permission to establish a lookout and signal station so that they could watch for the approach of enemy warships.

The meteorologists must have reported the arrival of the German ships, because the following day saw the arrival of a small Japanese government boat to inspect them. Moving quickly to keep the Japanese from boarding the *Orion*, Captain Steinkrauss sent one of his boats to greet the officials and invite them aboard the *Ole Jakob*. The beer flowed freely, and the Tripartite Pact between Germany, Italy, and Japan received many smiling toasts. The only sticky point came when one of the officials asked why the Rising Sun had been painted on the tanker's funnel. Steinkrauss evaded a direct answer, but promised to have it painted over immediately. This seemed to satisfy them, and after a few more beers, the Japanese officials departed.

Meanwhile, the crew of the *Orion* worked ceaselessly in the blazing sun and punishing heat. Everything that could be stripped down and cleaned or repaired was disassembled. Captain Weyher described his vessel as looking like a "huge demolition yard, littered with pipes, valves, parts of pumps and turbines." The return of the *Regensburg* on January 18 with fresh fruits and vegetables and, more important, 100 tons of drinking water, was greeted by all.

On February 1, the trio of German vessels was joined by the *Munsterland*. She arrived

During the month of January, U-boats sank 21 ships in the Atlantic. German aircraft accounted for another 15. To help replace them, President Roosevelt announced plans to build 200 cargo ships of identical design. They became known as Liberty Ships.

from Japan with another 200 tons of drinking water, additional foodstuffs and supplies, and 55,000 bottles of Japanese beer. Her most important contribution to the raider was a Japanese-made single float seaplane, a Nakajima. It had been purchased in Tokyo by the German Naval Attaché, Admiral Wenneker, after he had been assured that it would be able to take off and land safely in the broad swells of the Pacific. At last the *Orion* would have eyes in the sky that could spot potential targets or enemy warships beyond the horizon.

By the middle of February, the *Orion* was headed toward her new operational area, the eastern side of the Indian Ocean. It soon became obvious that the war at sea was turning against them. The Australians had acquired long-range bombers for reconnaissance purposes, American warships were prowling the area, and a Swedish ship had reported sighting the German ships at Maug Island. Things went from bad to worse as the raider made the 10,000-mile, month-and-a-half journey to her new area of operations. Planned meetings with supply ships failed to take place as each in turn fell victim to increased British and Australian naval activity.

The days and weeks went by once again without sightings of any value to the raider. By the end of April, as she logged her 102,500th mile at sea, she cruised off the African coast to little effect. On May 3 the seaplane alerted the ship to a vessel 120 miles southwest of Madagascar. The *Orion* rushed to the scene to intercept the ship only to have her identify herself as the American freighter *Illinois* heading from Calcutta to Cape Town with 10,000 tons of jute. Prevented from a closer examination by German naval orders, the *Orion* moved off. One hour later her radio operator picked up the following message from the *Illinois*: "Calling everybody. Nothing new here." It was obviously a coded message that she had been approached by a German cruiser. At the end of the month the raider was ordered to move its operational area to the southeast corner of the Atlantic

Ocean. Captain Weyher hoped for better pickings there because there continued to be a lot of traffic in and out of South African ports.

Long isolated from the rest of the war, the men aboard the raider understood how it had changed when on June 22, 1942, they learned that German and allied forces had launched a large-scale attack against the Soviet Union. In the Atlantic the U-boat war continued with sixty-one sinkings reported. But improved radar was making life increasingly dangerous for submarines. The latest innovation allowed detection of a periscope from over 1,000 yards away.

Things had changed in the South Atlantic since the *Orion* had last sailed her waters. The Royal Navy had stepped up its activities across the entire ocean. With the *Orion* limping slowly along on worn-out engines and knocking bearings, there was nothing left to do but head home. Captain Weyher was told that if his fuel supplies made it unlikely that he could reach Bordeaux, he could put his ship in at either Dakar, which was controlled by the Vichy French, or the Spanish-owned Canary Islands.

Weyher had no intention of ending his ship's war cruise hiding in a French or Spanish port. He was determined to reach Bordeaux. He sought help from the *Atlantis*, a modern diesel-powered cruiser that could run for a year on the amount of oil the *Orion* consumed in a month.

On July 1 the two raiders met, and the *Atlantis* pumped 580 tons of fuel oil into the *Orion*, which was all she could spare because she was scheduled to remain at sea for several more months.

On July 29 a ship was sighted about 20 miles away. The raider ran on a parallel course while she attempted without luck to identify the nationality of the unknown vessel. When darkness finally descended and the object of everyone's attention failed to turn on any lights, they knew they had an enemy ship almost within their grasp. Tension filled the raider, and many men had difficulty keeping their excitement in check. After all, it had been eight months since they had last sent an enemy to the bottom.

The *Orion*'s final victim was the British freighter *Chaucer* of 5,792 tons. She was on her way to Buenos Aires, sailing in ballast. At first the *Chaucer* ignored the *Orion*'s warnings as the raider approached. She immediately began broadcasting that she was under attack. To make matters worse, her 40-mm Bofors gun opened fire in response and did some minor damage to the *Orion*. In the end, the forty-eight crewmen abandoned their sinking vessel and were taken prisoners. It required several torpedoes and more than 400 rounds of 150-mm ammunition to send her to her final resting place.

The *Orion* suffered from the vibration of her own guns. Rivets were popping out of place throughout the ship, the electrical system began to break down regularly, and the propeller shaft knocked worse than ever. Now she avoided any potential contact as fuel was conserved and she headed toward a rendezvous with two U-boats off the Azores. The meeting took place on August 16. The U-boats escorted her through the Bay of Biscay disguised as a Spanish vessel. Finally, stripped of all disguises and flying the German naval ensign, the *Orion* entered the Gironde and limped up river toward Bordeaux where she received a noisy and joyous reception from some old comrades. The horns aboard the *Regensburg*, the *Ermland*, and the *Ole Jakob* blasted the quiet night air in welcome. The *Orion* had sailed 127,337 miles, the equivalent of more than five times around the world. Even though her results, in terms of number of vessels and tonnage sunk, were not among the highest of the raiders, she must be remembered for the remarkable achievement of her endurance. Renamed the *Hektor*, she was sunk by an Allied bomber on May 4, 1945.

KMS *Widder*: May 5, 1940–October 31, 1940

1. *British Petrol*; 2. *Krossfonn*; 3. *Davisian*; 4. *King John*; 5. *Beaulieu*; 6. *Oostplein*; 7. *Killoran*; 8. *Anglo Saxon*; 9. *Cymberline*; 10. *Antonios Chandris*. Courtesy of K. Rochford.

3

WIDDER ————————————————

THE RAM

Almost as ill suited to her task as the *Orion* was her sister ship, *Widder*, also known as Ship 21. Unlike the *Orion*, the *Widder* did not roam the seas, but was restricted to the Central Atlantic. She succeeded in sinking nine ships and taking one as a prize. *Widder* has the infamous distinction of being the only disguised commerce raider whose captain was charged and brought to trial for war crimes. Captain Helmuth von Ruckteschell was one of only two German naval commanders convicted as war criminals.

Captain Ruckteschell habitually demonstrated a complete disregard for the lives and well-being of the seamen who became his prisoners, in direct contradiction to the practices of the other raider captains. They would often remain in dangerous waters to rescue men in the water from sunken vessels and then did all in their power to see that these prisoners were well treated and received medical care. Ruckteschell thought nothing of setting prisoners adrift in small boats many miles from the nearest land when he felt that his ship was carrying too many of them.

Ruckteschell rarely fired a warning shot across the bow of a ship he was targeting. The *Widder*'s first shots were usually aimed at the vessel's bridge, and generally resulted in a number of deaths and injuries before the ship's captain knew he was under attack.

By all accounts, Ruckteschell was a moody and introspective man whom the crew of the *Widder* found it difficult to like. He suffered from severe migraine headaches and a nervous stomach. Gaunt and graying, he was forty-nine when he took command of the *Widder*. Not inclined to explain the reasoning behind his decisions, his own officers often were in the dark concerning what drove him and what his plans were. Artistic by nature and highly cultured, Ruckteschell was an avid reader and lover of classical music. During World War I he earned a reputation as an overly aggressive U-boat commander. This landed him on a list of sub commanders the Allies considered to have breeched the customs of war.

In the years between the wars, he left Germany to avoid the harassment suffered by former submarine commanders at the hands of the victors. For several years he lived in Sweden and Lapland, earning a living as a lumberjack and a surveyor. Recalled to duty in 1939, he was placed in command of an auxiliary minelayer. Although no official records exist to support the charge, it was rumored that Ruckteschell kicked an enlisted man, an act that left him few friends in the naval command structure.

The *Widder* had originally been the *Neumark* of the Hamburg-Amerika Line, a 7,851-ton freighter built by Howaldtswerke in Kiel in 1930. Converted to a raider in 1939 by Blohm & Voss, she was completed at the end of November. Her early trials gave an indication of how troublesome her power plant would be. The poor results delayed her departure until the following May.

On May 6, 1940, the *Widder* left German waters and headed up the Norwegian coast. It was exactly one month earlier that the *Orion* made the same trip. Unlike the *Orion*, which made the voyage during the peak of German and Allied operations along Norway's coast, these waters were now considered safer because they were almost completely under German control. Despite this, Ruckteschell had his crew remain at battle stations during the first night. It turned out to be a wise decision, for during that night a British submarine was sighted approaching the raider and her patrol boat escorts. The sub managed to fire two torpedoes at the raider before she was driven off by the escorts. The following day a second submarine approached, but was quickly chased away by the patrol boats. On the third day, May 8, the raider entered the harbor at Bergen and began the job of altering her appearance.

While this work was being done, the government of British Prime Minister Neville Chamberlain fell over the conduct of the war in Norway. Winston Churchill was selected to replace him.

On May 12, disguised as the Swedish freighter *Narvik*, the *Widder* left Bergen and continued her trip north to the Denmark Strait. The following day she encountered yet another British submarine. This time it was the famous HMS *Clyde*. The sub was running on the surface for some unknown reason when she was sighted by one of the *Widder*'s lookouts. Both ships fired a few rounds at each other as the raider turned away. The *Clyde* gave chase for about a half hour, but then gave up and disappeared in a rain squall. Why she did not take more aggressive action against the German ship is not known. As for the *Widder*, many of her crewmen were beginning to feel that she was a lucky ship, having survived three encounters with enemy submarines without any damage.

The raider made her way through the Strait and moved west along the polar ice pack, and then south toward her operational area. Just as her sister *Orion*, *Widder* consumed huge amounts of fuel oil and had to refuel from the supply ship *Nordmark* before reaching the Atlantic.

By the first week of June she was situated directly on the shipping route between Trinidad and the Azores, a heavily-traveled route in peace or war. Steaming along at 8 knots so as to conserve fuel, the *Widder* moved westward in hopes of encountering ships sailing out of Trinidad or even the Panama Canal. According to the ship's log, she reached the eastern edge of the neutrality zone, into which she was strictly prohibited from entering, when she reversed course and began patrolling the waters a safe distance from the zone that ran south along the American coast.

About 9:30 A.M. on June 13, a lookout reported seeing smoke on the eastern horizon. The raider, still in her disguise as a Swedish freighter, approached as if to pass the vessel at a safe distance. The oncoming ship was the *British Petrol*, a 7,000-ton tanker sailing in ballast for Trinidad, where she was to pick up a supply of oil. As the *Widder* drew closer, the tanker remained on course and took no evasive action. When the two vessels came within 6,000 yards of each other, the *Widder* suddenly, and without any warning, fired three salvos into the tanker. Two members of the crew were killed instantly as the bridge blew apart and burst into flames. Meanwhile, the raider's radio operator listened for any possible message from the tanker, prepared to jam it, but there was no message. The radio room had been among the first places destroyed in the shelling. Within minutes the tanker began to flounder, and the surviving crewmen started to lower her lifeboats. After the tanker's crew had been picked up, she was quickly sent to the bottom with a single torpedo. The *Widder* had made her first kill.

The following day Paris fell to the German army, and General Wilhelm Ritter von Leeb's Army Group C smashed through the vaunted Maginot Line. In the Mediterranean, French warships shelled the Italian ports of Genoa and Vado.

Four days later a large freighter was spotted steaming west. Ruckteschell kept his distance while he attempted to identify the vessel. Finally, fearing that it was an American ship and therefore not a potential target, he slipped away unseen. He did not want the American to see him and possibly alert the Royal Navy to his presence.

On June 24 the *Widder*'s aircraft, a Heinkel He 114B, made its last flight without sighting any enemy ships. On its return, the engine ceased functioning, and it was never able to be repaired. This left the *Widder* without eyes to search beyond the horizon. As with most of the float planes assigned to the disguised raiders, this one never lived up to its expectations. The aircraft were supposed to serve two major functions. First was to locate and identify ships that could be potential targets. The second was to keep a sharp lookout for enemy naval warships. Such ships, especially destroyers, were substantially faster than the *Widder*, and the latter risked its own destruction if it did not see the enemy long before they caught sight of her and gave chase. The raiders were heavily armed for combat against commercial vessels, even armed commercial vessels, but they were not real warships and lacked the armor plating needed to defend against the heavy shell fire of a destroyer or a cruiser. Without the use of a reconnaissance aircraft, Ruckteschell's area of vision was extremely limited.

To make matters worse, the following day it was discovered that the intake valves had become clogged with salt. The raider had to stop and remain without power for six hours while the engine room crew cleaned the valves. While this was being done, the radio room received a message that a Norwegian tanker, the *Sticklestad*, was in the area. She was sailing from Casablanca to Martinique. Ruckteschell was frustrated by his inability to seek out and destroy a target that had been identified for him by naval headquarters. He paced the bridge angrily until the repairs had been completed.

Shortly after the repairs had been done and the ship was prepared to resume her cruise, a lookout announced that a ship was approaching. Captain Ruckteschell watched her through his glasses and clearly saw a tanker sailing in ballast. He assumed that it was the *Sticklestad*, which was probably going to Martinique for a load of oil. He allowed the ship to pass astern of his raider, then uncharacteristically fired a warning shot. The tanker immediately came to a halt and made no attempt to radio for help.

The German boarding party discovered to their surprise that the tanker was not the *Sticklestad*, but another Norwegian tanker, the *Krossfonn* of 9,323 tons. The catch was almost as satisfying, for she was also out of Casablanca and heading to Martinique for oil. Ruckteschell decided that she would make a useful prize, so instead of sinking her, he sent her to Brest, newly occupied by German forces, to serve the Reich. Before doing so, he filled her tanks with seawater. This was intended to fool any passing Royal Navy warship into believing that she was heading to England with a shipment of oil. An empty tanker sailing toward Europe was almost certain to attract suspicion.

Keeping to the edge of the neutrality zone, the *Widder* kept up her hunt. Fed up with efforts to repair the ship's aircraft, Ruckteschell ordered that the plane's highly flammable fuel be dumped overboard. This was followed by about 200 bombs that were now totally useless without an airplane to drop them. The gas and the bombs were potential hazards if they were struck by enemy fire, so the disposal of them was for safety's sake.

On July 7 a Spanish freighter was stopped and boarded. Her papers identified her as the *Motomar*, traveling from New York to Rio with a load of manufactured goods and agricultural machinery. She was allowed to continue on her way.

> During the night of July 7, the German battleship *Richelieu* was damaged in an attack by a British commando unit while in Dakar Harbor. The next day additional damage was inflicted by a British torpedo bomber.

Three days later a heavily loaded freighter was sighted bearing down on the raider from the east. The 6,433-ton British-owned *Davisian* was carrying 4,000 tons of coal and 2,000 tons of chemicals for delivery at Barbados, Trinidad, and Grenada. T. J. Harrison, the freighter's captain, had no warning that the freighter he was approaching was an enemy warship until the latter opened fire. The first few salvos ripped away the *Davisian*'s antenna, preventing her from calling for help. Others smashed into the ship causing explosions and fires. Unable to defend himself against the *Widder* with a single antiquated 4-inch gun mounted on the stern, the *Davisian*'s crew was ordered to abandon the ship. What happened next has never been settled. According to one of the *Davisian*'s officers, John H. Jolly, the freighter signaled the *Widder* that she was being abandoned. Jolly claimed the raider continued firing into the vessel for another eight minutes after the signal was sent. In the German version of the incident, no such signal was received. In addition, several seamen were seen running toward the *Davisian*'s gun mount in an obvious attempt to bring it into action. These men were fired on and the decks swept by machine-gun fire as a result.

The result was that three of the *Davisian*'s crew were killed and a half dozen others were wounded. After removing as much foodstuff and tobacco as possible from the freighter, it was sunk by a single torpedo from the *Widder*.

There were now 100 prisoners aboard the raider. Her sick bay was full of wounded and ill seamen from the *Widder*'s first three victims.

On July 13 another freighter was sighted steaming west. As the British-owned 5,228-ton *King John* approached, she was fired on, probably as a warning to stop. She immediately began broadcasting an alert that she was under attack. Fortunately for the raider, the freighter's radio operator made a 150-mile mistake when he gave his ship's location. In response, the raider opened fire with several salvos. The bridge, in which the radio room was located, was heavily damaged, and live shells the freighter was carrying were hit and started several fires. Three men were killed in the firing and several more wounded. Another fifty-nine prisoners were added to the *Widder*'s collection.

This was far more than Captain Ruckteschell felt comfortable with. Especially bothersome to him were the twenty-one survivors from a Panamanian ship, the *Santa Marguerita*, which had been sunk earlier by a U-boat and rescued by the *King John*. He described this mixed group of Yugoslavs, Maltese, Portugese, and Spaniards as "dirty and lousy."

Ruckteschell now took an action that would have far-reaching repercussions. He put forty members of the *Davisian*'s crew and the men taken from the *King John*, with the exception of the captain, the chief engineer, and the wounded, into lifeboats. He gave them directions to the Lesser Antilles, some 240 miles away, along with supplies, and turned them loose.

The boats made landings on the seventeenth and the eighteenth, and reported all they had seen while aboard the raider. These were the first clear descriptions of a German disguised raider the British Admiralty had received. With over a dozen ships missing and presumed sunk, the British commander of the West Indies Station, Admiral Sir Charles Kennedy-Purvis, ordered a halt to all ships sailing independently, and altered the routes taken by convoys. He then sent every available warship under his command to search for the *Widder*.

Finding a single ship in the vast Atlantic was extremely difficult in those days. It was made more difficult in this case by the fact the seamen in the lifeboats reported that the *Widder* steamed north when they had been released, so this was where the warships concentrated their efforts. In fact, Ruckteschell did head north until the boats were out of sight, when he turned directly east and steamed away at maximum speed. He then took the precaution of altering the ship's appearance and identity. She was now the Spanish freighter *El Neptuno*.

It was time for a brief meeting with the tanker *Rekum* to refuel. After taking on 1,465 tons of oil and being disappointed by the fact that the *Rekum* had no fresh vegetables to pass along, the *Widder* returned to the hunt.

On August 4, an empty tanker was seen sailing toward the West Indies. During the daylight hours, the raider trailed behind the tanker, carefully staying just over the horizon. Evidently no one on board the 6,114-ton Norwegian tanker *Beaulieu* ever caught sight of the *Widder*, for she took no evasive action and did not radio for help. During the night the *Widder* slipped up to within 2,500 yards of the tanker, still unseen. The tanker made it easy for the raider to keep track of her because someone had carelessly left a door ajar through which an interior light could be seen on the otherwise blacked out vessel. Without warning the *Widder* opened fire, raking the unsuspecting vessel with shells. The captain and three crewmen were killed, but the remaining crew took to the boats and disappeared in the darkness.

A boarding party was sent to the crippled tanker to remove anything of value along with any surviving crewmen still aboard. Ruckteschell was later accused of disregarding the safety of the men in the boats. His defense was that he expected anyone who wished to be rescued to approach the boarding party boat. He also claimed to remain at the site for more than two hours, searching for survivors, although this may have been done under pressure from his own officers who claimed the raider's crewmen were complaining about leaving seamen in lifeboats in the middle of the ocean. The boats meanwhile beat a hasty retreat from the *Beaulieu*, evidently choosing a dangerous escape to imprisonment.

Any ship's ability to rescue seamen in lifeboats can be hampered by the victims themselves. When the potential rescuer is from the enemy ship that sank their vessel, the men in the lifeboats might not be anxious to be saved and made prisoners, as has often been the case. The rescue party runs the additional risk of survivors concealing small arms and preferring to fight rather than be rescued. In such a case the lives of the rescuers are endangered beyond that normally encountered by rescuers in the swells of the ocean. The charge brought against Ruckteschell after the war regarding the survivors of the *Beaulieu* resulted in one of the three guilty verdicts of the court. But, the confirming officer refused to uphold the verdict concerning the *Beaulieu* survivors and reduced the sentence of the court from ten to seven years.

The survivors were eventually picked up by the British tanker *Cymbeline* and taken to Gibraltar where they reported the attack. As for the *Beaulieu*, it quickly slipped below the waves after members of the *Widder*'s crew set a series of charges in her. Ruckteschell then turned his ship toward the busy shipping lanes that pass through the Azores.

It was close to noon on August 8, close to the Azores, when a lookout reported sighting a ship on the horizon. The *Widder* slowly moved away from the approaching vessel and slipped over the horizon to remain out of sight. It then began to trail what was later identified as the 5,059-ton Dutch freighter *Oostplein*. She had sailed from Cardiff with nearly 6,000 tons of coal and coke for Buenos Aires.

The *Widder* kept an eye on her target during the long afternoon, being careful once again to keep to the horizon with as small a profile as possible. When night finally darkened the sky, she moved into a position that put the *Oostplein* between her and the moon, silhouetting the target as clearly as if a spotlight were on her. Closing the range, the raider came to within 3,500 yards and then opened fire, again without issuing a warning. Though most of the shells missed their target, about a half dozen impacted near the bow of the freighter and caused several fires that burned out of control. When the distance between the two ships reached about 2,000 yards, the heavier weapons on board the raider stopped firing and the work was taken over by the lighter antiaircraft guns. Their primary targets were the bridge and the freighter's stern mounted gun.

With their ship burning beyond their control, and the enemy raking her decks with gunfire, the thirty-four crewmen on board the *Oostplein* had little choice but to take to her lifeboats. They lowered two lifeboats and clambered aboard. A short time later all were picked up by the *Widder*, and the freighter was sunk by a single torpedo. According to an entry in his log, Ruckteschell might not have taken the Dutchman's crew aboard but for the SOS signal sent from one of the boats. He also noted the success he was having with the night attacks, but was dismayed over the high level of fuel required to trail a target during the day to launch an attack after dark.

Three days later the *Widder* came on an old three-masted sailing barque flying the colors of neutral Finland. Two warning shots brought the sailing ship to a halt and a boarding party was sent to check her papers. She proved to be the *Killoran* of 1,800 tons. She was carrying 2,500 tons of maize and 500 tons of sugar, and had sailed from Buenos Aires for Las Palmas. Everything was in order, with the single exception that the ship's agent and the owner of the cargo were both British. As a result, the eighteen-man crew was taken aboard the raider and the ship sunk.

About this time, Ruckteschell began a program of training some members of the deck crew to work in the engine room. The engine room crews had been working almost without relief since the voyage started, nursing the ship's power plant to keep the ship going. They were having much the same difficulty as the engine room crew aboard the *Orion*. A weak power plant and a high rate of bearing failure caused the *Widder* to regularly stop in mid-ocean and drift for several hours while repairs or preventive maintenance was performed. Using men from the deck crew gave those below some relief to breathe fresh air and rest. Much as his counterpart on the *Orion* did, Captain Ruckteschell freely vented his frustrations in his war diary about the kind of ship he was given to use as a raider. "A steamship for this purpose," he wrote, "is and remains foolishness." He was correct of course. The ideal commerce raider was a sleek, fast motor vessel, not a sluggish steamship that required a long period of time to get up to speed and consumed enormous amounts of fuel oil. To this was added the delay caused when a boiler had to be shut down during repairs. It generally took as long as twelve hours for the steam pressure to reach a level to make the boiler useful for powering the ship. But, the German Navy was stuck using what was available and could be converted for wartime use.

The *Widder*'s next encounter, and the actions taken by her captain, proved to be Ruckteschell's undoing. The ship was the *Anglo Saxon*, a British freighter of 5,596 tons. The two met on August 21, 1940, not far from where the *Oostplein* had been sunk. For the raider it was the usual situation. The freighter was sighted during the day, so the *Widder* dropped over the horizon and waited as the freighter gradually drew closer. According to the raider's meteorologist, it would not be completely dark until 8:00, but the moon would rise at 8:18, leaving an eighteen-minute window for the attack.

The raider maneuvered into a position that put both vessels on opposite courses, and at exactly 8:08 in pitch black darkness she opened fire on the unsuspecting ship. At that point there was only 2,500 yards between them. One of the first targets was the gun mounted on her stern, which was hit in the first salvo. Also hit was the weapon's supply of ammunition, which exploded and set the stern ablaze. As the freighter's decks were swept by gunfire, a torpedo was fired into her hull and she quickly exploded and sank. In the darkness two lights were seen to flash back and forth, which the German's took to be two lifeboats signaling each other.

> The day before, the war at sea was altered by the announcement that North American British naval bases would be leased to the United States for use by the still neutral U.S. Navy. This could only mean increased naval activity by the pro-British Americans.

Then Ruckteschell made a mistake that cost him dearly. Instead of looking for the lifeboats, he ignored them and left the scene. He noted rather cavalierly that they were "only 800 miles from the Canaries," and they had the added advantage of favorable winds. One of the boats vanished without a trace, the other managed to reach the Bahamas seventy days later. Of the eight men originally on board this boat, only two survived to tell of their terrible ordeal. Although he could not be located to appear at Ruckteschell's trial, one of those survivors, Seamen Robert G. Tapscott, reported that the raider had fired at the lifeboats in an obvious effort to eliminate the survivors. Ruckteschell denied the charge. If anyone had fired at the lifeboats, he claimed, it was accidental. Although found guilty of this charge, it is hard to believe that the sailors manning the guns would knowingly fire at men in lifeboats, especially when we know that the crew was already complaining about their captain firing into vessels without first warning them, and his occasional failure to search more diligently for survivors. Every sailor, no matter what nation he represents, wants to believe that if his ship is sunk, someone, even an enemy, will rescue him from the sea.

During the afternoon of August 26, two ships were sighted at almost the same time. One was a freighter and the other a tanker. Ruckteschell decided on the tanker, but it proved to be too fast for him to catch. By the time he turned to pursue the freighter, it had gained a wide margin and also proved to be too fast for the raider to catch.

The *Widder* continued to cruise within her operational area, regularly forced to stop for repairs. Her time was drawing to a close, and her captain and probably most if not all her crew recognized this. Breakdowns were increasing each week, and there were times when she could make no more than 7 or 8 knots, a speed that meant that nearly everything on the sea could escape her.

Early on September 2 a tanker was sighted sailing in ballast for the West Indies. She was making about 12 knots, and as luck would have it, the boilers aboard the raider were working and she could actually catch her target. But, given the space between them, the captain realized that the tanker would have plenty of time to send out detailed radio signals if he suddenly turned in her direction and gave chase. Instead he waited until she was out of sight and then set his ship on the same course.

With all boilers working, the raider was able to make 14 knots, so she eventually caught up with the tanker a few minutes after 8:00 that night. At 2,600 yards' distance the *Widder* fired a star shell over the tanker and opened fire on her. The first salvo struck a boiler that exploded and covered the entire stern section in steam, making it impossible for anyone to man the gun mounted there. Following the explosion the raider ceased firing, but quickly resumed when the tanker's radio was heard to be broadcasting an SOS. Consequently the bridge was destroyed and those inside it killed.

Running a searchlight along the burning ship's hull, the Germans could read the name *Cymbeline*. She was of 6,317 tons and out of Liverpool, and had on her earlier voyage picked up the crew of the *Beaulieu* and taken them to Gibraltar. For some reason, perhaps under pressure from his own crew, Ruckteschell remained at the scene for four hours searching for survivors. Twenty-six men were rescued of the thirty-six man crew. Among the missing was the tanker's captain. A torpedo finally sent the burning hulk down. Actually, the tanker's captain, J. A. Chadwick, along with his first officer and third engineer managed to escape the scene in a lifeboat and were picked up fourteen days later by a tanker heading to South America.

> The next day, Hitler's headquarters approved the plans developed for the invasion of England. The invasion was scheduled for September 21.

During the next few days the raider was in its most vulnerable condition, engines shut down for repairs and adrift. The port engine was out of commission and every moving part in the power system seemed to be rattling or scraping against something. Many of the men began to wonder if she would be able to make it home.

The *Widder*'s final victim appeared during the night of September 8. She was the Greek tanker *Antonios Chandris* of 5,866 tons. In her holds were more than 6,000 tons of coal from Cardiff being taken to Buenos Aires. When a star shell was fired over her and she was signaled to stop, the freighter did as directed. A boarding party removed what foodstuffs they could transport back to the raider and set explosive charges throughout the vessel. The crew was put into the freighter's lifeboats to fend for themselves. Ruckteschell described the boats as "well founded," and added that they would have plenty of water because it was raining. With the crew sent on their way, the freighter was blown up and sank.

Later that month the *Widder* received a fresh supply of oil and additional provisions, but the war was over for her. Barely able to make 7 knots and hold together, she sailed for home, which in this case was the German-occupied French port at Brest. They arrived there on October 31, 1940. In six months she had sunk nine ships, taken one as a prize, and contributed enormously to the overall goal of creating chaos in the shipping lanes used by the Allies. For his reward, Ruckteschell was appointed as commander of another raider several months later, the *Michel*. As for the *Widder*, her armaments were removed and sent for the most part for use aboard the *Michel*. With the war's end the British took possession of her, renaming her the *Ulysses*. Later she was sold to a German shipping company and served as the freighter *Eichenheim*.

KMS *Thor*: First Cruise, June 6, 1940–April 30, 1941

1. *Kertosono*; 2. *Dalambre*; 3. *Bruges*; 4. *Gracefield*; 5. *Wendover*; 6. *Tela*; 7. Battle with HMS AMC *Alcantara*; 8. *Kosmos*; 9. *Natio*; 10. Battle with HMS AMC *Carnarvon Castle*; 11. *Trollenholm*; 12. *Britannia*; 13. HMS AMC *Voltaire*; 14. *Sir Ernest Cassel*. Courtesy of K. Rochford.

4

THOR ─────────────────

DEADLY BANANA BOAT

July 1940. The number of overdue cargo ships in the South Atlantic was increasing. This was a major concern for Rear Admiral Henry Harwood, the Royal Navy officer responsible for protecting Allied shipping in the area. Aboard the light cruiser *Hawkins* stationed off the coast of Brazil, Harwood received notices of overdue ships and copies of intercepts of German naval radio traffic. Both the notices and German radio traffic indicated that enemy raiders were active in the South Atlantic.

One disturbing message Harwood received concerned a group of seamen from several British vessels who had arrived in a number of small boats at the British West Indies island of Anguilla on July 17 and 18. The men reported that their ships had been sunk by a German raider disguised as a neutral freighter. They claimed that they had been set adrift by the raider's captain because there were too many prisoners for his ship to accommodate. The raider was the *Widder*.

Using the information provided by the seamen, Admiral Harwood surmised that the raider was working its way south. He ordered the Armed Merchant Cruiser *Alcantara* to search for the raider. Armed Merchant Cruisers were civilian passenger and cargo vessels that had been hastily converted for wartime use. These conversions were usually little more than placing antiquated guns on the ships and manning them with navy crews. Many of the guns were left over from World War I. The 22,209-ton *Alcantara* had formerly been a Royal Mail passenger liner. Her main armaments were eight

6-inch guns and two 3-inch guns as well as a selection of lighter antiaircraft weapons. The AMCs were a far cry from a man-of-war, but they still remained formidable foes for anything less than a full-blown warship.

At about 9:00 A.M. on Sunday, July 28, with clear skies and a calm sea, the *Alcantara* located an unidentified ship off the coast of Argentina. The stranger reacted to the *Alcantara*'s approach in a way that made the AMC's captain J.G.P. Ingham, suspicious. At a distance of 28,000 yards the other ship turned and sped away at what Ingham guessed was a speed of about 17 knots. Because his own ship could reach 19 knots, Captain Ingham placed the *Alcantara* directly on the other vessel's wake and went to full speed. It was only a matter of time before even the slight difference in speed would allow the cruiser to close on her target.

Aboard the other vessel, which was the German commerce raider *Thor*, disguised as the Yugoslav ship *Vir*, alarm gongs called all hands to their battle stations. The captains of the disguised raiders were under orders to avoid contact with enemy warships at all reasonable cost, so the *Thor* was doing as ordered. A sea battle with an enemy warship was considered counterproductive to a raider's twin missions of sinking cargo ships and disrupting the transportation of supplies vital to the Allied war effort.

The two ships sped across the ocean's surface for several hours. As each hour passed, the *Alcantara* gradually drew closer to the *Thor*. When the distance between them was reduced to 20,000 yards, the *Alcantara* sent a coded radio message that was not understood by the raider's radio operators, but was partially jammed by them. The Germans correctly surmised that the ship speeding after them had been signaling other ships in the area of its actions.

A few minutes before noon, with the enemy ship now less than 15,000 yards directly astern, the raider captain decided he had no choice but to fight. He was not about to outrun what he could now clearly see was a British Armed Merchant Cruiser. He also feared being trapped between the AMC and other British warships that might be approaching from other directions.

At 12:57 the raider reduced speed to 15 knots and began quickly turning so as to fire a broadside at the approaching enemy. At almost the same moment the *Alcantara*'s signal light requested the identity of the vessel it was pursuing, the German naval ensign bearing the swastika was raised on the *Thor*'s mast.

The *Thor*'s answer to the *Alcantara*'s question came at once from the raider's four guns broadside. The *Alcantara* also turned so that she could respond with her own broadside. By now both ships were less than 14,000 yards apart. The German gunners had the advantage of having the sun at their backs, while the British gunners were forced to aim and fire into the afternoon's glaring sun. *Thor* fired two more salvos in quick succession.

Aboard the cruiser, Ingham received reports of several hits including one that disabled his number four gun and another that damaged the engine. The latter caused his ship's speed to slow dramatically. When their fire control system was damaged by another shell, the British gunners continued to fire independently at the enemy. The loss of the fire control system was a severe handicap for the British gunners, who now had to rely on their own judgment of the enemy's range while at the same time loading, aiming, and firing their guns. One of the *Alcantara*'s shells passed through the raider's hull. Although it failed to explode, its impact damaged a forward gun ammunition hoist, temporarily putting the gun out of action. Another shell exploded when it smashed against the raider's boat deck. In addition to killing three men, the explosion damaged the fire control system for the *Thor*'s torpedo tubes, making it impossible for the raider to fire torpedoes at the cruiser.

The smallest of the disguised commerce raiders, the *Thor* was originally the 3,144-ton banana boat *Santa Cruz*, owned by the Oldenburg-Portuguesische Line. She was also the only disguised raider to successfully complete two tours at sea. During the 1930s the German Navy subsidized several Central American banana plantations in order to have fruit ships built by German companies that could later be quickly converted to wartime use. Banana and other fresh fruit ships enjoyed two distinct advantages as commerce raiders. They were faster than most other merchant ships, and because they were small and sat low in the water, they offered a small target for enemy gunners.

One other characteristic distinguished the *Thor* from her sister commerce raiders aside from her low profile and a top speed of 17 knots, the latter being exceeded by only one other raider, the *Kormoran*. At 379.9 feet she was the shortest raider with the exception of the *Komet*. Her war record was outstanding. By the time the raider war ended, the *Thor* sank eighteen enemy vessels, an accomplishment equaled by only one other raider, the *Michel*. She took four enemy ships as prizes, a number beaten only by the *Pinguin*, whose total included a large number of whaling boats. Her total of 653 days at sea was unmatched by any other disguised raider. But by far the *Thor*'s crowning achievements were the successful battles she waged against three British Armed Merchant Cruisers.

In a move that recognized the strength of the Luftwaffe in attacking British warships in the English Channel, the Admiralty announced on July 28 that all destroyers were withdrawn from the Channel between Dover and Portsmouth.

The *Thor*'s captain for her first cruise was Otto Kahler. A twenty-five-year veteran of the German navy, Kahler was forty-five years old when he took command of the former banana boat in October of 1939. Tall and well built with a square face sporting a thick Vandyke beard, he was a practical man who remained cool in the most trying situations. During World War I, Kahler served in Germany's U-boat fleet. Between the wars, his career led him to both sea duty and shore stations. His sea duties included command of the two sailing ships Germany used for training purposes. Kahler also commanded the navy's fast patrol boat fleet. He went from this post directly to command of the *Thor*. He was an avid cigar smoker who was routinely seen on deck chomping on one of his "stogies." Kahler was one of those sailors who had the sea in his blood. His father had served as the captain of a merchant ship. Kahler's superior seamanship and his manner with subordinates and prisoners earned him the respect of the *Thor*'s crew.

The *Thor* and the *Alcantara* continued to fire at each other. Kahler soon realized that he had the advantage of speed as the AMC gradually slowed, so he began to pull away from the cruiser. By 1:30 the ships were too far apart for their guns to be effective, and the shooting ceased. The crews of both vessels were busy fighting fires and repairing damage caused by the shelling. With the enemy out of range and soon to be out of sight, Captain Ingham turned his damaged vessel around to limp back to its base. Once out of the cruiser's sight, Kahler ordered his crew to change the raider's appearance just in case he was approached by another British warship. By now he was sure that the cruiser had radioed a description of the *Thor* to other warships in the area. The wounded were tended to and the dead given proper military burial at sea.

In his report on the action, Kahler indicated that he would have liked to turn and attack the badly wounded cruiser and perhaps finish her off. It would have certainly been a glorious kill for the raider, but Kahler allowed his better judgment to rule. Had he returned to the *Alcantara*, which was severely damaged and temporarily incapacitated, one lucky shot by the British gunners through the right section of the *Thor*'s thin hull might have sent her to the bottom in a series of mine and ammunition explosions.

The *Thor* began her first cruise on June 6, 1940. She steamed out of the naval base at Kiel and headed north for the cover of bad weather. She was escorted by a small armada of warships that included destroyers and minesweepers and even had that rarity, Luftwaffe air cover. At the time, the Allies were busy withdrawing more than 24,000 British and French troops from Harstad in Northern Norway. Because the raider would have to pass through the same area, there was some concern that the *Thor* might be intercepted by British warships escorting the troop carriers home.

The weather was terrible. The route through the northern reaches of the Norwegian Sea was comprised of constant fog and endless snow. It was ideal weather for a raider to sneak through, which the *Thor* did without incident. Disguised as the Soviet freighter *Orsk* sailing from Odessa, the raider reached the open seas of the North Atlantic on June 16. After passing south of the

Azores the following week, she altered her identity to that of the *Vir* out of the Yugoslav port of Split.

It was in that disguise that the *Thor* came on her first victim on July 1, 1940. Sailing from the Carribean to Freetown with a cargo of asphalt, machinery, and gasoline, was the Dutch freighter *Kertosono*. Totally unarmed, the freighter could do nothing but stop when ordered to do so by the raider. A warning shot fired across her bow aided the decision. Kahler concluded that the cargo and the ship were worth saving, so he put a prize crew aboard with instructions to head to France. The ship arrived in the German occupied port at Lorient on July 12.

On July 7, shortly after the *Thor* crossed the equator, a ship was seen off the port-bow as she turned away in an apparent attempt not to subject herself to the approaching stranger. For two hours the raider gave chase, gradually drawing closer to the other ship until at about 8,000 yards' distance Kahler ordered a broadside fired at her. The first two salvos fell short, but the third found its mark, and the British-owned *Delambra*, 7,032 tons, carrying hides and cotton intended for Liverpool, stopped. After a thorough inspection of the vessel, the forty-four members of the crew and the ship's single passenger, all British, were transported to the *Thor*. The freighter was sunk with a series of demolition charges.

Two days later it was the turn of the Belgian freighter *Bruges*. The 4,983-ton cargo vessel was transporting nearly 7,000 tons of wheat to Freetown when she had the misfortune to encounter the *Thor*. The crew of forty-four men was taken to the raider and their ship sent to the bottom.

> Overnight the battleship *Richelieu* was attacked and damaged by British forces while in Dakar Harbor. The following night the damage was increased by a torpedo from an aircraft flying off the aircraft carrier *Hermes*.

As the last few moments of daylight were receding over the western horizon on July 14, the *Thor* came on yet another British freighter. This time it was the 4,631-ton *Gracefield* sailing from Montevideo with more than 7,000 tons of wheat and bran. A shot across her bow convinced her Captain Brimmer to bring his vessel to a halt. A German boarding party sent her thirty-six member crew back to the raider. Once the freighter was abandoned and any documents the German's thought might be of value were removed, two torpedoes were fired at the *Gracefield*. One badly damaged her while a second failed to hit the stationary target, instead it circled the ship until it ran out of fuel. Several well-placed shells finally sent all that grain and the vessel down.

Two days later the *Thor*'s lookouts spotted a ship trailing a large plume of smoke from its funnel. The vessel, which was the British-owned *Wendover* of 5,489 tons, was heading toward Buenos Aires with a full cargo of coal. Concealing his raider in the smoke trail behind the freighter, Kahler pulled up to within firing range. It was then he noted that the freighter had two guns mounted on her stern for defense. He decided that it would be prudent to avoid a battle, so instead of warning the freighter, he fired several salvos at her. One hit near the stern and started a fire. In response to the attack, the *Wendover*'s radio operator began broadcasting an alert that his ship was under attack by a raider. In addition, several of the *Thor*'s crewmen reported seeing a man running toward one of the stern guns, evidently bent on returning fire.

Unfortunately for the *Wendover*'s radio operator, his bravery cost him his life. Another round of shells was fired by the *Thor*'s 5.9-inch guns. One made a direct hit on the radio room, silencing the freighter's call for help.

With several fires now spreading throughout his vessel, the *Wendover*'s captain had no choice but to slow to a stop and order his crew to abandon the ship. Seeing this, Kahler ordered a cease-fire. He then sent a boarding party to investigate and set demolition charges in the hull of the wounded freighter. The charges caused the *Wendover* to turn completely over so that only her hull was exposed above the water, but she did not sink. This had to be accomplished by a final shell from one of the *Thor*'s guns. Thirty-eight members of *Wendover*'s crew of forty were rescued. The remaining two, including the radio operator, were killed in the shelling. Two others, wounded during the shelling, died of their injuries while aboard the *Thor* despite the German medical staff's best efforts to save them. The two were buried at sea with full military honors, as was the custom on most raiders when an enemy seaman died.

The following day, July 17, 1940, yet another ship was sighted and sunk. This was the Dutch freighter *Tela*, carrying 5,451 tons of grain destined for England. In this case it took a simple shot across her bow to stop her. Her crew of thirty-three men was transferred to the increasingly crowded *Thor*, and the *Tela* was sunk.

In seventeen days she sank six ships totaling 35,201 tons. One consequence of this was the severe overcrowding of prisoners, who now numbered 194.

For ten days following the sinking of the *Tela*, the *Thor* remained in the same general area of the South Atlantic. She steamed parallel to the Brazilian coast without sighting another ship. Life on board the raider was settling down to a routine for both crewmen and prisoners. Each day the accumulated British, Arabian, Dutch, and Belgian seamen and officers were awakened at 6:00 A.M. After washing and eating breakfast, they stood roll call at 9:00 A.M., and then were allowed on deck in shifts of sixty to seventy each to breathe some fresh air and enjoy the sun.

Their luck held out on the morning of July 28. When the *Thor* encountered the British AMC *Alcantara*, it took a decided turn for the worse. Not too long after the unknown ship was brought to Captain Kahler's attention, he surmised that there was a strong possibility it was a British Armed Merchant

Cruiser searching for his raider. Reminding himself of the standing order to avoid a battle with any enemy warship, even an AMC, he turned his raider away and attempted to elude the approaching vessel. Shortly before noon, Kahler calculated the enemy's speed and knew that the raider would soon be within range of the British ship's guns. His only option was to turn and fight and hope to cripple the enemy enough to allow him to escape. Kahler gave the order to fire a broadside.

After the battle left the British Cruiser badly damaged and momentarily idle in the water, Kahler raced away south as fast as he could. With repairs being made, the best speed the raider could do was 5 knots over the next few days, but it was better than waiting around for additional British warships to arrive. Work parties labored around the clock, and, at the same time, the Captain allowed the engineers to conduct some badly needed boiler maintenance.

On August 25, the *Thor* made a scheduled rendezvous with the supply tanker *Rekum*. A month earlier the tanker had replenished the fuel supply for the *Widder*, but had disappointed the crew because it carried no fresh fruit. Now it was the turn of the *Thor*'s crew to be disappointed over the lack of fresh produce.

The next month passed without incident, other than the stopping and inspection of a Yugoslavian ship. Yugoslavia was a neutral, and the freighter carried no British-owned goods, so the ship, the *Federico Glavic*, was allowed to proceed. Kahler made extensive use of his spotter plane, an Arado 196A-1, sending it aloft every day that weather permitted.

Finally, on September 26, the Arado found a Norwegian ship. One hour later the *Thor* fired two shots across the bow of the whale oil tanker *Kosmos*, bringing her to an immediate halt. At 17,801 tons, she was the largest vessel yet taken by the *Thor*. Her cargo, 17,662 tons of whale oil, loaded while she acted as a whaling factory ship, was an extremely valuable prize. Ordinarily, Captain Kahler would have either sent her to a German-occupied French port with a prize crew, or used her as a supply ship for his and the other raiders in the Atlantic. One serious problem existed that led him to decide to sink her. She was due at her destination, Curaçao, in a short time. Her failure to arrive there, or report the reason for her delay, would be reported to the Royal Navy authorities who would then alert British warships to keep a sharp eye for her and her valuable cargo. Because of the unusual configuration of her two large funnels, set side by side instead of the customary one behind the other, the *Kosmos* would prove virtually impossible to disguise as another ship.

Kahler did not want to send the ship and her oil to the bottom of the ocean, but he had to weigh his options carefully. He finally arrived at his painful decision to sink the tanker after deciding that the vessel had little hope of reaching Europe without being stopped and taken by a British warship. On the other hand, those two funnels would prevent her from staying out in the ocean as a supply ship without being seen and identified, no matter what the Germans did to disguise her. Either way, the odds, as the Captain saw them, were great that she would fall back into the hands of the enemy and that the oil would be used against Germany.

Given these facts, as he saw them, he ordered her sunk. Kahler came under some criticism for this from Naval headquarters, where it was felt that such a valuable cargo was worth the risk of not making the passage through the British blockade of occupied Europe. In addition, some of Kahler's superiors felt that he overestimated the effectiveness of the blockade. In the end, the ship and her more than 17,000 tons of whale oil went to the bottom. It was a decision with which no one, including Kahler, was happy.

The *Thor*'s next victim was the 8,715-ton British refrigerator ship *Natia*. This time Kahler had no choice but to sink his prey. The *Natia* was sighted at noon on October 8, at a position 60 miles north of the equator. She was sailing on a course indicating that she was heading toward South America, where in all likelihood she was scheduled to pick up a load of Argentinian beef to help feed the U-boat blockaded population of Great Britain.

The following day, September 27, Germany, Italy, and Japan signed a treaty pledging that each would declare war on any nation joining the war against any one of the three. It is best known as the Tripartite Pact.

The raider chased the *Natia* for nearly one and one-half hours, jamming her radio calls for help. Captain J. W. Carr, who in one of those ironic twists that sometime result from war would become a close friend of Kahler in the postwar years, tried to outrun the raider. The pursuing ship, with its German ensign now clearly visible, slowly drew closer. Carr knew the only chance of saving his vessel was if his broadcasts for help were received by a British warship that could arrive before the *Natia* was within gunnery range of the raider.

At 1:27 P.M. that range was reached as the two ships came to within 9,000 yards of each other and the *Thor* opened fire. In the next half hour the *Natia* took eight or nine hits from the 175 rounds fired at her. Captain Carr soon concluded that he was only risking the lives of his eighty-five crew members in a "hopeless struggle" to outrun the raider, and ordered his ship halted, and his men to prepare to abandon the ship. Kahler watched his victim begin to slow and immediately ordered a cease-fire.

Eighty-four men were picked up by the *Thor*, one crewman having been killed in the attack. Another man who had been wounded died the following day and was given a naval burial. Kahler, along with most of his senior officers, attended the services and offered his condolences to Carr and his crew for their loss.

With the arrival of the *Natia*'s crew, the number of prisoners aboard the little banana boat outnumbered the crew. The overcrowding was getting critical and potentially dangerous should any of the prisoners decide to rise up against their jailors. Kahler radioed his superiors with an urgent request for relief. He had two additional problems that also required their attention. For some reason his engineers were unable to identify, boiler gauges were failing at an alarming rate. The *Thor* needed an extra supply to keep her at sea, or at least until they could determine the cause of these failures. Then there was fuel. In order to operate with full latitude and continue ranging throughout its assigned area, the *Thor* required refueling at least once every three months.

Help came in the form of the *Rio Grande*, a German supply ship that had been delayed at a Brazilian port by local authorities. The delay actually helped the *Thor*'s situation, because the *Rio Grande*'s captain was ordered to purchase additional boiler gauges while still in port. After this he was either permitted to sail by the locals, or simply broke from the port for his planned meeting with the *Thor*. The ships rendezvoused on November 9. In order to keep the prisoners from knowing the true identity of their new prison, and from where it had sailed, the ship's name was changed to the *Belgrano*, and some cursory alterations where made to her. The *Thor* received badly needed supplies, including the extra gauges, and the prisoners were transferred to the *Rio Grande*. Perhaps because he feared that so many prisoners accompanied by their captains might prove a security risk to the lightly armed supply vessel, Kahler decided to keep the four British captains on board the raider.

On November 16 the two ships parted. The *Thor* steamed south to search along the heavily traveled route between the African coast and the River Plate. The *Rio Grande* headed east for the French port of Gironde. Following its arrival on December 16, the prisoners were transported to a POW camp in Germany, where most remained until the war's end.

The day before, in what was an ominous sign for the German Navy, the United States began flying ocean patrols out of Bermuda using U.S. Navy flying boats.

Life aboard the raider changed substantially for the prisoners, primarily because there were now so few of them. Rations increased, as did the time they were permitted on deck. In addition, each week they were presented with a gift of a bottle of whiskey with the compliments of their German captor.

For the crew, life also changed from the hectic pace of their first months at sea. During the next few weeks, things slowed down to a more or less boring routine with no sightings being made.

Late in the month, Kahler received several messages informing him that the South Atlantic was alive with British warships. On November 22 the battleship *Resolution* was reported off Freetown, and the cruisers *Canberra*, *Cornwall*,

Delhi, Devonshire, Dorsetshire, Dragon, Shropshire, and *Vindictive* were active throughout the eastern half of the ocean. Off the coast of South America, closer to the *Thor*'s operational area, at least two more British cruisers were reported, the *Enterprise* and the *Hawkins*. Supporting these was an unknown number of Armed Merchant Cruisers. This clearly indicated that the enemy was taking serious action to reduce the number of raider and U-boat sinkings in the South Atlantic. It was becoming an increasingly dangerous place in which to operate a German vessel.

The boredom ended in the early morning hours of December 5. At 5:30, while steaming through a thick morning mist, a large ship was sighted approaching the raider. She was about four miles off, and kept drifting in and out of sight in the haze. Despite the visibility problem, two things were clear to the watching Germans. First, she was heading their way, and second, she was a very large ship. The vessel turned out to be the Armed Merchant Cruiser *Carnarvon Castle*. At 20,122 tons, she dwarfed the *Thor*, and with a maximum cruising speed of 19 knots, she had the added advantage of speed.

Kahler quickly surmised the as yet unidentified ship was the *Carnarvon Castle*, which he had assumed had replaced the *Alcantara* on patrol. Mindful of his orders to avoid combat, he ordered the raider turned hard to port and tried to slip away, using the mist as cover. The *Carnarvon Castle* was now astern of the raider, and for a few moments it appeared that the two might actually lose track of each other in the thick covering that hovered just a few feet above the ocean's surface. But luck was not with the German skipper that morning, at least not at first. After a few minutes of drawing away from the larger vessel, it became clear that she had turned directly toward him, and she was gradually closing the gap between them. She was steaming down the center of the *Thor*'s wake with an obvious determination.

Suddenly, as the German crew, now called to battle stations, watched, the *Carnarvon Castle*'s searchlight began signaling a message to the smaller vessel it was pursuing. The AMC ordered the ship it was following to stop and identify itself. The *Thor* did not respond. The order was repeated again, then again, but still there was no response. Finally at 7:01, Captain Hardy decided that his prey needed further coaxing, so he ordered a single shell fired from his forward 6-inch gun. The shot fell 300 yards short of the *Thor*, close enough for Kahler to realize that he no longer had any options; he had to turn and fight. He ordered the German ensign run up, and all camouflaging removed.

For the next half hour the ships circled around each other at a range alternating between 7,000 and 8,000 yards. Despite the disparity of their size, the two would-be warships were more or less evenly matched. Armed Merchant Cruisers like the *Carnarvon Castle* were vessels quickly converted from peacetime use as passenger liners or cargo ships. In the case of the *Carnarvon Castle*, she had been a passenger liner sailing out of South African ports. Like the disguised German merchant raiders, the Armed Merchant Cruisers received mostly old, even antiquated weapons, and little or no added protection than had been originally built into their hulls. The *Carnarvon Castle* had eight 6-inch guns, four each as broadside batteries, two 3-inch guns, and an assortment of lighter weapons such as machine guns. Unlike her adversary, she carried no torpedoes.

The two ships continued their circling. Both fired at irregular intervals, depending on range and opportunity. The *Thor* made as much smoke as she could to obstruct the British gunners' visibility. Kahler ordered two torpedoes sent into the water, but neither struck its target. Then the German gunners found the range and scored five direct hits on the *Carnarvon Castle*. Fires erupted in three separate locations, two aft of the bridge and one forward.

The AMC suffered a blow when her fire control system was damaged, leaving individual gunners without a fire control center, and left to their own devices in aiming their guns. Meanwhile, the much smaller target made by the *Thor* remained undamaged, with not a single British shell finding its mark. The two ships continued their macabre water dance, each trying to gain the advantage of putting the rising sun in the eyes of the other.

Finally at 8:05, with his ship hit by at least eight enemy shells, and fires reported throughout, including in his distinctive fat squat funnel, Captain Hardy ordered the *Carnarvon Castle* turned away from the battle, and three smoke floats dropped off the stern to cover her retreat. Aside from the fires, which would quickly be gotten under control, he was especially concerned that his ship was beginning to list to port. Hardy had little choice but to head toward the nearest port, Montevideo, and make repairs. Six of the AMC's crew had been killed in the battle, and thirty-two wounded.

As for the *Thor*, she had not been hit by a single shell. The only damage she suffered was that several of her guns had overheated and jammed, something that could be repaired while she steamed south at full speed. Kahler was anxious to exit the area as quickly as possible, for he had little doubt that other British warships were on their way to aid the *Carnarvon Castle*. He was correct. The Royal Navy had responded to calls from the *Carnarvon Castle* by ordering an immediate large-scale hunt for the raider. The primary hunters were the cruisers *Cumberland*, *Enterprise*, and *Newcastle*, any one of which could have easily blown the *Thor* out of the water.

An inventory of the *Thor*'s supplies found that over two-thirds of her shells had been expended in the battle with the *Carnarvon Castle*, and an unusually high amount of fuel. A replenishment of fuel was obtained from the tanker *Eurofeld* on December 21. On Christ-

On the same day, December 5, Adolf Hitler approved a draft plan for a future massive invasion of the Soviet Union. This would throw Germany into what most German military leaders feared, a two-front war.

mas Day they were joined by the Pocket Battleship *Admiral Scheer*. The *Admiral Scheer* had just completed a highly successful cruise as a raider in the North Atlantic, sinking or taking as prizes eight ships in two months.

A few days later, the small flotilla was joined by a ship the *Admiral Scheer* had taken as a prize on December 18, the British refrigerator ship *Duquesa*. It was a truly unique prize, for the *Duquesa* carried a cargo consisting of 15,000,000 eggs, and 3,500 tons of frozen meat. The Germans who lived off her cargo called her the Commissary Department Wilhelmshaven South. Later that same day the tanker *Nordmark* arrived.

A series of Christmas and post-Christmas parties were conducted on the ships. While these were in progress, Kahler met with the *Admiral Scheer*'s Captain Krancke to discuss the possibility of the two raiders working in conjunction. The two quickly realized how impractical it was. The pocket battleship had a cruising speed of 26 knots, much too fast for the *Thor*'s eighteen knots to either keep up or help scout potential targets. In the end they decided that both raiders would operate independently in the South Atlantic during the coming month. The *Admiral Scheer* was assigned the area north of 30°, the *Thor* south.

Replenished with fuel and ammunition, as well as seven tons of frozen meat and 62,000 eggs from the *Duquesa*, the *Thor* departed on January 2. The *Admiral Scheer* did the same, and the supply vessels continued their endless voyages around the South Atlantic, waiting for their next rendezvous and avoiding enemy ships. The *Nordmark* took the *Duquesa* in tow to save fuel.

Most of the next three months were spent in never ending fruitless searches for potential targets. The *Thor* and its crew settled down to long monotonous days interrupted only by periodic practice drills that were Kahler's attempt to keep his men sharp. The boredom was broken in early February by a rendezvous with one of the supply ships stationed in the area. Resupply inevitably brought some excitement, because it usually took place in high seas or bad weather, and there was always the danger of being caught in midtransfer by an enemy warship. The most difficult part of replenishing a raider was the transfer of torpedoes. Because of their size, the only way they could safely be moved from a supply vessel to a raider was to secure each torpedo to a rubber lifeboat and pull it along a line tied to each ship. It was always a tricky maneuver, because a sudden gust or wave might tip the dinghy and send the torpedo to the bottom.

By early March the raider was working an area southwest of the Cape Verde Islands. The naval command had hoped that the *Thor* might find some victims here because U-boats were active to the east of Cape Verde, and their presence might send lone merchant ships toward the west to avoid them. But the days and weeks slipped by with no meaningful result. Then the raider hit a jackpot on March 25, 1941.

At 7:00 that Monday morning a lookout spotted dark smoke on the horizon to the northeast. The raider turned toward the sighting and ran her speed up to 15 knots in an effort to catch her. About fifty minutes later, when the ships were about 11,000 yards apart, with the raider still flying a Yugoslav flag, the other vessel suddenly turned north and increased speed. Kahler could see that the large passenger liner he was pursuing had a gun mounted on her stern, so there was no doubt that it was an enemy ship. The liner, the 8,799-ton *Britannia*, had left Liverpool on March 11 with 527 people on board, including her crew of 200.

As the *Britannia* attempted to pull away, she made increased smoke to cover her escape. She also began evasive maneuvers that indicated that whoever was at her helm knew what he was doing. With no reason left to hide his true identity, Kahler ordered the Yugoslav flag brought down and replaced by the German ensign. When the distance between the two closed to 10,000 yards, the raider opened fire. The smoke and the actions of the liner made marksmanship difficult, and the raider fired continuously.

Making as much smoke as she could, and constantly altering her course, the *Britannia* proved a tough target. In addition, her gun crew returned fire as best they could, for they also were partially blinded from their target by their own smoke. In the liner's radio room a constant alert was sent out giving the ship's location and the fact she was being shelled by an enemy raider. Attempts to jam the broadcast were futile because the liner's transmitter was extremely powerful. The message was heard to be acknowledged and passed on by a shore station the Germans believed to be in Sierra Leone.

Finally, after the *Thor* had fired 159 shells, with only a few actually hitting their target, several fires could be seen aboard the liner. The *Britannia* slowed to a stop and ran up a signal message that she was surrendering. Kahler returned the message with a signal of his own ordering that the liner be abandoned. The passengers and crew began immediately taking to the lifeboats. Unfortunately, the crew was made up of mostly Pacific Islanders whose actions made the evacuation difficult when they pushed passengers aside to reach lifeboats. What should have been a nearly routine evacuation turned into a battle between the passengers, many of whom were Royal Navy and Royal Air Force officers, and the unruly crew.

While the *Britannia* was being abandoned, the raider stood by waiting. Kahler intended to sink the vessel and then pick up the people in the lifeboats. His plans were suddenly changed when his radio operator informed him that he had picked up a signal from another ship. The signal was intended for the *Britannia*, and appeared to indicate that the ship was a little more than 100 miles away and heading toward the scene. Kahler interpreted the message the only way he could, that a British warship was racing toward him. He quickly estimated that if the approaching ship was a cruiser, she would arrive in no more than four or five hours. It would take him at least that long to pick up the hundreds of people in lifeboats and rubber dinghies that were at that very moment pulling away from the wounded liner. It was then that Otto Kahler made a decision he would long regret.

Once all the lifeboats and rubber rafts were far enough from the *Britannia*, the raider fired over a dozen shells into the liner's hull at her waterline, sending her down in a huge burst of flames. Kahler then ordered his ship turned hard away and fled the scene. Although not completely comfortable with leaving the liner's survivors in the water, he expected that the approaching British warship would arrive soon and rescue them. He wanted to be long gone before that happened, and he did not want any of the survivors getting a good look at the *Thor* so that they could provide an accurate description to the Royal Navy. Indeed, this was the explanation he passed to his crew when he learned many of the men were upset about leaving people in the water in a part of the ocean that was a known habitat of sharks. As the *Thor* raced away, Kahler sent a signal to naval headquarters explaining that about 500 hundred people were adrift, and why he had left the scene. He hoped his coded message would then be rebroadcast in clear language to be picked up by other potential rescue vessels. It wasn't.

Only one member of the liner's crew was picked up by the raider. He had clung to a small raft that drifted close to the *Thor* while the *Britannia* was being abandoned. When hauled aboard, he explained that he had been swept overboard during the chase.

On the same day, March 25, representatives of the government of Yugoslavia were forced to meet Hitler in Vienna and sign the Tripartite Pact, committing their country to the Axis side of the war. Yugoslav citizens demonstrated in the streets of Belgrade against their government's capitulation to Hitler's demands.

For those the *Thor* left behind, life became a living nightmare. Starvation, thirst, and sharks took a dreadful total. One boat traveled 1,500 miles over a twenty-three-day period before reaching a shore. Others were picked up by various ships transiting the area over a period of time. In the end, only 331 people survived the ordeal. It was not until March 29 that Kahler learned of the fate of the passengers and crew of the *Britannia*. During that evening his radio room received a message from a Spanish freighter, the *Cabo de Hornos*, announcing that it had plucked a total of 79 people from lifeboats and rafts out of the water, and that they were from the *Britannia*. The Spanish ship was alerting others to the presence of possibly hundreds of people adrift in the area. Kahler was horrified. It was unimaginable that the British warship he believed was on the way had not found all those people. As it turned out, no one ever identified the vessel that sent that message. It was a tragic event that cost 195 lives.

A few hours after leaving the scene of the *Britannia* sinking, the *Thor* came across a Swedish freighter, the 5,047-ton *Trollenholm*. The raider stopped her with a shot across the freighter's bow. Kahler was taking a chance stopping a ship of a neutral country. If she were carrying an innocent cargo, he would have to let her go and deal with the possibility that she would report his location and appearance to the enemy. An inspection found that the *Trollenholm* was carrying coal from Newcastle to Port Said under charter to the British Admiralty. After transferring the thirty-one crewmen to the raider, demolition charges were set and the vessel sunk.

A few days later another ship was sighted at around midnight, but because she had all her lights on it was assumed that she was American, so the raider kept her distance so as not to be seen.

Life aboard the raider settled down to the routine of searching the vast ocean and sighting nothing day after day. Many of the crew, including the captain, were haunted by the specter of hundreds of people stranded in the ocean being attacked by sharks. They were images that would never quite leave most of the men, even long after the war was ended.

On April 4, the sun slipped out of the eastern ocean at about 6:05 in the morning. There was no forewarning that the events of this day would provide the *Thor* with an indelible entry in the annals of the commerce raiders.

Ten minutes after the sun rose, a lookout aboard the raider reported seeing smoke on the horizon to the southwest. The *Thor* was then about 900 miles west of the Cape Verde Islands. Captain Kahler quickly appeared on the bridge and studied the distant horizon through his binoculars. What he saw he judged to be, from the large amount of visible smoke, a coal-burning ship. Below the cloud of smoke was a single tall funnel and two masts. Kahler decided to investigate, and so turned his ship toward the southwest. Both vessels were now heading toward each other, with both going at a high rate of speed.

The oncoming ship had a narrow prow, which Kahler took for belonging to a passenger liner. He was partially correct. It had been a passenger liner, but it had recently been converted for the Royal Navy into an Armed Merchant Cruiser. Because she did not appear to be taking any evasive action in the face of an unknown ship approaching, Kahler thought she was most likely a neutral.

The two ships continued to race toward each other, rapidly closing the wide gap between them. The *Thor* remained in her disguise as a Greek freighter. At 6:21 Kahler ordered his men to battle stations. A few minutes later the AMC *Voltaire*, with a crew of 269, began flashing a signal asking the *Thor* to identify herself. Fearing the worst, that the vessel was an AMC, Kahler hauled down the Greek flag and ran his own up. He then fired a shot across the bow of the *Voltaire*. Just as he did, the two guns mounted on the ship's bow came clearly into view, and the German captain knew he was in for a fight.

A minute later the raider opened fire from her port battery. The 13,245-ton *Voltaire* immediately returned fire from two of her eight 6-inch guns. Aboard the *Voltaire*, Captain J.A.P. Blackburn realized even before the German ensign was raised that he was encountering one of the enemy commerce raiders that had been stalking the Atlantic. He had been on patrol for only five days, having sailed from Trinidad on March 30, and he knew about the damaging battles two other AMCs, the *Alcantara* and *Carnarvon Castle*, had with German raiders. The Admiralty, he had been told, suspected that both AMCs had fought with the same disguised raider. Blackburn suspected that was the same vessel from which he was now receiving fire.

When the shooting began, the ships were slightly more than 9,000 yards apart. The *Thor*'s first salvo hit home, starting several fires on the AMC. Among the first hits were the *Voltaire*'s radio room and her generator. This meant that she could not send radio messages for help, and the loss of electricity hampered her fire control system. Her gunners gallantly fought back as best they could, aiming and firing without the aid of the fire control system.

The raider kept up a withering fire as the large liner erupted in flames throughout, and yet the British gunners kept returning the fire, although their shots fell short of their target. As the Germans watched, the liner, which was periodically consumed in flames and smoke, continued to fight back. At one point it appeared that the liner was turning on them to either ram their ship or fire a torpedo. This caused Kahler to order his helmsman to turn away. He soon realized that the liner was not aiming for him, but her steering had been damaged and she was beginning to circle the battle area as flames poured out from her on all sides. He was right. Unable to control his ship, Blackburn watched in disbelief as she turned in a large circle with her engines running at 13 knots. Still his gunners kept up their efforts to sink the raider, although most of them were blinded by the smoke from their own burning ship. Captain Blackburn took personal command of one of the few operational aft guns.

The battle continued, with broadsides from the raider slamming into the *Voltaire* and her own gunners returning fire as best they could as they fought the fires that were consuming their vessel. The *Thor* was firing so many shells so quickly that her guns were seizing from the intense heat. At about 7:40 she could no longer fire any of her larger weapons, so Kahler decided to fire a torpedo into the burning liner from which shells continued to be fired. Just as he prepared to do so, he saw white flags being waved by men who had received Blackburn's order to abandon the ship. The firing stopped. By now the liner was a mass of flames.

When Kahler realized that the liner's lifeboats had all been either shot away or consumed by flames, he pulled the *Thor* in as close as he dare to the burning ship and put his own boats in the water. This time, there would be no one left behind if he could help it. For the next five hours the *Thor*'s boats swept the area, pulling sailors, some barely alive, from the sea. Everyone was covered with oil. Of the 269 men aboard the *Voltaire*, the *Thor* managed to rescue 197, including Captain Blackburn. As for their ship, she was put out of her misery at about 8:30 when she sank beneath the oil soaked waves.

The men taken aboard the *Thor* were in extremely bad condition. Over half were wounded and required immediate medical treatment. The raider's medical officer, Dr. Jurgen Harms, was joined by *Voltaire*'s medical officer, who had luckily survived the battle, and the *Thor*'s corpsmen, worked all night to treat the men. Two British seamen died during the night. The following day they were buried at sea with full honors, with their captain and Captain Kahler in attendance.

Kahler did not hide either his respect or admiration for the officers and men of the *Voltaire*. They had put up a valiant fight, and had behaved well even after being forced to abandon their ship. His feelings even found their way into his log when he wrote: "I expressed my admiration for the courage and heroism the captain and his men displayed during the fight and later in the water. The behavior of that crew, which faced certain destruction, was truly exemplary."

After fifty-five minutes of heavy shelling, the *Thor* suffered no damage other than having her radio mast shot away. Many of her guns required repair, as did their mountings, but all that could be taken care of with a few days' work. Kahler's biggest problem was that the battle with the *Voltaire* had consumed half his ammunition supply.

The United States took another step toward participation in the war against Germany on this day when President Roosevelt agreed to allow Royal Navy warships to be repaired in American ports, and to refuel there while on war patrols.

Ten days later the raider refueled from a German tanker and headed for home. On the way she came across her twelfth and final victim of this, her first cruise, the Swedish ore ship *Sir Ernest Cassel*. The crew was transferred to the *Thor* and the 7,739-ton vessel sunk.

Ordered to return to Europe so that his ship could be overhauled for a second voyage, Kahler turned the *Thor* northeast, heading for the coast of occupied France. Following a brief stopover at Cherbourg while a storm raged in the English Channel, the raider was escorted home to Germany by a flotilla of gunboats and minesweepers. At 5:00 P.M on April 30, 1941, the *Thor* was tied up to the dock at Hamburg where she would undergo her overhaul. Despite the Navy's attempt to keep her arrival secret, so the British would not learn that there was one less raider in the Atlantic, the ship and her crew were welcomed home as heroes.

The *Thor*'s first cruise lasted 329 days. She sank eleven ships, including an Armed Merchant Cruiser, took one freighter as a prize, and fought successful battles against two other Armed Merchant Cruisers. All together, the *Thor* accounted for 96,547 tons of enemy shipping.

The 57,532 miles the little vessel had sailed during her time at sea had taken a toll on her machinery. The former banana boat was turned over to the Deutsche Werft AG, the same firm that had converted her for her wartime mission.

> While the *Thor* was being prepared for her second cruise, Germany expanded the war by launching a massive three-pronged attack against the Soviet Union on June 22, 1941.

Exactly seven months later, on November 30, 1941, the newly refurbished *Thor* steamed out of German waters and headed south, hugging the French coast. Her old guns had been replaced with more recently manufactured weapons, and she now sported her own radar searching system. This was the raider's second attempt to put to sea, something that surely disturbed the naturally superstitious natures of seamen. On the first, weeks earlier, she had slammed into an anchored Swedish ore vessel, sending that ship to the bottom. Luckily no one on either ship was injured, although the *Thor* had to return to her dry dock for repairs.

Severe storms delayed her in the Bay of Biscay through the Christmas and New Year holidays. Finally, on January 14, 1942 she headed out into the Atlantic and turned south toward the Antarctic Circle in search of enemy whaling ships. The crew, nearly four dozen of whom had served on the first cruise, must have been given an extra warning to keep a sharp lookout, for the *Thor* now faced a new and potentially dangerous enemy in the Atlantic. A month earlier the Imperial Japanese Navy launched a surprise attack on the U.S. Naval base at Pearl Harbor in Hawaii, bringing the United States into the war.

The *Thor* was now under the command of Captain Gunther Gumprich. A tall, handsome, regular navy officer, Gumprich knew he was destined to operate in the Indian Ocean, where he was to replace the *Kormoran*.

Unlike most of his fellow commerce raider commanders, Gumprich was to make extensive use of his vessel's aircraft, an Arado 196A-1. The *Thor* arrived inside the Antarctic Circle on February 25, and quickly began regular air searches for enemy whalers. Despite having listened in on several shortwave conversations that intimated that whaling activity was underway in the area, several days of searching by both the raider and her airplane found nothing.

Finally Gumprich decided that he was wasting his time and returned north in search of potential targets in the busy South Atlantic shipping lanes. In the predawn hours of March 23 the lookouts spotted smoke that at first was thought to be from the supply ship *Regensburg*. The *Thor* was due to meet her soon. But it soon became clear that the smoke was not from the four-masted motorboat the Germans used to supply the raiders, but from a small Greek freighter. The raider bore down on the 3,492-ton *Pagasitikos*. Not wanting to

KMS *Thor*: Second Cruise, January 14, 1942–October 9, 1942

1. *Pagastikos*; 2. *Wellpark*; 3. *Willesden*; 4. *Aust*; 5. *Kirkpool*; 6. *Nankin*; 7. *Olivia*; 8. *Herborg*; 9. *Madrono*; 10. *Indus*. Courtesy of K. Rochford.

endanger his own crew in a fruitless effort to attempt an escape, the Greek captain did as instructed, stopped his ship, and sent no radio signal. The thirty-two men and one woman who made up the crew were transferred to the *Thor*, and their ship sunk by a single torpedo.

The following day the *Regensburg* appeared and replenished the raider. She then steamed around the *Thor*, acting as a target for the raider's radar operators to practice on. Radar was a recent addition, and the men were constantly in need of practice and a means to evaluate the system. The results were mixed. The *Thor* continued her cruise.

On March 28, the *Thor* spent more than three hours trying to catch up with a ship whose masts had appeared on the horizon, but the unknown vessel was faster and succeeded in escaping. Gumprich left no record of why he failed to use his aircraft to halt the vessel, so we can only assume that it was suffering some mechanical failure and under repair at the time.

Two days later the aircraft was back in action. In early midmorning the pilot and spotter returned with news that a British cargo ship was steaming in the same direction as the *Thor*, just over the starboard horizon. Gumprich increased his speed once the aircraft had been lifted aboard, and put the raider on a course that would gradually draw the two vessels closer together. The pursuit went for several hours without the cargo ship, the 4,649-ton *Wellpark*, suspecting anything. Finally at about 1:00 P.M. the *Wellpark* caught sight of the *Thor* as the latter drew up on her port beam. The freighter's master, Alexander Cant, ordered his Second Officer to keep a close watch on the stranger in case she meant them harm. Meanwhile the ships continued to sail on parallel courses that were slowly converging. Tension built on both vessels as the predators tried to approach their prey without causing alarm, and the officers aboard the *Wellpark* tried to determine if the ship they were watching was just another freighter passing by on its peaceful mission, or if it intended to attack them.

A few minutes after 3:00 Gumprich sent his aircraft aloft again, this time with orders to destroy the British ship's radio antenna. When Captain Cant heard the deep throb of the aircraft's engine, he knew that the odds of the stranger being an enemy had increased dramatically. He ordered his antiaircraft gun crew to prepare their weapon for action.

Cant listened to the approaching plane. Then he saw a seaplane suddenly dive out of the clouds and head for his ship from her starboard beam. As the plane drew closer, he saw what he at first thought might be a torpedo drop from her and splash into the ocean. He then realized it was a long wire hanging from the plane's underbelly. Attached to the wire was a series of hooks with which the pilot intended to pull down his radio antenna.

As the Arado approached the freighter, it opened fire with its twin 20-mm cannons. The *Wellpark*'s gun crew immediately returned fire. With its guns blasting the freighter's bridge, the Arado dragged its line across the mast bearing the aerial and ripped it from its brackets. The *Wellpark* was now unable to call for help.

The seaplane and the freighter continued firing at each other. In minutes the *Thor* came within range, and she too opened fire. The first few rounds fell short of the target, but then once the German gunners found their range, the freighter was doomed. The *Wellpark*'s hull was penetrated just above the waterline by one shell, while another exploded near the boiler room. In less than fifteen minutes the *Wellpark* slowed to a halt, and Cant ordered the vessel abandoned. Seeing his victim slowing, Gumprich ordered a cease-fire. The *Wellpark*'s crew was plucked from their two lifeboats. A few more shells sent the freighter down.

The next day the Arado searched for another victim, but found none. Better luck was had the following morning when an early flight discovered yet another British freighter. The seaplane returned to the *Thor* about 8:00 A.M. and reported her finding. Once the plane was aboard the raider, she headed toward the unsuspecting target. At noon the craft was once again lowered into the sea and sent aloft to confirm the location of the freighter, which she did.

The pursuit of the unseen enemy continued until shortly after 5:30 P.M., when the freighter finally came into view. Meanwhile, aboard the 4,563-ton *Willesden*, sailing from New York to Alexandria, Egypt, no one realized that they were being trailed by a German raider bent on their destruction.

With the enemy now in sight, Gumprich once again sent his aircraft off. This time he ordered the pilot to tear down the freighter's radio aerial so that she could not send for help or alert the Royal Navy to its location. The Arado lifted off from the calm waters at 6:20, after positioning herself so that she approached the enemy from the setting sun, she flew directly for the freighter. Hoping the enemy was blinded to his approach by the sun, the pilot dropped his weighted line with its hooks and aimed for the aerial. As he flew over the ship, the pilot also released two bombs that he hoped would ensure the aerial's destruction. The bombs missed their target, but the hooks succeeded in pulling down the aerial. To his surprise, the freighter opened fire on him with an antiaircraft gun. Although the plane was not hit, it was now obvious that the British sailors were aware that they were under attack.

Leaving the seaplane aloft, Gumprich pulled the *Thor* within range of his guns and opened fire. The *Willesden* returned the *Thor*'s fire, but her smaller caliber guns could not make the range. The British shells fell into the sea between the two ships, where they exploded harmlessly.

The *Willesden* was carrying a cargo of oil drums on her deck. The *Thor*'s first salvos struck these and set the deck ablaze. The freighter's gun crew was able to get off no more than six shots while their fellow crewmen were abandoning the burning ship. Finally they too had to leave the ship. The survivors were picked up by the raider after her aircraft was taken aboard. One of the British crew, the boatswain, was killed during the attack, and six others wounded. One of the wounded men died the following day of injuries he sustained when he was hit by a piece of shrapnel, fell from the ship, and crashed into a lifeboat. He was buried at sea with full military honors.

The incredible string of good luck experienced by the *Thor* and her Arado floatplane continued. Two days after sinking the *Willesden*, on April 3, 1942, the aircraft once again found a target. This time it was a Norwegian coal-burning freighter, the 5,630-ton *Aust*. The same routine was followed as before. The airplane pulled down the freighter's radio aerial with her hooked wire, and the raider fired a few rounds into the ship. Almost immediately, the unarmed vessel stopped, and the crew abandoned the ship. A German boarding party found nothing of value, so the ship was scuttled with demolition charges.

The weather and high running seas on April 10 prevented the Arado from being used. Instead, all attention was focused on the *Thor*'s radar system. It was the first radar placed aboard a raider and had not been used much on this cruise. Now it picked up a ship that was as yet still out of sight. Throughout the day the *Thor* trailed the vessel that appeared on her radar screen, not yet knowing if she were friend or foe, cargo or warship. After nightfall the raider slipped up on the unknown ship. She could now be seen through glasses as a darker shadow in the darkness. It was assumed that she was an enemy because she was running without lights, and her profile did not fit any of the German supply ships. Gumprich fired a torpedo at her from a range of about 2,420 yards. It missed.

In a move that would significantly improve the Royal Navy's operational status, two U.S. warships, the aircraft carrier *Wasp* and the battleship *Washington*, joined the Allied fleet at Scapa Flow.

As the range closed, he opened fire with several salvos from his 5.9-inch guns. One shell exploded near the target's wheelhouse, and set the bridge on fire. The firing came as a big shock to the crew of the 4,842-ton *Kirkpool*, a freighter of British registry. The vessel's captain, Albert Kennington, had no hint that a raider was drawing up on his ship in the darkness. As the fire spread across the decks of the *Kirkpool*, the order to abandon the ship was passed among the men. The crew attempted to lower the lifeboats, but they had either been severely damaged in the shelling, or blown away completely. With no real choice left, the men jumped into the water and began swimming away from the burning ship. A lucky few managed to take small rubber rafts with them. Most were picked up by boats sent out from the *Thor*. Of the forty-six men on the crew, thirty were rescued. When it appeared that all survivors had been taken aboard the *Thor*, the freighter was then sunk by a single torpedo.

Six days later the Arado found another ship, but unsure of her identity, the pilot took photographs of her. The Germans were to rendezvous with a tanker in this general area and did not want to take a chance on attacking the wrong vessel. In addition, Gumprich knew that another raider, the *Michel*, was operating in the area. The last thing he wanted to do was slip up on her and start a fight that might cost Germany two raiders at a time when she needed every one she could put to sea. When the photographs were processed, the ship's identity remained a secret, so the Arado was sent out once more to take additional pictures. As darkness closed in over the ocean, Gumprich decided to let the unknown vessel go rather than risk a night attack. He had still not determined who the vessel was.

A short time after this near encounter, the *Thor* received orders to leave the South Atlantic and head for the Indian Ocean. It was hoped that the raider could continue her amazing string of successes there. In less than one month she had sunk five freighters for a total of 23,176 tons.

The *Thor*'s passage around the Cape of Good Hope, which she accomplished on April 22, and her entry into the Indian Ocean was uneventful. Arrangements had been made with the Imperial Japanese Navy to reserve a portion of the Indian Ocean for the raider. The *Thor*, it was agreed, was to concentrate in the southeastern quadrant of the ocean so that she would avoid contact with Japanese submarines working along the East African coast.

She did not sight another vessel until she drew near Australia. The first sighting, made on May 4, turned out to be the German supply ship *Regensburg*. The raider traded some badly needed foodstuffs for 162 prisoners.

A few minutes after 8:00 A.M. on May 10, the Arado sighted a large coal-burning passenger ship about 1,500 miles off the western coast of Australia. The 7,131-ton *Nankin*, owned by the Eastern and Australian Steamship Company, was bound for Bombay with nearly 350 passengers and crew. The aircraft was seen by the *Nankin*'s lookouts, and the rest of the morning was spent drilling the passengers and crew in taking to the lifeboats, because it was assumed that the plane might be from an enemy ship.

At 2:35 that same afternoon the *Nankin*'s Second Officer was informed that an aircraft could be heard approaching from the port bow. This was almost immediately followed by news that a ship was sighted off the starboard bow heading directly for them. He immediately sent word to Captain Stratford, who was in his cabin, and turned the ship hard to starboard to avoid what he suspected was going to be a torpedo attack from the aircraft. The Captain needed no alert, for within seconds his cabin was riddled with machine gun bullets from the Arado as it flew over dragging its grappling line. It failed to catch on the radio aerial. Once on the bridge, Captain Stratford ordered his chief engineer to increase speed to the maximum as quickly as possible, and simultaneously to prepare to scuttle the ship if that became necessary. He would try to outrun the approaching ship for a short time, but realized that the chances of success were small.

Still firing its twin machine guns, the Arado circled the liner and prepared for another attempt at tearing down the *Nankin*'s radio aerial. As the craft headed in for her second attempt, she was greeted by a hail of bullets from the ship's machine gun and an assortment of rifles and handguns fired by members of the crew and several passengers. The passenger list included twenty-three men from the Royal Navy and Army who were presumably armed. By now they all knew the plane's mission was to silence the *Nankin*'s radio, which was sending out continuous alerts that she was under attack.

Meanwhile the *Thor* sped toward the liner, her gun crews at their stations awaiting orders to open fire. Her radio operators struggled to jam the *Nankin*'s distress calls, but had great difficulty because the liner's radio operator kept changing frequency in an attempt to prevent the jamming.

Finally, at 2:38, just three minutes after the action had begun, the raider pulled to within 13,000 yards of the *Nankin* and fired a salvo from three of her 5.9-inch guns. All three fell short of the target. Captain Stratford responded to the cannon fire from the raider by ordering his helmsman to commence zigzagging, the age-old defense against enemy shelling. With the enemy to his rear, Stratford ordered the crew of his own stern gun to open fire. Their shells also fell short.

For twenty-two minutes the two ships continued to fire at each other, but not a single shell fell on its target. The *Nankin*'s engineers fired their boilers beyond the margin of safety to gain as much speed as possible. The raider's did the same. The Arado approached as best it could under almost constant fire, but failed in its attempts to pull down the liner's radio aerial. Then at 3:00, nearly one-half hour after the first firing began, the German gunners found the range and shells began bursting all over the *Nankin*, pouring shrapnel over the ship. When one shell pierced the hull near the number one hatch, Captain Stratford knew that the game was up. At 3:05 he ordered the gun crews to cease fire and sounded the abandon ship alarm. The courageous crew of the passenger liner had hurled twenty-eight shells at the enemy raider, but their gun could never reach the required range.

"Nankin abandoning ship Latitude 26 degrees 43' South, 89 degrees 47' East." It was the last radio message the ship sent. Stratford ensured that all code books and Naval documents aboard his ship were secured in a perforated steel box that was dropped into the ocean before he boarded the last lifeboat.

On May 10, 1942, the last remaining American resistance to the Japanese invasion of the Philippines came to an end when General Sharp issued the surrender order to his troops.

The crew and passengers of the *Nankin* were picked up by the *Thor*. A prize crew was put aboard the *Nankin*, and repairs were made to the engines that had suffered only mild damage from the scuttling attempt. The shell hole near the bow was temporarily patched, and a portion of the cargo, which included frozen foods, wool, and walkie-talkies, was removed to the raider. A few days later the prisoners and some of the supplies were transferred to the *Regensburg* when it arrived. Then the German supply ship and the British liner were sent to Japan.

The next month passed quietly for a raider and her crew previously used to regular action. It was obvious that the section of the Indian Ocean the Japanese had allowed them to patrol was not anywhere as busy as the South Atlantic they had traveled earlier.

The next genuine contact occurred on the evening of June 14. The still somewhat primitive radar picked up a ship at slightly less than 10,000 yards' distance. The *Thor* altered course slightly so as to converge with the course of the target. As the unknown vessel drew closer, it was identified as a tanker. Unable to use the Arado to assure radio silence because it was too dark, Gumprich decided instead to put a few salvos into her in hopes of damaging her radio room. The salvos actually did more damage than intended, for the oil-filled vessel, the 6,307-ton Dutch Shell-owned tanker *Olivia*, burst into flames from bow to stern. One shell damaged the tanker's steering mechanism, locking her into a large circle.

Their guns now silent, the German sailors looked on in horror as the *Olivia* turned into "a floating wall of flame." For long agonizing minutes the tanker steamed in its death circle as it lit up the sea and the sky with its flames. The ship had been carrying a crew of forty-six. It appeared that all but one man perished either on the burning vessel, or in the blazing oil-covered sea around her. The single known survivor, J. D. Fischer, was plucked from the burning waters by the raider's rescue boat.

That night a solemn gloom descended over the *Thor*. Fighting a gun battle with another ship was what war was about to the men of the *Thor*, but what they had witnessed was something different. Many of them said what had happened, although not intended, was not to their liking at all. It seemed to some more like murder than war. For many of the men aboard the raider, the burning of the *Olivia* would be recalled as the most horrible memory of the war.

Unknown to the men of the *Thor* and to Fischer, one lifeboat actually did manage to escape from the *Olivia*. On board were four Dutch and eight Chinese seamen. Three of the Dutchmen suffered injuries that restricted their movements. According to the report of the *Olivia*'s Third Officer, W. A. Vermoet, most of the Chinese sailors refused to take actions at self-preservation. As a result, all but one died during the month the small boat sought the safety of land. One of the Dutch sailors also perished before the battered boat with its four remaining survivors washed up on a beach in Madagascar on July 13, nearly one month after their ship had burst into flames.

While the survivors of the *Olivia* struggled to reach land, the war continued. Five days after the sinking of the *Olivia*, a Norwegian tanker fell prey to the *Thor*. This time it was the 7,894-ton *Herborg*. The ship's Captain and Third Officer watched with foreboding as an unknown ship steamed directly toward them. When they heard the sound of an approaching aircraft, they both realized that they were in trouble. The small seaplane dropped its grappling line and ripped down the tanker's radio aerial moments before the approaching ship fired several warning shots overhead. The *Herborg*'s only means of defense was an old 3-inch gun that both Dutchmen knew would be totally useless against the obviously heavily armed commerce raider that had them in her sights. The ship was stopped and the crew ordered to the boats.

> The same day the *Herborg* was taken, President Roosevelt and Prime Minister Churchill held an historic meeting in the United States at which they agreed to share atomic research and work together toward developing an atomic weapon.

A tanker full of oil was too good a catch to waste, so Gumprich put a prize crew aboard her and sent her to Japan. Before she left, he changed her name to *Hohenfriedburg*. The tanker arrived in Japan on July 7. On July 4 a second Norwegian tanker was taken. In an almost identical replay of the capture of the *Herborg*, the 5,894-ton *Madrono* surrendered without a fight. She was quickly renamed the *Rossbach* and also sent, with a prize crew aboard, to Japan. She arrived there on August 5.

The *Thor*'s next, and final, victim was a British refrigerated freighter. Unlike the Norwegian tankers, the 5,187-ton *Indus* was not about to surrender without a fight. The *Thor* caught sight of the *Indus* and recognized from a distance that she was an enemy vessel by the presence of a stern-mounted gun. It was 3:00 P.M. on July 20 when the freighter came within range and *Thor* fired her first salvos. It is not clear why Gumprich did not make use of the Arado, perhaps it again was being repaired. In any event, when the *Indus*'s Captain Bryan heard the gunfire, he ordered the engine room to maintain speed and the gun crew to return fire. The gunners managed to get off two shots before they had to abandon the gun. A direct hit from the *Thor* killed the chief gunner and damaged the gun beyond repair.

> The day before, the Battle of the Atlantic took a drastic course change when the last two U-boats operating off the U.S. coast were ordered withdrawn. Improved convoying had left them impotent against the growing might of the U.S. Navy.

Meanwhile, the *Indus*'s radio operator kept up a steady stream of alert signals that were picked up and responded to by several land stations. Despite a spreading fire, the man stayed at his station until he was killed by a shell that also set the bridge aflame. In the engine room, the crew, comprising mostly south Asian natives and islanders, abandoned their stations and fled to the deck. Most were cut down by shrapnel from the numerous exploding shells that pounded the ship.

When Gumprich saw the ship slow and received reports the radio had fallen silent, he ordered his guns to stop firing. The *Indus* was burning so badly that a German party was not sent aboard to search her. Instead survivors were picked up, and the raider sped from the area, expecting that warships might be on their way in response to the distress calls. Half the crew of the *Indus* was lost either in the shelling or from the fires that spread rapidly.

The *Indus* brought the total ships taken or sunk on the *Thor*'s second cruise to ten, for a total of 55,587 tons. The grand total for both cruises was twenty-two ships and 152,134 tons.

The *Thor* was a brave little ship that fought well in two of the world's oceans. Like the soldier who wants to die with his boots on, she deserved a better end than she met. Her ignominious death occurred on November 30, 1942, in Yokohama, Japan. Sent there to have his ship refitted for a third cruise, Gumprich arrived on October 10 and immediately set about trying to get Japanese cooperation in accomplishing the required work quickly.

The work was nearly completed when the German tanker supply ship, *Uckermark*, entered the harbor and tied up alongside the raider. She too was in need of some repairs. At about 2:00 P.M. on the thirtieth an explosion was heard coming from within the tanker. Chinese laborers were inside her scraping her tanks down, and either a spark or a lighted cigarette, no one knows which, must have ignited some gas within the confined area. The smaller explosion was almost instantly followed by another larger one, then another. The third was so powerful it blew the tanker's superstructure apart. A large portion of the tanker's bridge blew into the air and crashed down on the raider. Fire quickly spread across the *Thor*'s deck. Explosions continued to fill the basin in which both ships were tied as the flames consumed the tanker and the raider and spread across the surface of the water. The flames seemed to pursue the crew members who had leapt overboard to save their lives.

Gumprich, who was motoring across the harbor at the time of the blasts, returned as near to his ship as he dared and rescued as many men as he could before his boat was also threatened by the flames. The fuel-fed flames spread across the harbor and added to their toll. In addition to the *Thor* and the *Uckermark*, the British freighter *Nankin*, which the *Thor* had taken as a prize on May 10 was consumed by the flames, as was a Japanese freighter, the *Unkai Maru 3*. Thirteen members of the *Thor*'s crew were killed in the incident, as were fifty-three of the *Uckermark*'s crew, and an unknown number of Japanese and Chinese workers.

The *Atlantis* disguised as the Norwegian freighter *Tamesis*. From David Woodward, *The Secret Raiders: The Story of the German Armed Merchant Raiders in the Second World War* (New York: W.W. Norton & Company, 1955).

HMS *Devonshire* entering Freetown harbor shortly after sinking the *Atlantis*. From David Woodward, *The Secret Raiders: The Story of the German Armed Merchant Raiders in the Second World War* (New York: W.W. Norton & Company, 1955).

Boat alongside—men from a ship sunk by the *Atlantis*. From Ulrich Mohr as told to A. V. Sellwood, *Atlantis: The Story of a German Surface Raider* (London: Werner Laurie, 1955).

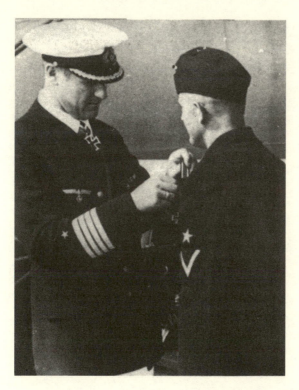

Captain Rogge of the *Atlantis*. From David Woodward, *The Secret Raiders: The Story of the German Armed Merchant Raiders in the Second World War* (New York: W.W. Norton & Company, 1955).

Admiral Eyssen of the *Komet*. From David Woodward, *The Secret Raiders: The Story of the German Armed Merchant Raiders in the Second World War* (New York: W.W. Norton & Company, 1955).

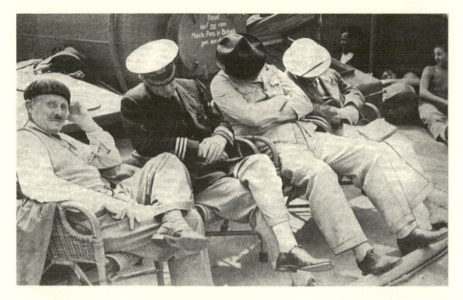

Prisoner-Captains aboard the *Atlantis*. From Ulrich Mohr as told to A. V. Sellwood, *Atlantis: The Story of a German Surface Raider* (London: Werner Laurie, 1955).

Atlantis crew comes home via U-boat. From Ulrich Mohr as told to A. V. Sellwood, *Atlantis: The Story of a German Surface Raider* (London: Werner Laurie, 1955).

The *Komet* and the *Orion* at a Pacific rendezvous. From David Woodward, *The Secret Raiders: The Story of the German Armed Merchant Raiders in the Second World War* (New York: W.W. Norton & Company, 1955).

The *Balzac*, the beginning of the end. From Ulrich Mohr as told to A. V. Sellwood, *Atlantis: The Story of a German Surface Raider* (London: Werner Laurie, 1955).

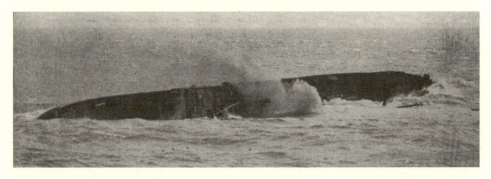

The *Balzac* sinks. From Ulrich Mohr as told to A. V. Sellwood, *Atlantis: The Story of a German Surface Raider* (London: Werner Laurie, 1955).

KMS *Pinguin*: June 15, 1940–May 8, 1941

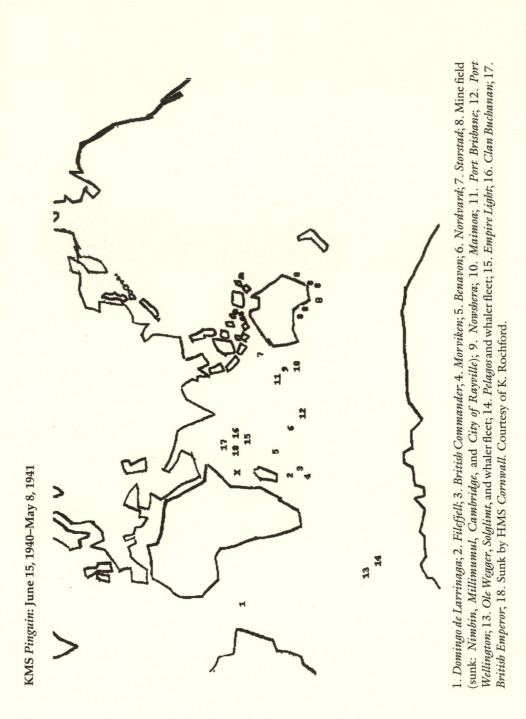

1. *Domingo de Larrinaga*; 2. *Filefjell*; 3. *British Commander*; 4. *Morviken*; 5. *Benavon*; 6. *Nordvard*; 7. *Storstad*; 8. Mine field (sunk: *Nimbin, Millimumul, Cambridge,* and *City of Rayville*); 9. *Nowshera*; 10. *Maimoa*; 11. *Port Brisbane*; 12. *Port Wellington*; 13. *Ole Wegger, Solglimt,* and whaler fleet; 14. *Pelagos* and whaler fleet; 15. *Empire Light*; 16. *Clan Buchanan*; 17. *British Emperor*; 18. Sunk by HMS *Cornwall*. Courtesy of K. Rochford.

5

PINGUIN —————————————————

THE FIRST CASUALTY

On July 17, 1940, the Greek motor ship *Kassos* encountered the German U-boat UA in the mid-Atlantic. The U-boat, commanded by thirty-two-year-old Hans Cohausz, had just recently sunk a 5,800-ton Norwegian freighter. It was Cohausz's third victim. The U-boat's commander requested permission to return to Europe because he had been experiencing serious engine troubles. His request was denied by Admiral Donitz because there was a shortage of U-boats in the area. Instead, Cohausz was instructed to meet the Greek freighter.

The *Kassos* was in reality the disguised German commerce raider *Pinguin*. The latter had brought a supply of torpedoes, food, and fuel, as well as items that the U-boat might need to make engine repairs. The submarine could not tie up alongside the raider because Cohausz feared that his small vessel might be damaged if she was driven against the raider's hull by the high seas. The torpedoes and other goods had to be moved from the raider to the submarine along lines strung between them, with everything resting on flotation devices. The transfer took seven days.

Built in 1936 by the Weser Werk of Bremen for the Hansa Line, the 7,766-ton *Pinguin* was originally known as the *Kandelfels*. In late 1939 and early 1940 she was converted to an auxiliary cruiser. On February 6, 1940, she was commissioned as the KMS *Pinguin*. Most of her weaponry, which included six 5.9-inch guns and a selection of

The day before the two German vessels rendezvoused, Adolf Hitler issued his Directive 16. In it, he announced his decision to begin preparations for an invasion of England.

7-mm, 37-mm, and 20-mm guns, as well as four 21-inch torpedo tubes, was removed from the obsolete battleship *Schlesien* before she was scrapped. The *Schlesien* was an old pre–World War I dreadnought, one of eight such capital ships left to the German navy by the Peace Treaty that ended that war.

When the *Pinguin* departed Gotenhaven on June 15, 1940, she was disguised as the Soviet vessel *Petschura*. Making her way up the Norwegian coast, she hoped to give the impression that she was heading for the Soviet port of Murmansk. Built to withstand heavy seas, she outpaced her smaller escort vessels, and they soon fell so far behind that they abandoned their mission and returned home. The heavy seas also turned away an unidentified submarine that surfaced nearby in an effort to ascertain the ship's identity. Tossed around in the violent seas, the sub gave up and slipped beneath the waves. She was not seen again.

Captain Ernst-Felix Kruder was glad to have the high seas, but he would have been happier had the weather been a little worse. Bad weather, especially fog and rain, allowed ships like the *Pinguin* to slip past enemy warships unseen. The *Pinguin* had the misfortune to be sailing in clear weather with not a cloud in the sky. Matters were made worse by the fact that it was the time of the year when the night never actually grew dark in the far north, but instead maintained only a dusklike atmosphere all night. This meant that the raider could not hide in the dark of night and run without lights.

Now a slender forty-three years old, Kruder had volunteered for duty with the Imperial Germany Navy in 1915. He saw duty in the Black Sea and at Jutland. During the years between the wars, he had served in various administrative posts in the training and construction bureaus, and had become something of an expert in mines and minelaying.

Kruder was proud to be given command of one of Germany's daring raiders. Although he might have preferred guns that were less outmoded, he was otherwise pleased with his new command. She was more than 485 feet long, and was powered by twin 6-cylinder diesel turbines with a combined 7,600 horsepower. The *Pinguin*'s top speed was 17 knots, but her refitters at Deschimag claimed that she could run for 207 days at 12 knots without a break if so required. All in all, she was a fine ship for the duty she, her captain, and his 420-member crew had been assigned. That assignment was to disrupt Allied shipping in the Indian Ocean off the coast of Australia until late November, then head south and wreak havoc among the whaling fleets that normally operated in the Antarctic from December through March. One mission that Kruder and his navigator, Lieutenant Wilhelm Michaelson, looked forward to was to use their 300 mines to sink ships entering and leaving Australian and Tasmanian ports.

But before reaching the Indian Ocean, the *Pinguin* had first to make her way through the Denmark Straits and then down both the North and South

Atlantic Oceans. One bit of good news was that the surrender of France on June 22 had resulted in the withdrawal of French warships from service alongside those of the Royal Navy. This left the British with increased areas to patrol and French ports to keep watch on should their former allies turn on them.

On July 10, the *Pinguin* altered her disguise to the Greek freighter *Kassos*. This was required for her meeting with the submarine, but also because it was unlikely that a Soviet vessel would be sailing in the Atlantic. The sight of one would draw unwanted attention to the raider.

Once the transfer between the *Pinguin* and the UA was completed, the raider took the submarine in tow and proceeded south. Using the larger vessel to tow the smaller saved the U-boat's fuel, and returned her to her own operational area off the coast of Sierra Leone. Leaving the submarine behind, the *Pinguin* continued her journey south.

As the raider neared the isolated Ascension Island, some 1,200 miles off the west African coast, on July 31 a ship was sighted off the port bow at about 9:00 A.M. Both ships were traveling in opposite directions, but on parallel courses. Because of the clear weather, they sighted each other at about the same time.

Fearing that the unknown ship was one of the German commerce raiders known to be operating in the South Atlantic, the captain of the 5,538-ton British freighter *Domingo de Larrinaga* quickly turned away. When he saw the other vessel turn toward him, he ordered his radio operator to broadcast the alert that they were under attack by a raider. He also sent his gun crew to prepare the freighter's antiquated stern gun for action, and raised the British flag up the mast.

Captain Kruder watched the freighter's actions and ordered full speed to give chase. After nearly two hours of racing across the ocean surface, the raider closed the gap between the two ships from the original 4 miles to slightly more than 2, and opened fire. Meanwhile, his radio room tried without success to jam the freighter's distress calls.

Several shells struck the freighter and started a fire near the bridge. At that point the abandon ship order was given and thirty-two crewmen lowered three lifeboats. They left behind the bodies of four dead comrades. An inspection of the freighter found that she was carrying more than 7,000 tons of grain destined for Great Britain. The freighter was then sunk by a torpedo after several demolition charges failed to do the job. Having taken her first victim, the *Pinguin* resumed her journey south and rounded the Cape of Good Hope to enter the Indian Ocean.

On August 26, the raider was off the coast of Madagascar when Kruder ordered one of his two Heinkel He 114B seaplanes aloft to search for targets. The aircraft was disguised with British markings so as not to alert any ships that might see it. At 12:50 P.M. the plane spotted an obviously full tanker with no visible nationality identification. Flying low over the tanker, the plane dropped a weighted package containing a message purporting to be from a Royal Navy officer. The note warned the tanker captain that a German raider was in the area and instructed him to alter his course and keep his radio silent. The tanker appeared to follow the instructions as the seaplane flew away. The altered course would send the 6,901-ton Norwegian tanker, the *Filefjell*, directly toward the *Pinguin*. She carried a full load of 10,000 tons of gasoline and 500 tons of oil consigned to Cape Town. At that time the tanker and the raider were about 140 miles apart.

The aircraft returned to the *Pinguin* and was lifted aboard to be refueled. The raider continued on her course with the as yet unknown tanker her destination. By 5:00 P.M., Kruder was becoming concerned. His lookouts should have spotted the tanker by now, unless the ship changed course once the seaplane was out of sight. He decided to send the plane aloft once more to locate the tanker. The aircraft returned and reported that the tanker could not be found. Angered by the tanker's betrayal, the captain ordered the *Pinguin*'s radio operators to scan all frequencies and keep a watchful ear for any signal that might originate from her.

A short time later, fragments of radio messages were intercepted indicating that the tanker was making a dash for the safety of the nearest port. After determining the tanker's location, Kruder sent the aircraft after her with instructions to tear down her radio aerial. He ordered the pilot to then land as close to the tanker as possible and maintain visual contact with her until the raider arrived on the scene. He realized that approaching darkness would make this a dangerous assignment for the two men aboard the plane, but he did not want to lose the tanker again, especially because she was getting close to the African coast where she could find sanctuary.

On board the *Filefjell*, the Norwegian skipper had not been fooled by the first message originally dropped by the seaplane. Although the plane had British markings and the message was written in English, he knew almost immediately it was false. The message was written in extremely poor English, not the kind of language one would expect from a British pilot. Because he was sitting atop a ship load of highly inflammable liquids, gasoline and oil, he had no desire to face the possibility of being shelled by a German or Italian raider. One well-placed shell could blow him, his ship, and his crew into the next world. So, after the plane disappeared, he ordered his engines at full speed and decided to get as far away as possible. If he could reach a neutral or Allied port at either Madagascar or mainland Africa, he might actually survive this cruise.

It was about 5:50 when the *Pinguin*'s aircraft finally located the tanker. The pilot dropped his line with the grappling hook and ripped down the *Filefjell*'s radio aerial on the first pass. On a second pass he machine-gunned the tanker's bridge to make sure the captain knew he meant business, and dropped another message. This one was also written in English, and simply instructed the ship to stop immediately. Fearing for the safety of his crew and himself, the tanker captain did as he was ordered.

The plane landed, although it proved to be a difficult task as the seas were picking up, and came as close to the large ship as it safely could. Using a signal lamp, the pilot instructed the tanker's captain to remain stopped and to put the ship's lights on. The captain did as instructed. By now he guessed that plane was really German, and that they were waiting for a German ship to arrive. One hour later the *Pinguin* joined them, guided by the lights of the tanker.

The *Filefjell*'s crew was replaced by a German prize crew as soon as Kruder was informed of the extremely valuable cargo the tanker carried. Meanwhile the *Pinguin*'s radio room picked up a signal from another ship, the *Bernes*, claiming that it was being stopped by a passenger liner. Shortly after, the *Bernes* signaled that it was returning to cruising speed and resuming her voyage. It was obvious to the Germans that the passenger liner could only be a British Armed Merchant Cruiser. They hoped that it wasn't nearby.

During the predawn hours of August 27, with both the *Pinguin* and the *Filefjell* still and without lights, another blacked out ship was seen not too far off. Kruder fired up his engines and took off after her. A little over an hour later, at about 4:20, the raider signaled the tanker she was chasing with instructions to stop. The *British Commander*'s Captain Thornton did as he was ordered, but his radio operator kept broadcasting a continuous alert message giving the ship's location and the fact she was being stopped. In order to halt the radio, the *Pinguin* began shelling the tanker. Not one to be deterred, the *British Commander*'s radio operator continued, only altering the message to indicate that his vessel was being shelled. The radio finally ceased broadcasting when Thornton and his crew abandoned the *British Commander*. The forty-six member crew was taken aboard the raider, and the empty 5,008-ton tanker was sunk.

A few minutes later another ship came into view. When the ship drew within range, the *Pinguin* fired a warning shot, and the 7,616-ton Norwegian freighter *Morviken* immediately came to a stop. Her crew of thirty-five, who thought they were heading to Calcutta, was removed and she was sent to the bottom. The little *Pinguin* was getting extremely crowded with so many prisoners.

A hour after the *Morviken* was sunk, the prize crew aboard the *Filefjell* signaled the *Pinguin* that they had seen yet another freighter passing by. Kruder would have loved to give chase to what could possibly be his fourth ship in less than six hours, but thought better of it. He knew that the alert sent out by the *British Commander* had been picked up by at least one land station, that at

Walvis Bay, because the station had repeated the signal. This meant that the Royal Navy was aware of his presence and that at that very minute British warships might be speeding toward him. He decided to let the unknown freighter pass. Instead, Kruder ordered the prize crew off the *Filefjell*, and the tanker sunk. His feeling was that it was unlikely that the prize crew could make it back to Europe unmolested by the Royal Navy, and he didn't want to have the ship trailing along behind him, especially if he was chased by warships.

In a major effort to increase convoy protection, on August 27, 1940, the Royal Air Force Coastal Command established an air base on Iceland. In coming months the base would be greatly expanded and disrupt the U-boats' dominance of the North Atlantic.

Kruder's assumptions about the Royal Navy were correct. Two cruisers and two Armed Merchant Cruisers had been dispatched to attempt to locate the source of the *British Commander*'s alarm. When the AMC *Kanimbla* arrived at the spot where the tanker had been sunk, all that remained was an oil slick and a small amount of debris. On August 28, 1940, the day after the three ships were sunk, the *Pinguin*'s radio operator picked up a signal from a British patrol aircraft that came very close to the raider's location, but not close enough to be seen.

The following week Kruder had the appearance of his vessel changed from a Greek freighter to the Wilhelmsen Line's *Trafalgar*. He hoped that this would afford him additional protection, because one of the Norwegian officers told him he knew his ship was in trouble when he spotted the *Pinguin* because the Greeks did not have such fine vessels in this part of the world.

Calamity struck on September 5. The Heinkel seaplane was irreparably damaged by high seas and sank. The pilot and observer had to be rescued by one of the raider's boats. This significantly reduced the *Pinguin*'s ability to operate by eliminating her ability to tear down the radio aerials of targeted ships. Loss of the aircraft meant that Kruder would have to be prepared to use his guns to silence any ship he approached that sent out an alarm. This increased the possibility that lives would be lost if a ship sought help when it realized that it was being approached by a German raider. He preferred being able to silence an enemy's radio by tearing its aerial down, but his options in this area were now greatly limited. The second plane could only be brought out of storage and assembled in extremely calm seas. Weather forecasts held no promise for the near future.

First to suffer from the *Pinguin*'s new method of stopping and silencing an enemy ship was the 5,872-ton British freighter *Benavon* on September 12. She was carrying a load of hemp and rubber destined for Great Britain. Still operating off the coast of Madagascar, the raider's lookouts caught sight of the freighter's smoke just after dawn. Kruder called his crew to battle stations and headed directly for his target on the horizon.

On board the freighter, Captain Thomson was called to the bridge when the unknown ship was sighted. He arrived, still in his pajamas, and watched as the other vessel closed the gap between them to about 1 mile. He ordered his helmsman to turn to avoid a possible collision and then prudently sent his gun crews to man the *Benavon*'s single 4-inch cannon and the 3-inch antiaircraft gun, just in case.

When Kruder saw the freighter begin to turn away, he signaled her to stop and fired a warning shot. He was surprised when instead of obeying his command, the *Benavon* returned his fire. One shell from the freighter's cannon pierced the *Pinguin*'s hull and entered the crew's quarters close to where the supply of mines was stored. It was the kind of shot that raider skippers had nightmares about. One lucky shell in the right place and the entire ship would disappear in a huge fireball of exploding mines. Hardly anyone on board could survive such an incident. To Kruder's relief, the shell from the *Benavon* failed to explode. Crewmen worked quickly and carefully to throw it overboard.

The *Pinguin* turned to enable her to fire broadsides at the freighter, and within a few minutes both her bridge and gun mount were hit. Captain Thomson and several of his officers were killed, along with most of the gun crews. The freighter's guns fell silent, as did her radio, which was being successfully jammed by the raider. She slowed to a stop. The *Pinguin* ceased her firing. Of the forty-nine crew members that sailed aboard the *Benavon*, only twenty-eight survived the brief battle. These men had to be rescued from the sea because the freighter's lifeboats had been destroyed by the shelling and they were forced to jump overboard. Their ship was sunk by a few more well-placed shells. *Pinguin* had now taken her fifth victim in six weeks. Three days later Kruder decided to leave the African coastal region and head toward Australia. He sent a coded message to naval command with his decision.

Taking a possible German invasion of England seriously, the Royal Navy ordered several of its most powerful ships to patrol likely invasion routes beginning on September 13. Included were the battleships *Rodney* and *Nelson*. They joined the *Hood*, already at Rosyth, and the *Revenge* at Plymouth, as well as several cruisers and destroyers.

Kruder's decision to use one of the more popular sea routes between South Africa and Australia had almost immediate results. On September 16 the raider came upon and stopped the Norwegian motor ship *Nordvard* without firing a shot. The freighter was carrying more than 7,000 tons of Australian wheat. Because she had given no radio alarm, Kruder had some time to think about what he was going to do with the ship and her valuable cargo. With the sinking of the *Filefjell* still on his mind, he decided to put a prize crew on the *Nordvard* and send her to occupied Europe. The decision also allowed him to get rid of the almost 200 prisoners who were crowded below decks. She arrived in France on November 22.

Continuing toward the Australian coast, Kruder and his navigator, Lieutenant Wilhelm Michaelson, began studying charts of the waters around Australia and Tasmania for likely locations to lay minefields. Tasmania is an island of about 26,383 square miles located 150 miles off the south coast of Australia. Originally part of New South Wales, Tasmania became a separate state of the Australian Commonwealth in 1901. Between Australia and Tasmania lies the Bass Strait, a busy water route that leads directly to New Zealand and the Pacific Ocean.

Kruder and Michaelson together developed a plan to mine six Australian and Tasmanian channels with the fewest number of mines in the least possible time. Their plan was hailed by the naval operations staff as "outstanding." Their goal was to cover as many of the shipping channels as possible with the mines they had on board as quickly as possible, since detection of the sinking of a ship by a mine would result in Australian minesweepers searching the channels. This effort would halt all shipping in the channels until they were swept. Kruder hoped to lay as many mines as possible with forty-eight-hour time delays, so that there would be no premature explosions. The plan had one major flaw: Two ships were required to accomplish it. This meant that the *Pinguin* would have to capture an enemy vessel intact and convert her to a minelayer.

The solution to their problem steamed into view on October 7, in the form of the 8,998-ton Norwegian tanker *Storstad*. Loaded down with 12,000 tons of diesel oil and 500 tons of coal, the unarmed tanker's captain thought it wise to follow the order to stop sent to him via flags by an approaching ship that had already fired a single warning shot. He also decided it would be unwise to draw more fire by attempting to transmit a message that he was under attack. The *Storstad* was sailing from the British possession of North Borneo to Australia, where she was to unload. The tanker had several advantages as an auxiliary minelayer, not the least of which was the oil she carried. In addition, few coast watchers would suspect a tanker of being a pseudo German warship, a role normally given to freighters. Tankers were extremely common in this part of the world, where a lot of oil reserves were to be found, so she would fit into the shipping lanes easily.

Kruder changed the tanker's name to *Passat*, which means trade wind in German, and sent a work party on board to make alterations for her new assignment. Over the next several days, bulkheads were torn out and rooms prepared for the storage of mines. Then 110 mines were transferred from the raider to the tanker. Each mine was placed on a mattress and gently rowed from one ship to the other to avoid an accident. In return, the *Pinguin* topped off her fuel tanks with more than 1,000 tons of oil from the tanker's cargo. The *Passat*'s new commanding officer was Erich Warning, who had been staff captain of the 51,700-ton passenger liner *Bremen* when she made a famous run through the Allied blockade in 1939 on a return trip from New York.

When the work of converting the tanker to a minelayer was completed, both ships continued the journey to the Australian coastal waters. The plan devised by Kruder and Michaelson called for the *Pinguin* to mine the channels around Sydney, Newcastle, and Hobart. The *Passat* was to mine both the eastern and western approaches to the Bass Strait, and the Banks Strait. The whole operation went off without a hitch. The Germans were amazed at the lax attitude demonstrated by the Australians when they found lighthouses in full operation, and thus able to be used as navigational markers for the laying of mines. In some cases the German vessels came so close to land they could see the lights of homes and businesses ashore. It was as if Australia was not at war, or the Australians thought the war was so far away that special precautions were unnecessary.

The *Pinguin* began laying her mines in the channel approaches to Sydney during the night of October 28. The following night the *Passat* began laying hers at Banks Strait. During the night of October 30, the converted minelayer placed forty mines across the eastern approach to Bass Strait, then sailed through the Strait and put another forty at the western entrance. On the night of November 7, as the *Pinguin* was mining the entrance to Spencer Gulf, the raider's radio room picked up a message that the 10,846-ton British freighter *Cambridge* had struck a mine at the eastern approach to Bass Strait and sunk. The next day at the western end of Bass Strait the 5,883-ton American-owned freighter *City of Rayville* became the first U.S. ship sunk in the war when she too hit one of the *Passat*'s mines. The result of these two catastrophes was as the Germans expected, Australian ports were closed, and the coastal waters were swept for mines. Aircraft sent out to search for the vessel or vessels that had laid the mines found no trace of either the *Pinguin* or the *Passat*, both of which were steaming southwest at top speed.

On October 28, the German submarine U-32 sank the famous 42,328-ton British passenger liner *Empress of Britain* off the Irish coast. The ship had been damaged two days earlier in an attack by a Luftwaffe bomber. She was the largest ship sunk to date in the war.

Two other ships were sunk by the mines laid by the raider and her cohort. One was the 1,052-ton coastal freighter *Nimbin*, the other a 287-ton trawler, the *Millimumul*. A third ship that struck one of the mines was the 10,923-ton

113

Hertford, which put her out of service for repairs for almost one year. In an accident related to the mining, the minesweeper *Goorangai* was lost with all hands when it collided with a freighter while searching for mines left by the Germans.

The *Pinguin*'s original orders included a foray into the Antarctica whale hunting grounds in search of Norwegian whalers and their valuable cargos of whale oil. They had at least one month before they were to head south, so Kruder decided to head back into the Indian Ocean in search of prey. The two ships, the *Pinguin* and the *Passat,* operated in tandem. Using their recently supplied shortwave radio systems, with a maximum range of 100 miles, both ships could maintain a distance of seventy to eighty miles and still keep in touch with little fear of their transmissions being overheard by the enemy.

It was in this way that the *Pinguin* took her next victim. It was a British freighter of 7,920 tons, the *Nowshera.* The freighter's smoke was first spotted by the raider's lookouts during the late afternoon of November 17. At the time, the raider was stopped with her engines shut down for some overhaul work that was nearing completion. As soon as the engines could be brought back into service, the raider sped off in search of the vessel whose smoke had been seen. It wasn't until close to midnight that the *Nowshera* was found.

The raider suddenly appeared out of the darkness and swept the freighter with her spotlights, at the same time ordering her to stop and not use her radio. The freighter complied with the instructions. Once on board, the German boarding party found 113 crew members, as well as 4,000 tons of zinc, 3,000 tons of wheat, and 2,000 tons of wool. The mostly Indian crew was transferred to the raider, along with enough provisions to feed them, and the ship was sunk. The boarding party had been surprised to find a Japanese manufactured 4-inch gun mounted on the freighter, and defensive precautions taken to protect the ship's bridge and radio room in the form of stacks of sandbags and extra steel plating. They had assumed that the freighter was unarmed because she had stopped and followed orders without resistance.

On the following day, November 18, 1940, an important event in the Allied war against the U-boats occurred in the North Atlantic when a German submarine was detected approaching a convoy by a flying boat using the new Air to Surface Vessel radar system.

On November 20 a similar incident began in the same way, but ended quite differently. Early that morning the raider's lookouts could see smoke from a vessel on the horizon. With one engine requiring some run-in time because of its recent overhaul, Kruder decided to follow the ship along for a while until he could get up more speed without endangering the engine.

On the horizon, Captain H. S. Cox of the British freighter *Maimoa* had also seen smoke. He was concerned that the ship that appeared to be trailing him in the distance might be an enemy warship or a commerce raider, so he kept a close watch. His 10,123-ton refrigerated ship was carrying a load of frozen meat, butter, and eggs, all destined for Great Britain.

Aboard the *Pinguin*, Kruder pondered his ability to catch the unknown ship. His speed was greatly reduced because of that engine needing to be broken in, so he realized that the only option he had was to send his aircraft aloft to tear down the ship's aerial and order her to stop. He could not give chase for any period of time without alerting the vessel to impending danger and giving her plenty of time to radio for assistance. Luckily, the sea was running calm, so the plane was removed from its space in the hold and lowered into the water.

Captain Cox saw the aircraft rise into the air at about 1:20. Now there was no doubt that the unknown ship in the distance meant trouble. He increased his speed to the maximum of 11 knots, and turned away from the approaching raider. Next he sounded the freighter's alarm, sending the crew scattering to their stations.

The Heinkel swept low over the freighter and caught the radio aerial, lifting it away as the aircraft climbed. On a second pass it dropped a weighted package with a written message ordering the ship to stop and not to use its wireless. It also contained a warning that failure to obey would result in the ship being "bombed and shelled." Just for good measure, the plane dropped two bombs into the sea nearby.

Unlike the captain of the *Nowshera*, Captain Cox was not about to be intimidated, nor was his crew. Cox had the boilers banked for more speed, and told his chief engineer to make as much smoke as possible to cover their escape. Meanwhile on deck, crew members began firing at the aircraft with the few weapons they had. Engineer Ernest Howlett fired his rifle at the aircraft in an attempt to shoot the pilot. More effective was the crew manning the Lewis machine gun. They found a running battle with the plane, which circled several times firing back at them.

While the battle ensued, several crewmen located a spare radio aerial the ship was carrying and managed to raise and secure it to the mast. The *Maimoa* immediately began broadcasting a continuous alert that she was under attack. She gave her present location, her speed, and the direction in which she was heading. After a while the Heinkel had to break off the battle and return to the raider as she was running low on fuel and her floats had been pretty badly shot up by the freighter.

Kruder was distressed by the fact his radio operators were unable to jam the freighter's signal, but he realized that at her current speed he would catch her in about two hours. With no time to lose bringing the seaplane aboard, he lowered a boat with supplies to remain with her in case he couldn't return until the next day and continued chasing the freighter. Finally, at 7:45 the raider came within range of the freighter and fired two salvos at her. With the big guns firing at him, Captain Cox decided that the time had come to surrender. At 8:15 that evening the ship, her crew of eighty-seven having been removed, was scuttled.

Returning to pick up the seaplane and the boat he had left for it, Kruder received a report of another ship in the area. Fearing that the Australians were sending warships in response to the *Maimoa*'s signals, he decided to wait until dark when he could slip up on the vessel without giving alarm and force her to stop.

The *Pinguin* was now trailing another British refrigerated freighter, the 8,739-ton *Port Brisbane*, carrying a full load of frozen meat, along with butter and cheese, for Great Britain.

The *Pinguin* followed the *Port Brisbane* the entire day of November 21, being careful to stay as far away as possible so as not to alarm the freighter's crew, but the crew was already alarmed. They had been between 60 and 70 miles from the last location given by the *Maimoa* when she broadcast the alarm that she was under attack by an aircraft and was being approached by a raider. After picking up those signals, the *Port Brisbane*'s captain, H. Steele, doubled the number of men on watch and altered his course northward to take his ship as far away from the area of the attack on the *Maimoa* as possible. At 9:00 P.M., with no ships having been seen by his crew, he felt secure enough to reduce the watch to its normal size, return his freighter to its planned course, and retire for the night. At about the same time, the raider's crew was being sent to battle stations to await the order to attack.

The order came shortly after 10:00, when the raider slipped up on the freighter in the dark and suddenly illuminated her target with her searchlight and sent her a signal lamp message to stop and not broadcast. The first response from Captain Steele and the crew of the *Port Brisbane* was to prepare for a battle, even though every man on board knew that the three antiaircraft guns she had been armed with were no match for a commerce raider. Captain Steele ordered the radio operator to send an alert that the ship was under attack by a raider. The German radio operators moved swiftly to jam the signal, and Kruder ordered several salvos fired at the location of the radio room and the bridge.

To the surprise of those in the *Pinguin*'s radio room, the freighter's signal was promptly repeated by someone else, and the signal was so strong it indicated that whoever was repeating the distress call was not far away. The *Port Brisbane*'s bridge was destroyed with the first few shells, and her radio room so severely damaged, that her transmissions quickly ceased. Realizing that resistance was futile, Steele dumped all valuable papers overboard and ordered the ship abandoned.

Two of the *Port Brisbane*'s lifeboats were picked up by the raider, containing sixty-one of the freighter's crew members. A third boat disappeared in the darkness. Kruder would have loved the opportunity to remove some of the freighter's cargo of frozen meat and butter and cheese for his crew's use, but time was an important factor if he was going to make a speedy departure. He knew that enemy warships were responding to the *Maimoa*'s distress calls, and quite possibly to the signals of the *Port Brisbane*, so once the two boats were emptied, the freighter was sunk and the raider left the scene. The twenty-eight men in the third boat were left to their fate, because they had obviously decided to avoid being rescued by the raider. Fortunately, the men on that boat were rescued by the Australian heavy cruiser *Canberra* in less than twenty-four hours.

Anxious to be as far away from the enemy warships that were converging on the scenes of his last two encounters, Kruder sped first south then west. The *Passat*, which had lingered around the edges of the encounters, and had since resumed her original identity as the *Storstad*, followed along behind the *Pinguin*.

Once far out of range of Allied patrols, the *Pinguin* stopped for some additional work on her engines. This was done in anticipation of receiving orders to proceed south onto the waters of Antarctica in search of whaling fleets. Those orders arrived on November 24, along with a plan for the raider to proceed to the west coast of India for minelaying operations in late January. The overhaul was completed on November 28, as well as alterations to the ship's appearance. Much of her hull and structure was painted black. She then began her voyage toward the expected locations of the whalers with the tanker close by.

Shortly before noon on November 30 the tanker reported seeing a ship on the horizon. It was too far off to be identified, so Kruder sent the tanker away with instructions to rendezvous in three days, and he began a long gradual approach toward the unknown ship. He decided to wait until dark and see if the ship ran with or without lights. Running without lights at night was a sure sign that her owners were from a belligerent nation.

The ship turned out to be the *Port Wellington*, sister to the *Port Brisbane*. In fact, her relationship to the raider's last victim was even stronger, since her First Officer, F. W. Bailey, was the brother-in-law to the *Port Brisbane*'s Captain Steele. The 8,303-ton refrigerated vessel was taking more than 4,000 tons of frozen meat, butter, and cheese, as well as other goods, to England.

The *Pinguin* trailed the freighter all day. When darkness fell and she failed to put her lights on, Kruder knew that he had his next target. By 10:30 that night the raider was within a mile of the *Port Wellington*. The German skipper decided not to risk another protracted engagement in which an enemy vessel alerts all within radio range of her location and situation, so he opted to slip up on her and immediately open fire on her radio room. In this way he hoped to both force the vessel to stop and prevent her call for help.

The first shells killed the *Port Wellington*'s radio officer at his post and severely injured the captain. With flames consuming the control center of the ship, First Officer Bailey assumed command and ordered the vessel abandoned. Eighty-one crewmen, including the captain who would soon die of his injuries, and seven women passengers were plucked from the boats, and their ship sunk. Kruder would have preferred to transfer some of the food in her refrigerated holds to his command, but once again time was the intervening factor. He feared the possibility that the flames and smoke from the freighter could attract an enemy warship that might be in the area.

On December 17, 1940, President Roosevelt held a press conference at which he outlined his plan to provide additional aid to war-torn Britain. It later became known as Lend Lease.

There were now more than 400 prisoners aboard the *Pinguin*. This was a totally unsupportable number of prisoners that made life difficult for everyone on board. Kruder decided to send the *Storstad* to Europe with the prisoners. The fact that Germany could use her cargo of oil in the war effort was an additional consideration. The two ships parted as the *Pinguin* went off in search of the Norwegian whaling fleets. The prisoners and the oil arrived in France on February 4, 1941.

For the first few weeks the search of the waters around Antarctica produced nothing more than icebergs and a few whales. Then on Christmas Eve, the same evening that Kruder was notified that he had been awarded the Knight's Cross of the Iron Cross, the raider's radio picked up wireless messages between whaling boats and their factory ships. Kruder increased speed and headed west, the location of the sources of the messages.

By December 29 the raider was prowling among the drifting ice of Antarctica. The whaling fleet was acting as if there was no war going on; radio transmissions were made without the use of codes, and the whale catching boats, usually between 250 and 350 tons each, kept their factory ships constantly aware of their locations.

By listening to the transmissions, the Germans were able to determine that there were two factory ships close by, with nearly a dozen whalers operating in the icy cold water. According to an international agreement signed in 1937, whaling fleets had only a three-month period in which they could hunt their prey. Whaling had always been a dangerous occupation, but two recent innovations in the centuries old trade contributed to making it less hazardous, and commercially more viable, even after the 1937 accord. The invention of the explosive harpoon in the late 1800s gave the small boats added advantage in hunting the faster whales, and the advent of factory ships in the early twentieth century meant that each whaler could kill more whales and have them processed almost immediately. The whalers chased down and killed the whales, then towed the dead animals back to the factory ship where they were stripped of their meat and processed in much the same manner it had been done on shore stations for centuries. This got the whaler back to the hunt quicker.

For three weeks the *Pinguin* kept track of the Norwegian whaling fleet operating in the area. By constantly monitoring their radio traffic, it was learned that the factory ships were the *Ole Wegger*, of 12,201 tons, and the *Pelagos*, of 12,083 tons. On January 3, Kruder heard that the *Pelagos* was almost out of fuel and her skipper complained that a tanker meant to refuel her was now two weeks overdue. The *Ole Wegger* had plenty of fuel left to stay on station, but her whale oil tanks were nearly full, meaning she could not process many more whales until she could pump some of that whale oil into a transport tanker. Both ships desperately needed that overdue tanker.

A wireless signal was sent by one of the factory ships to the tanker company inquiring about the vessel's location and when it could be expected. From that transmission, which was made to New York City, Kruder surmised that the tanker was American. This meant that he would have to strike before the tanker's arrival so as to avoid causing an international incident by having an American ship in the middle of his action against the Norwegians.

The situation was changed by a simple request from one of the whalers working off the *Ole Wegger*. The man asked if there was time to include one more piece of mail with the mail packet to be given to the *Solglimt* when she arrived. A quick check of their record books informed the Germans that the *Solglimt* was a 12,246-ton Norwegian whale oil transport tanker. This meant that the tanker they were waiting for was not American after all. Kruder decided to wait for the tanker to arrive before striking. In the meantime, the raider silently steamed around the huge icebergs and kept herself hidden in snow and fog banks as best she could.

During the month of January 1941, twenty-two German U-boats were operational in the North Atlantic. They sank a total of twenty-one ships for 126,800 tons. The Battle of the Atlantic was joined by German aircraft, which claimed an additional fifteen ships.

On January 6 a transmission indicated that the *Solglimt* was about 400 miles southwest servicing another Norwegian factory ship. Meanwhile, the whalers went about their work of killing and collecting whales and bringing their catch to the two factory ships.

The *Solglimt* arrived on January 13 and tied up alongside the *Ole Wegger*. Care had to be taken in approaching the ships because if the alarm were given, every whaler and the other factory ship would know there was a problem. In the half darkness of the next morning the raider moved in. A sudden snow squall momentarily blinded the men aboard the *Pinguin*, but when it passed a few minutes later they were almost on top of the two Norwegian ships. The whaling ships were tied together with several whales floating between them waiting for processing. The scene was well lighted by the deck and work lights of both vessels as the raider slipped alongside the *Solglimt*. Two boats were lowered and the armed parties quickly boarded the Norwegians and took command of them. In a matter of forty-five minutes both ships were under German control. The officer who took them was Erich Warning, the same man who had commanded the *Passat* during her minelaying duties. Warning had his men gather the crews into the mess halls and told the two Norwegian captains, Evenson and Andersen, to remain calm and to continue their work. He promised them that they would be paid by Germany. A boat was also sent out from the raider to round up and bring in the whalers, which it did.

Later that night the *Pelagos* was captured in similar fashion, along with her whalers. In all, it was an impressive haul for a single day's work. Three large ships, each exceeding 12,000 tons, along with eleven whalers, were taken. The greatest prize of all though was the whale oil, some 20,000 tons of it whose value exceeded one-half million pounds sterling. There was also another 10,000 tons of fuel oil that could be used by raiders and submarines.

On January 10, Germany and the Soviet Union signed accords setting frontiers in Eastern Europe and establishing trade in raw materials for manufactured goods between the two nations. The trade continued up to the very day Germany invaded Soviet territory in Operation Barbarossa.

It took two weeks to sort through several hundred prisoners, and decide who among the *Pinguin*'s crew could be spared to return to Europe with the prizes. Kruder emptied the *Ole Wegger*'s whale oil into the *Solglimt*'s storage tanks, and sent her, the *Pelagos*, and ten of the whalers back to Europe. He suggested that the smaller boats could be used for close-in antisubmarine warfare. The name of one whaler was changed to *Adjutant*, and it was converted into an auxiliary minelayer.

Unfortunately for the Germans, several of the whalers had managed to escape, and evidently warned the *Thorshammer*, for when the raider went to locate her, she could not be found. It was assumed that she headed home after being warned about a German warship in the area.

On February 18 the supply ship *Alsteror* arrived to restock the *Pinguin*'s larder and give her a new supply of torpedoes, mines, and a replacement aircraft. Again time was taken to work on the raider's power plant and do some painting to alter her appearance. When they were finished, the German raider was called *Tamerlane*, a Norwegian freighter. She now traveled in the company of the former whaler *Adjutant*, which was fully outfitted for minelaying operations Kruder planned for the waters around Karachi.

The following month, having sighted no potential targets, the *Pinguin* rendezvoused with the *Ole Jakob*, a Norwegian motor tanker that had been taken as a prize by the raider *Atlantis* several months earlier and was pressed into service supplying fuel oil to the raiders operating in the Indian and Pacific Oceans. Life for a raider in the Indian Ocean was becoming a routine of daily frustration. Most Allied ships were keeping close to shore, where they could be offered protection by British aircraft patrolling from a variety of land bases. Further away they were guarded by Royal Navy ships on convoy duty. Those ships not part of convoys appeared to be avoiding the usual shipping lanes in favor of circuitous routes that increased their ability to avoid detection.

By mid-April the raider and her consort were off the coast of Madagascar, not far from the Mozambique Channel. Early on the morning of April 24, the *Adjutant*, which was under the command of Ensign Hans-Karl Hemmer, reported the location of a vessel of 6,000 to 8,000 tons to the *Pinguin*. The raider was experiencing mechanical difficulties and did not arrive on the scene until shortly after 5:00 the following morning. The whaler spent the entire day trailing the ship, which was the 6,828-ton *Empire Light*, trying to remain below the horizon and out of sight of the freighter's lookouts.

The day before, April 23, 1941, the disguised commerce raider *Thor* entered the German occupied harbor at Brest after completing her first cruise. She sank ten merchant ships, took another as a prize, sank one Armed Merchant Cruiser, and severely damaged two others.

On board the *Empire Light*, the whaler had been spotted and reported to the captain, who debated whether or not to report the presence of a whaler in the Indian Ocean so far away from the whale hunting grounds. Whatever his reasons, the captain failed to report the whaler to any naval authorities. It was an act that might have saved his ship, because the Royal Navy was now aware that a German raider had been at work among the Norwegian whaling fleets to the south. Without question a warship would have been sent to investigate, and might have arrived on the scene before the *Pinguin*.

In any event, when Kruder did arrive, his ship sped past the whaler at full speed and opened fire on the freighter with a single salvo. The mast with the radio aerial was struck and broken off, and the steering mechanism was damaged. The German gunners were becoming increasingly adept at hitting the masts of enemy vessels in order to silence them quickly. Kruder had been hoping to capture an enemy ship intact that he could convert to an auxiliary minelayer the way he had with the *Storstad*. His preference was for a tanker, because it would seem less suspicious to the enemy. But because there were few tankers sailing alone these days, a freighter would have to do. He was disappointed to learn from his boarding party that the *Empire Light*'s steering mechanism had sustained damage too extensive for a speedy repair. The crew of seventy-one men were brought aboard the raider; the freighter and her cargo of hides and ore were reluctantly sent to the bottom of the Indian Ocean.

Using both the converted whaler, the *Adjutant*, and the Arado AR 196A-1 floatplane he had been given by the *Alsteror*, Kruder resumed his search for a tanker. He could now sweep an area in excess of 200 miles with the help of the plane and the boat.

During the afternoon and evening of April 28, the aircraft spotted two ships, each sailing alone. Kruder picked the one closest and gave chase. After five hours of pursuit he was about to resign himself to the possibility that his best speed was not quite good enough to catch the vessel, when the Arado reported another ship, one much closer and not moving as quickly. The *Pinguin* changed direction and chased after this third vessel. The pursuit went on during the entire night as the raider gradually drew closer to the British freighter *Clan Buchanan*. The 7,266-ton vessel was carrying a cargo of military supplies and equipment that had been loaded in an American port and intended for delivery to British forces in India.

The freighter's First Officer was on watch when the *Pinguin* opened fire from a distance of 5,000 yards at 5:15 A.M. Until that moment, the ship had no idea it was being tracked by a raider. Two salvos were fired at the *Clan Buchanan*, bringing her to a halt. Her radio aerial had been brought down probably by the first salvo, and her steering gear severely damaged by the second, which also destroyed her one stern-mounted 4.7-inch gun. Surprisingly, no one was seriously injured or killed in the attack. All 110 people aboard were transferred to the *Pinguin*. Several of the freighter's officers had attempted to destroy code books and other items by throwing them overboard in weighted containers, but the quick work of the *Adjutant* managed to save some of the material. Among the items recovered was some code information, the war diary of the British Cruiser *Hawkins*, and information concerning the ships that had been sunk by the mines laid by the *Pinguin* and the *Passat* around Australia. Once again the damage done to the steering prevented the ship from being of use to Kruder for his minelaying plans, so she was scuttled.

The Germans had some minor concern over a radio signal that had been sent by the *Clan Buchanan* after her aerial had been shot down. Her radio officer had used an auxiliary transmitter that Kruder decided had emitted a signal far too weak to have been picked up by anyone. He was wrong.

Kruder decided to get as close as he could to the entrance to the Persian Gulf, where he expected to find that tanker he so badly wanted. Fearing the high level of Royal Navy activity in and around the Gulf, he sent Hemmer and his boat away with instructions for a future rendezvous.

Those faint distress calls from the *Clan Buchanan*'s auxiliary transmitter had been heard by two British land stations. Word was immediately passed to all Royal Navy bases in the area that a raider was active, and the position of its latest victim. Warships immediately began to converge on the area. From the base at Colombo rushed the New Zealand light cruiser *Leander*. From Mombasay came the British aircraft carrier *Eagle*, the light cruiser *Hawkins*, whose war diary was in Kruder's possession, and the heavy cruiser *Cornwall*.

Meanwhile, the *Pinguin* drew closer to the Arabian Peninsula in Kruder's search for a tanker. At dawn on May 7, as Allied warships swept the area south of them, the Germans caught sight of a small tanker. It was the 3,663-ton *British Emperor*, and Kruder hoped to capture it intact. She refused all attempts to make her stop, and relentlessly sent a continuous barrage of messages that she was under attack by a surface raider, and included her position. Under a series of salvos the tanker caught fire and quickly began to sink. Despite the fact she was burning and sinking, the man at the radio remained at his station sending the alarm.

The signals from the *British Emperor* were heard by just about everyone who might be interested, from the British warships in the Indian Ocean to German Naval command in Berlin. Two additional cruisers, the *Liverpool* and the *Glasgow* sped toward the position given by the tanker. But, the most consequential person to hear the last cries for help from the *British Emperor* was Captain P.C.W. Manwaring aboard His Majesty's Ship *Cornwall*.

The *Cornwall* was about 500 miles south of the *British Emperor*'s position. Manwaring immediately turned north and began the process of getting his ship up to full speed. Just past dawn the following morning the *Cornwall* launched her two seaplanes to expedite the search. A few minutes after 7:00 A.M. one of the aircraft reported a freighter about 65 miles from the cruiser. Returning to the *Cornwall*, the pilot reported what he had seen, a vessel bearing the name *Tamerlane*. A second plane made another pass over the raider three hours later and reported that the ship flew the Norwegian flag and resembled the *Tamerlane*. A third aircraft was launched at 1:45 P.M. with instructions to keep track of the freighter's movements.

At 4:07, with the freighter in sight, the *Cornwall* asked her identity. In response, the *Pinguin* did what any Allied cargo ship would do under similar circumstance, she radioed her name, her position, and that she was being challenged by an unknown ship. The signal, allegedly from the *Tamerlane*, caused some anxiety aboard the *Cornwall*, for they began to fear that perhaps they were chasing a Norwegian ship after all, and not a German raider.

The *Cornwall* fired a warning shot over the top of the freighter, which she appeared to ignore. As the warship drew to within 11,000 yards of the *Tamerlane*, she fired another warning shot. This time the freighter turned sharply as the German naval ensign flew up her mast. By now Kruder knew he had no chance of escaping and little choice except to stand and fight, even though he was carrying a full load of mines. The raider fired several broadsides at the cruiser, but did not have the range. The shells passed harmlessly over-head.

The battle began in earnest. The *Cornwall*'s main armament was slow in joining the action over a faulty electrical system, but in a matter of time her guns bore down on the *Pinguin*. Kruder fired two torpedoes, but both missed. Then at 5:26 P.M. a four-gun salvo from the *Cornwall* shook the *Pinguin* like a toy boat. One of the shells smashed through the hull and exploded right in the mine storage hold. The resulting explosion sent flames and smoke thousands of feet into the air and scattered pieces of the raider across the surface of the sea. As what was left of the ship began sinking, an unknown German officer unlocked the door behind which most of the prisoners were secured, thus saving many of their lives.

The *Cornwall* had suffered some damage to her electrical system in the bat-tle. As a result, her engine rooms became so hot one officer died of heat stroke and the rest of the engine room crew had to abandon the spaces until the fans could be put back on line. When this was finally done, the cruiser sent boats af-ter the survivors. Twenty-two prisoners and sixty German crewmen were res-cued from the water. Two hundred and three of the *Pinguin*'s prisoners and 342 of her crew were lost, including her captain.

6

Komet ──────────────────────────

THANK YOU STALIN AND LENIN

She was known as Ship 45. She set no record for sinking enemy ships, for she sank only three on her own and only seven when working in conjunction with the *Orion*. Her major achievement was in the way she sailed from her home port to her operational area in the Pacific Ocean, through the Northeast Passage. One other unique item about her cruise was that she was the only disguised raider to shell a shore installation. At 3,287 tons, the *Komet* was the smallest of the raiders, but her armament was almost identical to her larger sisters. Her captain had personally selected her for his command.

On November 14, 1914, the German cruiser S.M.S. *Karlsruhe* mysteriously exploded and sank, taking 263 members of her crew with her. Among the 150 survivors was a twenty-two-year-old ensign named Robert Eyssen. The son of a coffee plantation owner in Guatemala, Eyssen joined the navy three years earlier. After hostilities ceased, Eyssen served in a variety of posts that included command of a survey ship and staff positions in Berlin. With the outbreak of World War II, Captain Eyssen volunteered to serve as commander of a commerce raider, and decided himself on the smallest of the vessels being prepared for that duty.

The *Komet* was built in Bremen in 1937 for the North German Lloyd Line. The freighter's original name was *Ems*. Two years later she was pulled out of service and underwent extensive conversion to serve as a light auxiliary cruiser. She was less than 359 feet long, slightly more than 50 feet wide at her beam, and drew less than 20 feet of water. Her two 6-cylinder diesel powered engines

KMS *Komet*: July 3, 1940–November 30, 1941

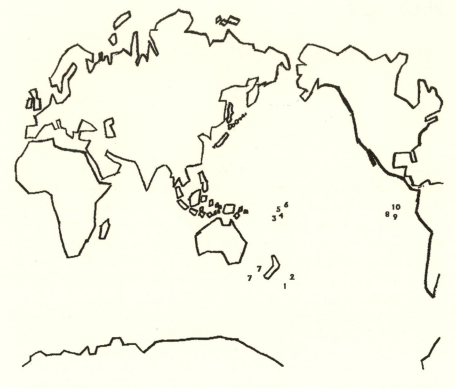

1. *Holmwood*; 2. *Rangitane*; 3. *Triona*; 4. *Vinni*; 5. *Komata*; 6. *Nauru Island*; 7. Mine field; 8. *Australind*; 9. *Kota Nopan*; 10. *Devon*. Courtesy of K. Rochford.

gave her a cruising speed of 16 knots. When the work on her conversion was completed, the *Komet* was provided with one Arado AR 196A-1 floatplane, and a motor launch christened *Meteorit*.

The Nazi-Soviet pact in August 1939 provided Germany with the ability to use several far north Soviet ports, including Murmansk, as bases from which to supply warships operating in the North Atlantic. The following month two German ships arrived in Murmansk. They were assigned to act as supply depots for auxiliary surface raiders, the disguised commerce raiders. In anticipation of large-scale raider activities in the North Atlantic, the Germans requested permission to locate repair facilities near Murmansk to service their fleet. The response came from the Soviet Foreign Minister himself, Vyacheslav Molotov, who suggested that some other location might be more suitable, a location where foreign vessels did not call. His suggestion was a port further east from Murmansk, Teriberka.

Germany's lead man on this subject was the naval attaché assigned to Moscow, Captain von Baumbach. Following an inspection of facilities at Murmansk, Teriberka, and other ports with access to the Arctic Ocean, von Baumbach informed Berlin that it was his opinion that none of these ports was suitable for what the German Navy had in mind. He said it would not be possible to keep secret the fact that repair work was being done to German warships in supposedly neutral Soviet facilities, and once the enemy became aware of this, the Soviet government would come under tremendous pressure to halt the work. Besides, he suggested that the work done in Soviet ship repair facilities was not comparable to German dockyards and not up to German standards.

Although exactly who first came up with the idea of German ships sailing across the top of Russia, through what is commonly called the Northeast Passage, is not known, it is very probable that it was von Baumbach. In a message to Naval headquarters dated October 8, 1939, he suggested the possibility of using that route to bring home from the Pacific region some thirty-five German cargo ships stranded there at the outbreak of the war. He offered the opinion that these vessels might be able to be brought back to Germany during the following summer. Most of the year this route is completely blocked by the Arctic ice pack.

In January 1940, von Baumbach was instructed to learn more about the use of the Passage by ships and to feel out the Soviet government concerning its use by German ships. The obvious advantage of the Northeast Passage, if it was a viable route and the Soviets would give permission, was that German ships could pass from the Atlantic to the Pacific, and back again, unmolested. At the same time, several German shipyards then engaged in converting cargo ships for use as commerce raiders were instructed to strengthen the hulls of those ships for possible use in polar regions where ice would be a factor. One of those vessels was the *Komet*.

The Soviet government became nervous about the possible reactions of Great Britain and France to a German naval base in Soviet waters, so the Germans were never able to establish what they had begun calling Basis Nord. But the passage of German ships across the top of the world, with the assistance of Soviet icebreakers, was still possible, although the Soviets remained somewhat apprehensive about this as well.

German Naval Command was determined to get at least one ship through, a disguised commerce raider if possible, to see if it could actually be done. Ever the advocate of the plan, von Baumbach did some research and discovered that the Soviets had experienced dramatic improvement in their ability to send ships through the Passage during the 1939 season. Previous years had seen many failures, but he expressed the opinion that most of those failures were caused by human factors and that the Soviets appeared to have learned from their mistakes. Additional impetus came from the Japanese naval attaché assigned to Berlin who offered the friendship of the Imperial Japanese Navy to German raiders working in the Pacific. While still technically neutral, Japan was interested in demonstrating her friendship with Germany, especially at a time when the Germans appeared to be winning their war.

When informed of the plan to send a raider into the Pacific through the Northeast Passage, Captain Eyssen expressed confidence that he and his small ship could accomplish the task. Among the things in favor of his selection was his experience in the Arctic waters around Iceland and Greenland during his captaincy of the survey ship *Meteor*.

Orders were soon issued for the *Komet*. She was to sail across the top of Europe and Asia, with Soviet help getting through the ice fields, and steam into the Pacific Ocean. In addition to the Pacific, her operational area would include the Indian Ocean and possibly the whaling regions along the coast of Antarctica. The plan called for her, accompanied by a supply ship, to rendezvous with a Soviet icebreaker near Vaigatch Island in the Kara Sea on July 15, 1940.

The *Komet* steamed out of Gotenhaven, formerly the Polish port of Gdynia, on July 3. She was soon joined by the supply tanker *Esso*, which carried fuel oil for the raider and fresh water for her crew. The plan called for the *Esso* to follow the *Komet* through the Northeast Passage and into the Pacific to keep her supplied with fuel and water. If all went well, the *Esso* would make the return trip with a load of whale oil captured from Norwegian or British whaling fleets in the Antarctic. Unfortunately, things did not go well from the beginning for the tanker. After a brief stop at Bergen, Norway, the two ships headed north, with the raider flying the Soviet flag and disguised as cargo ship *Deynev*. Somewhere along the way the *Esso* damaged her hull and had to return to Bergen. The *Komet* was forced to make the trip to the Pacific on her own.

The next bit of misfortune came in a message from von Baumbach in Moscow. The Soviets had informed him that the ice melting season was behind schedule and the Passage was not yet available even to icebreakers. The Soviets suggested to von Baumbach that the German vessel put in at Murmansk and wait there until passage could be accomplished.

The Germans did not like the idea of their disguised raider sitting in Murmansk where Allied spies were certain to spot her, so instead they decided she should stay far from any port. For the next month, from July 15 to August 13, the *Komet*, still disguised as a Soviet ship, remained in the frigid waters of the Barents Sea. In order to save fuel, she spent most of that time drifting with the currents or whenever possible, at anchor. At this time she changed her disguise from that of a Soviet ship to the German cargo freighter *Donau*.

Captain Eyssen put the time to good use. In addition to training the crew in proper warfare techniques, he provided them with instructions concerning what they could expect during their passage through the ice fields that lay ahead of them. In addition, the cargo she carried was regularly checked to make sure it remained secure. In her holds, the *Komet* stored just about everything a ship with a crew of 270 men would need to stay at sea for an extended period of time. There was more than 35 tons of meat, 30 tons of potatoes, 60 tons of flour, 38 tons of vegetables, 5 tons of marmalade, 3 tons of coffee, 12,000 cans of milk, 10,000 eggs, 100,000 liters of beer, 5,000 bottles of liquor, 25,000 bars of chocolate, 1.2 million cigarettes, 46,000 cigars, 6,000 packages of cookies, more than 100 movies (which could be traded with other raiders met at sea), nearly 600 records, and a like number of books, an assortment of sports and exercise equipment, as well as skis and even reindeer sleds. For combat, the *Komet* carried thirty mines that were to be laid in the waters around Australia, 14,000 rounds of ammunition for her four 20-mm guns, 5,000 rounds for her twin 37-mm guns, 250 rounds for her single 60-mm gun, and 1,850 shells for her six 5.9-inch guns. There was also an assortment of light caliber machine guns, rifles, and handguns, as well as a small supply of torpedoes. Although she no longer had the support of the fuel supply stored in the *Esso*, the 2,180 tons of fuel in her own tanks would allow the *Komet* to remain self-sufficient for many months.

Finally, in the second week of August von Baumbach was told by the Soviets that the ice pack now appeared to offer more favorable opportunity for passage. He contacted Berlin, and the orders to move ahead were sent immediately to Captain Eyssen. Because of the unpredictable behavior of the ice pack, Eyssen was told that it was essential he proceed with all possible speed. On August 13 the *Komet* left its last anchorage and headed east toward a planned meeting with Soviet ice pilots near the entrance to the Matochkin Strait that divides the island of Novaya Zemlya in half and leads into the Kara Sea.

The following morning the raider, still disguised as a Soviet vessel, arrived at the rendezvous. Two Soviet ice pilots were taken aboard from a small settlement, and the ship passed through the Straits and continued on eastward as quickly as it could. Time continued to be crucial, for the Soviet pilots explained to Eyssen that the ice pack could make itself impassable again at almost any time.

Once into the Kara Sea, and the southern edges of the West Siberian Sea, the *Komet* confronted an assortment of ice. Some was loose or in a semimelted stage and could easily be passed through, while other sections remained complete obstacles to a ship and the pilots had to navigate around them. The next day, after traveling 160 miles, they encountered an ice field of such size and density that it required the pilots to contact their superiors in the Northern Sea Route Administration. The Director of the Western Sector of the Sea Route was a man named Smolka, who maintained his headquarters on board the ice breaker *Stalin*. Smolka instructed the pilots to return to the Matochkin Strait and await further orders.

The *Komet* retraced her path and waited for the approval to try again. The nearest icebreaker was the *Lenin*, but she was engaged in other duties and unable to help the *Komet*, so the Germans could do little but wait. On the third day of waiting the pilots received orders from Smolka to proceed. He gave them very precise instructions for the route they were to use based on reports he had been receiving on the condition and locations of the ice.

On August 20, British Prime Minister Winston Churchill rallied the people of Great Britain with a speech praising the pilots of the Royal Air Force Fighter Command who almost single-handedly defended Britain from the German Luftwaffe. The speech lived on in history for its words: "Never in the field of human conflict was so much owed by so many to so few."

The following day they reached the same ice field that had prevented their passage earlier, but this time it was in an advanced state of decomposing, and they were able to push their way through it. In slightly more than two hours the raider cleared the ice field and was once again in open water. This was the first experience in Arctic waters for most of the German crew, and many of them must have been concerned about the screeching sounds that traveled throughout the ship from massive hunks of ice scrapping along the *Komet*'s hull, or the moaning of the ship herself as she pushed through the ice field. Few wanted to be on deck to look at the depressingly stark landscape or battle the bitter cold temperature and the icy arctic winds.

On August 23 the *Lenin* joined the *Komet* for the next leg of her voyage. The icebreaker was built in England in 1917. In her time she was the most powerful state-of-the-art icebreaker in the world, able to make 19 knots. In 1928 she enjoyed a brief period of international notoriety when she located and rescued the world famous Italian explorer Umberto Nobile after his dirigible had crashed and disappeared in the Arctic region. Nobile and American explorer Lincoln Ellsworth and Norwegian explorer Roald Amundsen were the first men to cross the North Pole in 1926.

The *Komet* trailed along behind the *Lenin* through the Vilkitsky Strait and at midnight on August 26, passed Cape Chelyushkin. Later that day they were joined by the *Stalin*, the flagship of the Soviet Union's Arctic Fleet. At 11,000 tons, the *Stalin* dwarfed the much smaller raider.

The two Soviet icebreakers and the disguised German commerce raider tied up together and Eyssen joined the Russian captains for a conference on board the *Stalin*. After discussing the general conditions ahead, the three retired for a traditional Russian gathering filled with vodka and other refreshments. None of them even dreamed that in ten months their two countries would be locked in a bloody conflict that would cost millions of lives.

Four hours later the *Stalin* took the lead and the *Komet* resumed her cruise toward the Pacific. The *Lenin* turned back toward the Kara Sea and additional duties there. The going was slow as the icebreaker worked its way through the thick ice pack, but they made steady progress. At about 6:00 that evening a thick fog bank moved in and reduced visibility to almost zero. This meant a corresponding reduction in speed since the pilot and helmsmen aboard the raider had great difficulty following the *Stalin*. They had to depend on her periodic fog horn blasts and the occasional dim sight of her spotlight. One thing they did find helpful was an oily trail the icebreaker left in her wake as she continuously was pumping her bilge.

On the twenty-eighth the *Stalin* lead the *Komet* into open and generally ice free water. This was as far as the icebreaker was to go. Smolka told Eyssen that the route ahead was generally ice free until he reached the area around Bear Islands. Should he run into any unreported ice, the Soviet official gave the German captain precise instructions concerning ways of skirting it. Once near Bear Islands, the *Komet* would enter the Eastern Sector of the Northern Sea Route Administration. The Eastern Sector Director, Eyssen was told, was named Meleshov, whose headquarters were aboard the icebreaker *Kaganovich*. Meleshov stood ready to come to the *Komet*'s assistance should she require it. Eyssen thanked the Soviet official for all his help and waved him a hearty good-bye as the *Stalin* retreated toward the west.

The next two days passed without serious incident as what ice was discovered was able to be navigated through or gone around. The raider was joined by the *Kaganovich* late on the thirtieth, and the voyage continued in her wake because the ice ahead was reported to be thick. The following day and night proved to be the worst part of the trip, as the raider became locked in the ice several times and it took the best efforts of the icebreaker, sometimes working under the searchlights of both vessels to break her loose. At one point the *Komet*'s rudder was damaged by the ice and required several hours of effort to be repaired.

On September 1, the worst of the ice behind them, the two vessels dropped anchors close to each other. The *Kaganovich* lowered a boat, and it transported Meleshov to the raider. Once aboard he regretted that he had been ordered by the authorities in Moscow to return the *Komet* to European waters. The Soviets had received reports of several American warships, including submarines, having been sighted in the Bering Strait. They were concerned that the Soviet Union could be charged with violating its own neutrality by escorting a German ship through the Passage and into the Pacific.

Captain Eyssen knew that he was about 400 miles from the Bering Strait; and from the two latest Soviet pilots on board his ship, he also knew that it was relatively ice free. He explained to Meleshov that he was not concerned about the presence of American warships. Eyssen assured Meleshov that he could get past them with little or no trouble. The two debated the issue until they reached a compromise. The icebreaker would accompany the German ship as far as Aion-Shelangski, where they would await further instructions. Eyssen recognized this for the ploy it was. From that point east there was no ice, and the *Komet* would not require any type of Soviet escort. If he continued the trip alone, without Soviet approval, the Moscow authorities could rightly claim that they had instructed him to turn back and he refused.

Having reached their destination the next day, Meleshov returned to the *Komet* for another conference. The German captain handed him a typed message that indicated quite clearly that he understood the warning the Soviet official had given him concerning the warships in the Bering Strait, and that Meleshov had been ordered to send the *Komet* back. He acknowledged the assistance he had received, and thanked the Soviets for it, but firmly stated his intentions to continue his cruise to the Pacific, "and take full responsibility for all consequences." It was all the Soviets needed to step aside and allow him to continue.

At 6:00 the following morning the *Komet* resumed its voyage alone. In the predawn hours of September 5 the *Komet* passed through the Bering Strait without being seen by whatever warships were there. The entire voyage of 3,300 miles had taken twenty-three days. Although it was a record setting cruise, Eyssen was the first to admit that he could never have done it without the help of the Soviet icebreakers. It was a trip, he wrote in his war diary, that he would not volunteer to do again.

On September 10, the *Komet*, once again disguised as the Soviet ship *Deynev* out of Leningrad, entered the Pacific Ocean and proceeded to her operational area in the far south. She still carried enough fuel to keep her at sea for up to eight months. Eyssen immediately resumed practice combat drills, something he had not wanted to do under the watchful eyes of the Soviets.

> On the same day, Hitler decided to postpone the invasion of England because the Luftwaffe had failed to win clear air supremacy over Britain.

The *Komet* ran into terrible weather in the North Pacific. Just after entering it, she was buffeted by powerful northwesterly winds. A few days later, off the coast of the northernmost Japanese Home Islands she ran into a heavy typhoon, but managed to survive each with only minor damage. On September 30 she reached the Caroline Islands without sighting another vessel that was not flying the Japanese flag.

Mystified and frustrated by not finding at least one potential target, Eyssen decided to send his seaplane aloft to widen the search area on October 2, 1940. The Arado was lost that day when it crashed while attempting to land, leaving the *Komet* without a scout plane.

Eyssen's original instructions called for the *Komet* to rendezvous with the supply ship *Weser* at the Ailinglapalap Atoll in the Marshall Islands, but that vessel had been captured by a Canadian cruiser while leaving a Mexican port. German naval authorities feared that the Canadians might have learned about the planned meeting, so instead they sent the *Komet* to Lamotrek Island in the Carolines to meet another supply ship that had recently stocked up in Japan, the *Kulmerland*. About this time Eyssen decided that a Soviet freighter this far south in the Pacific would be unusual and attract attention, so he changed the disguise of his raider to that of a Japanese freighter, the *Manyo Maru*.

The meeting took place on October 14. The following day the raider took on supplies and fuel from the *Kulmerland*, which also had altered its disguise to that of a Japanese ship, the *Tokyo Maru*. The two waited inside the beautiful lagoon that served as the island's anchorage for the arrival of the raider *Orion* and a second supply ship, the *Regensburg*.

At a few minutes before 5:00 on the evening of October 18, three other "Japanese" ships entered the lagoon in quick succession. It became an awkward situation, because one of them was actually Japanese—the passenger ship *Palao Maru*, which was loaded with camera laden Japanese tourists. Right behind her was the raider *Orion*, disguised as the *Maebasi Maru*, and the *Regensburg* disguised as the *Tokyo Maru*, the same name used by the *Kulmerland*.

The arrival of these ships in the small lagoon, and the formation of a small squadron consisting of the two raiders and the supply ships is detailed in Chapter 2. Working together for the next two months, the *Komet* and the *Orion* sank seven ships.

With the *Regensburg* returned to Japan to obtain additional supplies, the two raiders and the *Kulmerland* became badly overcrowded with prisoners. Earlier Eyssen and the *Orion*'s captain, Kurt Weyher, had received instructions from Naval Command not to send prisoners to Japan. Prisoners were to be returned to Europe whenever possible. For this minisquadron operating in the South Pacific, that was not a possibility, so Eyssen decided to put more than 500 hundred of them ashore on Emirau Island in the Bismarck Archipelago. They were provided with supplies, including four rifles for their protection, sufficient until they were rescued. The island was occupied by two British planters and their wives as well as some workers from nearby islands. The planters, once over the shock of seeing boats flying the German naval ensigns come ashore, agreed to look after the prisoners.

The following day the squadron disbanded. The *Kulmerland* headed for Japan for supplies, the *Orion* returned to Lamotrek to meet a tanker, and the *Komet* set off to accomplish a pet project of Eyssen, the destruction of the phosphate facilities on Nauru Island. The two raiders had approached Nauru twice in the past two months with the idea of landing men there and blowing up the loading platforms and oil storage tanks on the British-controlled island, but were turned away by high seas that would have made landing small boats difficult.

On December 25, the German cruiser *Admiral Hipper* attacked a British troop convoy 700 miles west of Cape Finisterre, but was driven off by the convoy's escort, consisting of three cruisers and two aircraft carriers. The *Hipper* was forced to return to port with only one sinking for a month-long cruise.

On December 27, the *Komet* arrived off the island and signaled to the operators that she was a German warship and that she was going to shell both the equipment used to load phosphate into ships and the oil storage tanks.

Eyssen advised them to evacuate the area immediately to avoid casualties. If they did not attempt to use their radio, he would not shell the buildings housing their offices and living quarters. The island had no means of defense, which is incredible when you consider that at the time Nauru shipped between 700,000 and 800,000 tons of phosphate annually, most of it to Australia and New Zealand. Phosphate's primary use was in the manufacture of fertilizers and in animal feed.

The warning was heeded. No radio signals were sent from the island, and those working in and around the loading facility withdrew from the area. The shelling lasted for one and one-half hours, and did considerable damage to the loading cranes and storage bins. The oil tanks were set ablaze, burning more than 13,000 tons of oil. Despite the extensive damage, there was not a single casualty among those on the island. As a result of the shelling, there were no shipments from the island for the next ten weeks, and it did not return to full production until long after the war was over.

The shelling of Nauru by a commerce raider created quite a stir around the world. In Tokyo, the Japanese government complained that Japan was also a customer of the phosphate facility and closing it down had an adverse effect on the nation's economy. The Japanese also complained about Eyssen's decision to release the prisoners. They claimed that some of those prisoners knew that German ships were obtaining supplies in Japan, and were disguising themselves as Japanese freighters. They feared that this information would be given to the Allies. As it turned out, they were correct.

The shelling was headline news in Australia and New Zealand. Much hand wringing was done, and questions were raised about the lack of protection for the vital installation. Fearing the apparent daring of the enemy ship, more ships were prevented from sailing alone and had to wait for convoy gatherings. The newspapers did note that although the German ship caused extensive damage, no lives were lost.

In Germany, the Naval authorities were not sure if Eyssen should be heartily congratulated on such a spectacular feat, or reprimanded for angering the Japanese and potentially putting his ship in jeopardy by exposing it to a shore installation that might have been equipped with batteries. In the end, they decided on some mild congratulations but followed it with orders to all raider captains to refrain from similar operations, especially anywhere near Japanese territory.

Eyssen defended his action by pointing out the damage he had done to the phosphate trade of the enemy, and that he had drawn considerable attention to an area he was rapidly leaving. He claimed to have accomplished one of a raider's primary objectives, to draw enemy warships into sectors where there were no German ships and force them to expend a great deal of time and fuel searching for ghosts. The *Komet* headed for its next operational area in the Indian Ocean.

The year 1941 began on a high note for Eyssen and the *Komet*, but then slipped into a prolonged dark period. On New Year's Day Eyssen was informed that he had been promoted to the rank of rear admiral. This made him clearly the highest ranking officer in the disguised commerce raider fleet.

Instead of being sent directly to the Indian Ocean, the *Komet* was sent further south to search for Allied whaling fleets along the coast of Antarctica. The raider reached the ice barrier on February 16, but the only radio transmissions it could pick up were those of Japanese whalers. There was no trace of either British or Norwegian whaling fleets. On the twenty-second Eyssen came upon the Japanese factory ship *Nisshin Maru*. The ever friendly Japanese traded some whale meat and acetylene gas to the raider for a quantity of German wine. A high point was reached when the radio room reported intercepting transmissions in English. After listening further, it was determined that the signals were not from a British whaler, but an American expedition team in Antarctica led by the famous explorer Admiral Richard Byrd.

The search for ships to sink or capture continued without success. In the hope of catching Allied whalers at anchor, *Komet* headed for the Kerguelen Islands where a whaling station existed. The raider dropped anchor in Royal Sound of Grave Island and put a party ashore. They inspected the bleak, barren island and found that the station had been abandoned for years. Taking the provisions that had been left there, the raider turned northeast for the Indian Ocean on March 10 and a meeting with the raider *Pinguin*. The rendezvous took place on March 12 about 120 miles east of the Kerguelens. Joining the two raiders was the supply ship *Alsteror*.

At that point in time the Indian Ocean was a busy place for German raiders. The *Komet* would have to share it with the *Pinguin* and her cohort the *Adjutant*, and several other disguised commerce raiders. Because of the high level of raider activity, it was becoming difficult to find ships sailing alone in the Indian Ocean. Because of this the next few months passed slowly and unproductively for the *Komet*. On May 9, while cruising off the coast of Western Australia, they picked up a Royal Navy broadcast announcing that His Majesty's cruiser *Cornwall* sank a German commerce raider south of the Arabian peninsula. Eyssen knew this was the area in which the *Pinguin* had intended work, and a small memorial service was held aboard the *Komet* for their fallen comrades. Eyssen sent a message to Naval Command asking that the former whaler now minelayer *Adjutant* be assigned to his ship.

May 1941 started off badly for the German Navy. On the seventh, a weather ship was taken by British raiders whose mission was to capture papers related to the Enigma coding machine used by the German Navy. Further Enigma data was gathered a few days later when U-110 was forced to surface and was boarded by the Royal Navy. The Germans assumed that the U-110 was sunk, and did not learn of its capture until after the war.

On the May twenty-first, the *Adjutant*, following orders from Europe, rendezvoused with the *Komet*. It was not a happy meeting for the young ensign Hemmer. Up to that time he had been acting as the skipper of the whaler. The *Pinguin*'s captain, the late Ernst-Felix Kruder, had given Hemmer a great deal of freedom, but Admiral Eyssen, and especially his executive officer, Josef Huschenbeth, was a bit more formal, and required tighter control over the *Adjutant*.

Eyssen wanted to strengthen the former whaler's combat effectiveness, so he had three light weapons mounted on her, one 60-mm and two 20-mm. In addition, she was equipped with a range finder and smoke-making equipment that would help hide her from enemy ships. She was also given a supply of magnetic mines. The following month she was sent to lay those mines at various places around several New Zealand seaports. Hemmer was replaced as commander of the *Adjutant* for this mission by the *Komet*'s mine expert, Wilfried Karsten. Hemmer went along as navigator. This situation, along with the tighter control exercised by Eyssen, caused a serious morale problem among the sailors manning the whaler. For months they had been virtually free to act as they wished, but they were now dragged back into the regular navy with all its protocol and regulations. The minelaying operation went off without a hitch, other than the grumbling of some of the *Adjutant*'s crew and some whispered threats to throw Karsten overboard. There is no record that any of the mines the *Adjutant* laid on this mission had ever sunk or damaged a ship.

On July 1, the little German warship that never saw Germany was sunk by gunfire from the *Komet*. Eyssen gave the order reluctantly, for an extra set of eyes that could range 100 or so miles from the raider was a valuable tool. The *Adjutant*'s engine had broken down, and the *Komet*'s engineers reported that it was beyond their ability to repair while at sea. The guns were removed, and Hemmer was allowed to take the whaler's wheel and bell before she was scuttled. Two days later Eyssen pinned a Knight's Cross to Hemmer's chest in recognition of his activities as commander of the *Adjutant* and a member of the crew of the *Pinguin*.

The *Komet* returned to the Pacific Ocean, where in late July her fuel tanks were topped off by a tanker sailing from Japan to Europe. On the twenty-fifth, Eyssen was told that he could enter the previously sacrosanct Pan American Neutrality Zone set up by the United States to offer sanctuary to British ships, and look for Allied ships on the Australia/Panama Canal route. The *Komet* headed for the Galapagos Islands, several hundred miles west of the coast of Ecuador. This was to be the first leg of the return trip home, for Eyssen was told that the *Komet* had to be back in Germany by October so that she could be refitted for a second cruise. It had not been a very successful cruise, and Eyssen was not anxious to return to Germany without a few more ships taken.

It had been nearly seven and one-half months since the men of the *Komet* had even caught sight of an enemy ship. It is therefore not hard to imagine the excitement that ran through the raider at about 3:30 on the afternoon of Thursday, August 14, 1941, when a ship was spotted less than 20 miles south of the Galapagos Islands. It was a British freighter, the 5,020-ton *Australind*, with a cargo of Australian dried fruit, honey, and zinc concentrate intended for Great Britain via the Panama Canal.

On board the *Australind*, Captain Stevens watched the approaching ship. He told his first officer that they could safely pass what he thought was a little Japanese ship on the port side. When the ships were about 5,000 yards apart, the raider dropped her disguise. The German naval ensign flew up her mast followed by the admiral's pennant, and canvas coverings dropped over the Japanese markings. The *Komet* immediately fired two warning shots. Instead of stopping, Stevens decided to try to outrun the raider. He told his radio operator to broadcast the alert that they were under attack by a surface vessel, and sent his gun crew to man the 4-inch gun on the stern.

The freighter's signal was weak and easily jammed by the *Komet*. Before the gun crew could get off a return shot, the two vessels had closed to less than 3,000 yards. Eyssen ordered his gunners to take out the bridge, the location of the freighter's radio room, which they did in short order. The resulting explosion killed Stevens and one of his officers, and severely injured another. As the freighter slowed, her boats began to be lowered and in less than one minute the encounter was over. The *Australind* was blown up and sunk after the mail it carried, its radio equipment, and some food supplies had been taken off. Forty-three prisoners were collected and put aboard the raider. The injured officer died shortly after and was given a burial at sea with full honors.

The brief incident raised morale among the *Komet*'s crew, for this was the first time since they had left Germany that their ship had sunk an enemy vessel alone. The previous sinkings had been while working in cooperation with the *Orion*. Eyssen decided to remain close to the Galapagos while he searched for more targets. The next day they gave chase to what they thought was a Dutch freighter, but she was too far off and moving too fast for them to catch her. The ship never even knew she was being pursued. That night the *Komet*'s radio room intercepted a message from the British refrigerated ship *Lochmonar*. It gave her position and the expected time of her arrival at the entrance to the Panama Canal. Plotting the ship's course, Eyssen guessed that she would have to pass close to his current position within the next twenty-four hours.

The entire following day was spent drifting, engines off and the men on watch told to keep a sharp eye out for a ship heading toward the east. After nightfall the engines were restarted to prevent the raider from being taken by surprise by the passing *Lochmonar*, and she cruised in a large circle. They never even saw the smoke of the lucky *Lochmonar*.

At about 9:30 A.M. on Sunday, August 17, a ship was finally sighted. It wasn't the *Lochmonar*, but it would do. Aboard the 7,322-ton Dutch freighter *Kota Nopan*, Captain Hatenboer was preparing to conduct church services when he was called to the bridge. On his arrival, the officer on watch pointed to a ship that was approaching from almost dead ahead. Hatenboer could see that she was wearing Japanese markings, but he knew this was no guarantee to her identity. As a precaution he had his ship immediately swung around and increased speed. He was heading toward the relative safety of a Galapagos harbor about forty miles away.

Seeing the "Japanese" ship turn and follow, Captain Hatenboer called his gun crew to battle stations and told his engineer to increase steam to full ahead. He explained that they were being chased by an unknown ship. The freighter's radio operator began broadcasting an alert identifying his ship, giving her position, and that they were being chased by another surface vessel. He quickly changed that to explain that they were being fired on by another vessel when the *Komet* raised the German flag and fired her first warning shot. The *Kota Nopan*'s crew returned the warning shot with two of their own, but both fell considerably short of their target.

A few more shells from the raider brought the *Kota Nopan* to a halt. Captain Hatenboer saw to it that any important or secret documents aboard his ship, including code books, were placed inside a heavy perforated metal box designed for this purpose, and dropped into the sea.

A boarding party rounded up the crew of fifty-one and reported her cargo back to Eyssen. The freighter was carrying tin, manganese ore, and rubber, an extremely valuable prize, especially to a nation at war. The Admiral would have loved to put a prize crew aboard her and send her home, except that she had only about 220 tons of oil left in her tanks, not enough to reach Europe. He radioed Naval Command for assistance in locating fuel oil for his prize, and began moving some of the most valuable of the cargo from the freighter to his own ship. This would make it less costly to scuttle the *Kota Nopan* if fuel could not be found, and gave him additional space for prisoners in the meantime. Her own crew, as well as the crew of the *Australind*, were put aboard the *Kota Nopan*, while Eyssen awaited a reply.

Eyssen was still waiting and still transferring cargo two days later when another ship was spotted passing nearby. Several of the *Komet*'s boats were in the water engaged in the cargo transfer, and the raider's engines were shut down. Not one to miss another target, Eyssen called the boats in and fired up the engines. It was almost a half hour before they were underway, but the vessel they were chasing, the 9,036-ton British freighter *Devon*, was a slow moving old coal burner.

When the *Komet* was within 8,000 yards from her prey, she opened fire with two warning shots. That immediately brought the *Devon* to a stop. The 144 crewmen were removed and the ship sunk with gunfire. Her cargo of miscellaneous goods was deemed of not sufficient value to save.

Five days later the Royal Navy warned that a German raider was suspected to be operating in the area of the Galapagos Islands. Radio broadcasts said that the United States was angered over the violation of the neutrality zone it had established, and American warships were reported speeding toward the area. Naval Command instructed Admiral Eyssen to leave the Galapagos, taking the *Kota Nopan* with him, and steam south. A rendezvous was established for the two ships to meet the raider *Atlantis* and the supply ship *Munsterland*. The latter was sailing from Yokohama.

At the meeting, which took place east of New Zealand, Eyssen and the commander of the *Atlantis*, Captain Rogge, argued over the supplies brought by the *Munsterland*. Because the *Komet* was heading home and the *Atlantis* was staying at sea, most of the fresh vegetables—something the crew of the *Atlantis* had not seen in almost eighteen months—were given to the latter. The *Komet* and the *Kota Nopan* each received enough fuel for the trip to Europe, and the meeting ended on September 24.

Once around Cape Horn and into the South Atlantic, the *Kota Nopan* was sent ahead because she was a faster ship and it would waste fuel to slow her down to the *Komet*'s speed. The raider saw several prospective targets on the trip home, but they proved to be either American or too fast to chase. Finally she arrived in Hamburg on November 30, 1941. A highlight of the return trip occurred on the day before her arrival when a British bomber roared overhead while she was in the English Channel and dropped four bombs on her. Three missed entirely, and the fourth did only minor damage.

The *Komet* had sailed 87,000 miles, crossed the equator eight times, and working alone and with the *Orion*, sank nine ships and took one prize. The most spectacular part of her cruise was her passage across the top of Europe and Asia. Now that Germany was at war with the Soviet Union, it was a feat that was never to be duplicated by another German warship.

The planned second cruise of the *Komet* was delayed time and again as repairs took longer than expected. On the night of October 7, 1942, she left Flushing under the command of Captain Ulrich Brocksien. Off the coast of Dunkirk, four of her minesweeper escorts were almost simultaneously blown up by mines. The area had been swept just four hours before, but obviously the British were quick to replace them.

The Royal Navy watched the attempts to get the *Komet* to sea, and made every effort to prevent it. Two combat groups were formed totaling nine destroyers and eight motor torpedo boats (MTB) with the express purpose of preventing the raider from breaking out.

After over a week of hiding in Dunkirk, the *Komet* made a run for the open sea late in the evening of October 13. She was escorted by four torpedo boats. Shortly after midnight they were sighted by the British, and a fierce gun and torpedo battle ensued. At 2:15 the *Komet* burst into flames from what was believed a torpedo fired from the British MTB 236. Within minutes she exploded in a huge ball of flames that shot hundreds of yards into the dark sky, and sank. Her career as a raider ended.

After leaving the *Komet*, Rear Admiral Eyssen served in a variety of posts, including naval liaison with Airfleet IV in Russia, from March 1942 through

August of that same year, and Chief of the Naval Depot at Oslo. His last post was as Commander of the III Military District in Vienna, from which he retired on April 30, 1945. He died in 1960, two days before his sixty-eighth birthday.

KMS *Kormoran*: December 1, 1940–November 19, 1941

1. *Antonis*; 2. *British Union*; 3. *Afric Star*; 4. *Eurylochus*; 4. *Agnita*; 6. *Canadolite*; 7. *Craftsman*; 8. *Nicolaos de L.*; 9. *Velebit*; 10. *Mareeba*; 11. *Stamatios G. Embiricos*; 12. HMS *Sydney* (sank by same); X. where *Kormoran* sank. Courtesy of K. Rochford.

7

KORMORAN ———————————————

DUEL TO THE DEATH

Visibility was unlimited across the Indian Ocean in the late afternoon of November 19, 1941. With less than three hours of light left, the day remained unusually bright, clear, and warm. A lazy, southwesterly wind prodded the ocean currents in a gentle swell.

One hundred and seventy miles west of Australia the Royal Australian Navy Cruiser HMAS *Sydney* was steaming home after escorting a convoy bound for Cape Town. The voyage had been largely uneventful. Their major threat, the German U-boat wolf packs that were sinking Allied ships daily in the Atlantic, rarely prowled the waters between Australia and the African continent.

The *Sydney* was the namesake of another cruiser that had won a memorable victory during World War I when it challenged and sank Imperial Germany's most notorious sea raider, the *Emden*. That famous battle had taken place in the same part of the Indian Ocean in which the present-day *Sydney* was now cruising.

HMAS *Sydney* had continued the illustrious reputation of her predecessor. During seven months' service in the Mediterranean, she fought off more than sixty attacks from Axis aircraft. On eight separate occasions the Italian navy claimed to have destroyed her. In a fierce battle she sank the Italian cruiser *Bartolomeo Colleoni*. The *Sydney* had sailed more than 80,000 miles since the war began, and fired more than 4,000 shells, all without the loss of a single crew member.

Although no one knows with any certainty what occurred aboard the *Sydney*, we can make certain assumptions based on the facts we do know.

At about 4:00 P.M. the *Sydney*'s lookout alerted the bridge that he spotted a ship in the distance. The duty officers may have routinely identified what appeared to be a Dutch merchantman of about 8,000 tons. Her Dutch flag was clearly visible. The *Sydney* signaled by lights for the merchantman to identify herself.

On board the Dutch freighter, Captain Theodor Detmers admonished his crew to be alert. The deck was crowded with shipping crates and seamen stood around talking in small groups that were visible from the *Sydney*'s bridge. Detmers' signalman at first failed to respond to the *Sydney*, because neither he nor the Captain understood the coded message: "N.N.J." Finally, when the warship demanded "What ship?" the merchantman hoisted the signal flags that identified his ship as the *Straat Malakka*. The flags became entangled as they swung aloft, making it impossible to read the merchantman's name clearly. The warship signaled that the message was unreadable and ordered, "Hoist your signal clear." The Dutch ship responded with a clearer signal.

While this time-consuming exchange continued, the *Sydney* gradually drew closer to the Dutch vessel. When the ships were about 3,000 yards apart, the *Sydney* signaled again, asking the Dutch ship's cargo and destination. Captain Detmers replied by ordering his radio operator to break radio silence and broadcast a QQQ signal, the Royal Navy's distress call for a ship that suspected it was under attack by a German raider. He also hoisted several more garbled flag messages.

The patience of the officers of the *Sydney* must have worn thin with what they saw as a waste of time when they were anxious to get home. They negligently allowed their warship to close to within 1,000 yards of the merchant ship.

Aboard the freighter, Captain Detmers watched intently as he stared into the muzzles of the *Sydney*'s eight 6-inch guns. He knew that those guns were capable of quickly blowing his ship apart. He tensed as the *Sydney* continued to approach. When Detmers saw that the cruiser's deck anti-aircraft guns were not manned and that members of her crew were actually lounging along the rail, he allowed himself to relax slightly. The two ships came even closer together.

Annoyed by the merchant ship's confused signals, the *Sydney*'s bridge officer finally flashed a signal for the Dutch vessel to give her secret call letters. Captain Detmers realized that someone on the *Sydney* had decided she should behave in a manner befitting a warship of a nation at war. Detmers shouted a command to his crew. Instead of hoisting the coded secret signal, the Dutchman released her colors. The Dutch flag plummeted to the deck as the swastika-decorated Nazi naval ensign was run up the foretop. The time was now 5:30. The cat-and-mouse game had been going on for one and one-half hours. All that time the Australian warship had closed on the unknown vessel, gradually coming within deadly range.

The crew of the *Sydney* must have gaped in shocked disbelief at the swastika banner as the panels that appeared to be part of the merchantman's upper hull dropped open and revealed the 5.9-inch guns of the German Auxiliary Cruiser *Kormoran*. The German crewmen who had been milling around the deck swiftly tossed open the false shipping crates placed strategically on the deck and manned the antiaircraft guns and machine guns that were hidden inside them.

In less than thirty seconds the seemingly innocent Dutch merchant ship was transformed into one of Nazi Germany's most deadly weapons of the naval war, a disguised commerce raider.

The *Kormoran*'s first salvo scored a direct hit to the *Sydney*'s bridge, setting it aflame. Detmers then fired a torpedo from one of the six tubes hidden below the *Kormoran*'s waterline. It caught the *Sydney* under her forward gun turrets and instantly knocked them out of action. A second torpedo lifted the Australian cruiser's bow out of the water as the German raider's antiaircraft guns swept the *Sydney*'s deck, killing the men who just seconds before had been standing at the rail. Though the *Sydney*'s two forward gun turrets were out of action, the third turret scored two hits. The first shot passed through the German's funnel, causing little real damage. The second scored a hit amidships, setting fire to the engine room.

During the next few minutes the Australian cruiser and the disguised German raider waged a savage battle. Suddenly the *Sydney* swung about as if to ram the German, but quickly lost speed and passed astern of the raider as flames swept through her superstructure. Meanwhile, the *Kormoran*'s guns blazed away at the crippled and dying warship.

The *Kormoran* had her own problems. Several of her deck guns had gotten so hot that the crew was forced to cease fire and cool them down with fire hoses. Then her power plants stopped as the blaze in the engine room grew and destroyed the electrical system. Smoke poured into the early evening sky from the vessels as the life was burning out of them both.

No longer firing at her enemy, the *Sydney* drifted away as flames consumed most of the deck spaces. *Kormoran* was unable to give chase and finish her off because her engines had stopped and the bridge had lost all contact with the engine room. Detmers watched as the *Sydney*, now not much more than a flaming hulk, slowly limped away. The burning cruiser drifted southward as if she were making for Perth. The flames created an aura over the helpless ship as darkness gathered around her. The German skipper wondered why the Australian cruiser had sent no radio signals about the encounter from the time the two ships first met, or, why she hadn't launched the airplane that sat on her catapult, or why she had allowed herself to be drawn so close to a ship that should have aroused her suspicions. These questions remain unanswered, and are at the heart of a controversy that rages in Australia to this day (see Appendix E).

The *Sydney* drifted off into the horizon a burning hulk. The Germans reported later seeing her flames leap into the sky, the apparent result of an explosion. The explosion ultimately sent her and her entire crew of 644 men to the bottom of the sea. Most of the German sailors paid little attention to the explosion. Their focus was on abandoning their own sinking ship and seeking the closest land.

The *Kormoran* was the largest and most modern of the Auxiliary Cruisers. At slightly more than 515 feet long, and 66.3 feet at her beam, the former Hamburg-Amerika Line freighter *Steiermark* could, when pushed, make 18 knots. Her power plant consisted of four 9-cylinder Diesel engines and two electric motors. On the day she confronted the *Sydney*, the raider had been at sea 352 days. In that time she had taken two ships as prizes and sunk nine others. The *Sydney* was her twelfth and final victim.

The *Steiermark* was built by Krupp-Germania Werft in Kiel, and launched in 1938. Two years later, after being taken over by the German Navy and converted to a warship, she was rechristened the *Kormoran*. On October 9, 1940, she was commissioned as an Auxiliary Cruiser and given the official designation of Shiff (Ship) 41. Two months later, on December 3, 1940, she began her cruise.

Like most of her sister raiders, the *Kormoran* was well equipped as a commerce raider. Her armament included six 5.9-inch guns that were each hidden behind covers that were counterbalanced so that they could be "very quickly swung away manually." Also included, and hidden away as well, were two 37-mm and five 20-mm guns, and five heavy machine-guns. One of the 37-mm guns had originally been an army antitank weapon. The other, along with the 20-mms, were antiaircraft guns. There were six torpedo tubes and an initial supply of fifteen torpedoes. Even though one of the 5.9-inch guns and several torpedo tubes had been lying around shipyards since the Battle of Jutland in World War I, all weapons systems were the best available. The German Navy was fully aware that a raider would be at sea, generally operating alone, for a prolonged period of time. Most of that time would be spent searching for targets with only brief interludes of action, so the ship had to be able to be self-sustaining for at least one year.

To beef up the raider's ability to find and destroy enemy targets, the *Kormoran* was provided with two Arado AR 196A-1 floatplanes and a motor torpedo boat for laying mines.

Lieutenant Commander Theodor Detmers was, at thirty-eight, the youngest man offered command of an Auxiliary Cruiser. He knew that naval regulations required that the post be given to at least a Captain, or under certain circumstances nothing less than a Commander. But, to his own surprise and joy, he was appointed to command the newest Auxiliary Cruiser. Detmers had fallen in love with the idea of commanding such a ship, partly as a result of reading everything he could find about the exploits of Germany's commerce raiders during World War I. The romance of sailing the seas alone seeking out and destroying enemy ships had become a part of his dreams. Despite his desire, he "had hardly dared to hope that I would be given command of such a vessel." In an ironic twist of fate, one of Germany's most famous and successful World War I raiders, the *Emden*, was destroyed in a battle with the Australian cruiser HMAS *Sydney* on November 9, 1914.

The choice of Theodor Detmers was an excellent one. A lean, tough, and practical man with long experience dealing with temperamental power plants, he managed to make the combination of electric and diesel power of the raider work well. He also understood that the success of any vessel, especially a raider working in isolation from a fleet, depended on a happy and harmonious crew.

Detmers joined the navy in 1921, when he was nineteen. It was the long dry period for the German military following the humiliating defeat of the Great War. He worked his way up the ranks aboard several of the tiny German Navy's mostly coastal craft, and at the Naval Staff in Berlin. Contacts made at Berlin served him well as the *Kormoran* was being prepared for her assignment and certain pieces of equipment or changes in timetables were needed. His most recent assignments had included command of a torpedo boat and a destroyer.

When the work of converting the *Steiermark* into the *Kormoran* was completed, and the trials run, Detmers was ready to take his ship out into the world. His operational area was the Indian Ocean and the waters around Australia. Before the *Kormoran* could begin its commerce raiding, it first had to break through the British blockade of Northern Europe.

There were two primary escape routes from which Detmers could choose his means of breaking out into the Atlantic. The fastest was to race through the English Channel. By this time—December 1940—France had surrendered, and the French channel ports were under German control. If Detmers kept close to the French coast, he could probably run the channel, under the protection of German shore batteries, in about fourteen hours. Unfortunately, the Luftwaffe was not able to guarantee control of the air along the coast. This convinced Detmers that although faster, the channel option was more dangerous. Instead, he chose the more traditional route, through the Denmark Strait.

Disguised as a Soviet ship out of Leningrad with the totally fictitious name *Vyacheslav Molotov*, the *Kormoran* took advantage of bad weather and high seas to slip through the Strait unseen. By midday of December 13, she was in the Atlantic and heading south. During this run for the open sea, the *Kormoran* was knocked around so badly that some crew members gave her the unofficial name, the Rollmoran.

As is usual for a lone ship hunting the world's seas, the *Kormoran* spent long weeks of sailing without coming across a single potential target. Her general direction remained south toward the warm water shipping lanes between Africa and South America. What they did see plenty of during this time period were ships with the American flag painted on them. At night these flags were brightly illuminated, and protected the ship bearing it from predators. Although Detmers would have liked to stop these vessels and verify that they were American, he was restrained from taking such actions by a Naval Warfare Department that feared that such actions might provoke the United States into entering the war against Germany. In fact, the German Navy had drawn a north/south line more than 600 miles out from the east coast of the United States across which no auxiliary cruiser was permitted to operate. Once inside this safety zone, a ship of any registry was safe from attack.

On December 18, Hitler issued his Directive 21, calling for the German armed forces to be prepared to "crush Soviet Russia in a rapid campaign." The planned invasion of the Soviet Union was code named Barbarossa.

Days went by without a sighting of any kind. Then suddenly there were too many ships, all bearing the American flag. While the German sailors were frustrated at their inability to attack or even stop a ship exhibiting this flag, they also knew that it was imperative to avoid contact that would lead the captains of these vessels from sending out signals warning of the presence of a German cruiser. Such a radio signal would invariably bring British warships rushing to the scene. Warships were something all Auxiliary Cruiser captains were warned to avoid at all costs. Despite the strong level of armament they carried, these thin-hulled ships were barely more than the cargo or passenger vessels they had been before the war, and were generally no match for a real warship. Their hulls and deck structures were not built to withstand heavy gunfire. Most British warships could stand off, out of range of an auxiliary's largest guns, and safely bombard the cruiser until it sank. This was the fate of the most famous Auxiliary Cruiser, the *Atlantis*.

Detmers worked diligently to keep life aboard the *Kormoran* interesting and pleasurable. Each afternoon a movie from the large supply provided by the navy was shown. The men attended the showings in a rotation that permitted everyone on board to enjoy the entertainment. Although attendance was voluntary, the room in which the movies were shown was always packed. The ship's pool was used extensively by men off duty, although later Detmers would have to close it when his men ignored his warnings about sunburn and too many had to be released from duty due to severe burns. A ban on hard liquor eliminated the potential for the problems often associated with its abuse. Additional officers and crewmen were assigned to lookout duties, so all felt that they were making a contribution to the vessel's progress. Routines for such activities as gunnery practice were established and adhered to, and the men were generally kept in shape for the action everyone knew was bound to come.

The war finally became a reality for the crew of the *Kormoran* on January 6, 1941. At 4:00 that afternoon, one of the lookouts reported seeing smoke in the distance off the starboard bow. Because both ships were on a course that would intersect, Detmers needed to take no action that might otherwise warn the prey. When they came within about 3,000 yards of each other, the *Kormoran* signaled by light for her to identify her nationality. Quickly the target vessel ran up the Greek ensign and signaled back that she was the Greek merchantman, the *Antonis*. Detmers had his own German ensign run up and the camouflaged guns exposed, and signaled the *Antonis* to "Heave to!" He also warned her not to transmit anything over her wireless. The Greek vessel followed instructions and waited for a boarding party sent by the *Kormoran*.

The *Antonis* was a small merchantman of less than 4,000 tons. She was carrying 4,800 tons of high-quality South Wales coal from Cardiff and was headed for Rosario on the River Plate in South America. A thorough search of the vessel uncovered three British-made machine guns and a thousand rounds of ammunition for them. The Germans also found seven live sheep aboard the *Antonis*. The twenty-eight officers and crew, one passenger, and the seven sheep were all transferred to the *Kormoran*. Part of each cruiser's refitting included quarters where the crews of ships sunk or taken as prizes could live in relative comfort. The men from the *Antonis* were locked into these quarters, and the sheep were readied for slaughter the following day. As the *Kormoran* prepared to leave the scene of her first success, the time bombs left aboard the *Antonis* exploded and within minutes she sank beneath the waves.

> On the same day the *Antonis* was sunk, President Roosevelt referred to the United States as the "arsenal of democracy" in an address before Congress.

About this time, the *Kormoran* began experiencing a problem that would plague her throughout her cruise. Three of her bearings had burned out, and Detmers' Chief Engineer, Lieutenant Hermann Scheer, blamed the problem on the soft white metal that had been used in manufacturing the casings. It was Scheer's opinion that the casings wore away prematurely, causing the bearings to burn. Unfortunately he did not have any harder steel from which to make new stronger casings, so was forced to use the white metal. Scheer expected to have continued trouble with the bearings. He was correct.

The *Kormoran* sailed near the center of the Atlantic, first cruising north, then turning south. Once again the days without an enemy sighting mounted. There remained the occasional ship flying the American flag. Other neutrals were also seen, including a ship from Spain. In all cases the *Kormoran* kept her distance so as not to provoke a radio message that would give her position away to the Royal Navy.

Then about 6:00 P.M. January 18, 1941, she came up behind what was identified as a British tanker sailing alone. She turned out to be the *British Union*, and Captain L. Atthill was not about to surrender without a fight. Detmers maneuvered his raider so that she was in the relative darkness of the oncoming evening, and the tanker was silhouetted against the setting sun. The tanker appeared to be following the British Admiralty's orders to all ships sailing alone, that is, to zigzag her course about three points so as not to continue following the same course she was on during daylight hours. The goal was to "minimize the possibility of pursuit by raider or submarine at night."

The *Kormoran* gradually drew closer to the *British Union*, always careful to remain in the increasing darkness behind her so that she would appear to be little more than a dark spot herself to any lookout aboard the tanker. Detmers ordered all camouflage to be removed and sent his crew to battle stations. As he watched the tanker grow larger in his field glasses, he noticed that she flew no flag. What gave her away as an enemy vessel was the fact that she did not turn on any lights as the darkness grew, which is something a neutral ship would do so as to light up her identifying colors, and there was the presence of a gun mount on her stern.

At about 6,000 yards, Detmers ordered the masthead searchlight switched on and a salvo fired at her. Suddenly the target disappeared from view as the smoke from the guns drifted back across the raider, blinding Detmers and the gunners for several minutes. Meanwhile aboard the *British Union*, the Royal Navy armed guard opened fire with the stern gun, but failed to get the range. Captain Atthill order a distress signal sent, and the tanker's radio operator sent the prescribed message, "RRR British Union shelled," and then gave his coordinates.

Kormoran then fired a star shell to light up the target. This done, the heavy guns resumed firing until the rear quarter of the tanker was ablaze and she ceased broadcasting the alert. With the spotlight turned back on, Detmers could see that the *British Union* had stopped and was lowering her boats, so he stopped firing.

Twenty-eight officers and men, one bird in a cage, and one pet monkey were recovered from the boats. Seventeen members of the tanker's crew were presumed to have died during the shelling. Once again time bombs were planted on the ship and set to explode once the German search party had left. The *British Union* had been sailing from Gibraltar to Trinidad where it was to pick up a supply of oil and return to the British colony on the tip of the Iberian Peninsula. The air in her empty tanks kept her from sinking completely as a result of the explosions, so Detmers decided to fire a torpedo into her. This did the job, and the vessel went down.

Fearing that a warship might respond to the *British Union*'s distress call, Detmers ordered the *Kormoran* to head west at full speed. It was a fortuitous decision, for unknown to the German raider, the light from her searchlight and the flames from the burning tanker had been seen by an Australian cruiser, the HMAS *Arawa*. The Australian was racing to the scene in response to the tanker's radio messages. By the time she arrived at the coordinates the tanker had broadcast, there was nothing left of her but some debris floating on the surface. The enemy vessel had vanished. Searching the area, the cruiser located a lifeboat with eight of the seventeen presumed dead crew members, whom they took aboard. The men were able to identify their attacker as not a submarine, as was originally believed, but a commerce raider. The *Kormoran* had been lucky, for she would have been no match for the heavily armed cruiser bearing down on what the Australians knew was an enemy ship.

> For a three-day period beginning on January 16, 1941, German Stuka dive bombers attacked the harbor facilities and airfields on Malta. Damaged in the attacks were the British aircraft carrier *Illustrious* and the cruiser *Perth*.

Although the quarters set aside for prisoners was becoming a bit crowded, life aboard the *Kormoran* had definitely taken a few steps up for the crew. They had now sunk their second ship, and could really feel that they were a part of the war.

Nine days later, as she sailed just a few degrees north of the equator, the *Kormoran* found her next two victims in quick succession. January 29 was a blistering hot day. In addition, there was a thick blanket of haze riding close to the ocean surface that made it difficult for the lookouts to see anything in the near distance. Detmers had just returned to his cabin at about 1:15 in the afternoon when the alarm bells rang throughout the ship. Rushing to the bridge, he was told that a ship could barely be made out on the horizon. At first, all Detmers could see through his glasses was the sun reflecting off a ship's wake. Then the vessel itself came into view. The image was extremely vague through the haze, but it appeared to be a very large ship.

In fact, it was an 11,900-ton refrigerated ship sailing from Buenos Aires to Great Britain. In her chilled holds was 5,708 tons of meat and 634 tons of butter, both extremely valuable commodities in England. In addition to the food supply, the *Afric Star* also carried a crew of seventy-two officers and men, and four passengers, all British citizens. Two of the passengers were women.

The two ships were about 16,000 yards apart, and moving in the same direction. The *Kormoran* gradually increased her speed and slowly eased closer to the *Afric Star*. Meanwhile, the raider's radio operators listened for a signal from the enemy ship, but there was none. Detmers found it hard to believe that the ship had not seen him and been alerted to the potential danger he presented.

After fifteen minutes the vessels were 10,000 yards apart. Although the ship flew no flag and displayed no nationality markings, the clearly visible gun mounted on her stern was all the proof Detmers needed to know that she was an enemy.

At about 9,000 yards' distance, the *Afric Star* suddenly began to turn away as if they had at last spotted the approaching ship. Now that he had been seen, Detmers ordered the camouflage dropped from his weapons and the German flag run up. He notified the radio operator to transmit the following instructions three times: "Stop. No wireless!" For good measure, a shot was fired across the *Afric Star*'s bow. The ship did the exact opposite of what she was told. The *Afric Star* increased her speed and began broadcasting a distress signal that she was under attack by a commerce raider.

The *Kormoran* responded by jamming the distress signal and firing into the ship. After a few minutes of this action, the *Afric Star* ceased broadcasting and slowed to a stop. Almost immediately her boats were lowered and those aboard began loading into the lifeboats. The raider pulled to within 2,000 yards of her target and lowered, her launch so that her boarding party could inspect and mine the vessel. When Detmers received a radio message from the boarding party reporting on the cargo, he would have liked to take the *Afric Star* as a prize and distribute the food among the other raiders, U-boats, and supply ships operating in the Atlantic, but she had been too severely damaged in the shelling to continue to operate, so he reluctantly gave the order to sink her.

Following some routine questioning and a thorough search for weapons, the male prisoners were placed in the prisoners' quarters below decks. The two women were given a cabin to share near the ship's hospital.

Slightly more than three hours had passed from the time the *Kormoran* first instructed the *Afric Star* to stop and the ship's disappearance below the surface. That was too long for Detmers' liking. The part of the ocean they were in was known to be heavily patrolled by the Royal Navy, and he was sure someone had picked up at least a garbled version of the *Afric Star*'s call for help. He ordered the raider to turn southwest and leave the area at full speed. As it turned out, the Freetown radio operator did not understand the *Afric Star*'s radio broadcast, but several other ships had picked up the vessel's distress call and they passed it on. Once again Detmers had made a wise decision to sacrifice one of his torpedoes to rapidly sink a victim so that he could abandon the area with haste.

Detmers had instituted a policy that the first man, officer or crew, who spotted a ship would be rewarded with a bottle of champagne, provided that two conditions were met. The first was that it had to be any enemy vessel; and second, the sighted vessel had to be either sunk or taken as a prize. The officer of the watch had been first to sight the *Afric Star*, and was still enjoying his reward when he again sounded the alarm. It was less than three hours after the *Afric Star* sank.

Once again Detmers, who had been enjoying a postbattle chat with several officers in the ward room, rushed to the bridge. Through his glasses he could make out a ship off the starboard bow. He recognized the vessel's single unusually large funnel as belonging to a merchantman of the Blue Funnel Line, a British shipping company. He immediately ordered the *Kormoran* to give chase.

As the raider closed in on the ship, Detmers sent her a lamp signal requesting her name. The response was that she was the *Eurylochus*. This confirmed Detmers' guess that she belonged to the Blue Funnel Line because all the vessels of that company were given names out of Greek mythology.

When the *Kormoran* pulled abreast of the merchant ship and was about 3,500 yards off, she radioed her usual instructions to a potential victim, "Heave to! No wireless!" The *Eurylochus* appeared to increase her speed, and began broadcasting an alert that she was under attack. The raider opened fire with her heavy guns. Much to the German's surprise, the single antisubmarine gun mounted on the *Eurylochus*'s stern returned fire. Within minutes the *Kormoran*'s gunners had found the range and the *Eurylochus*'s gun fell silent without its operators ever finding the range for effective fire.

With shells pounding his ship, the *Eurylochus*'s captain ordered his engines stopped, told his radio operator to cease broadcasting, and sounded the abandon ship. When Detmers saw that the enemy had shut down her power and received confirmation that she had stopped sending wireless messages, he ordered his own guns to cease fire. Both ships were now about 1,000 yards apart as the merchantman began lowering her boats.

The *Kormoran* rescued forty-two members of the *Eurylochus*'s crew from two waterlogged lifeboats. Three were British citizens, the remaining were Chinese seamen employed by the shipping company. According to one of the British officers, thirty-eight members of the crew, Chinese and British, were missing. Detmers assumed that they had either died in the attack, or their lifeboats were in better condition than the two the Germans had rescued, and they were out there in the dark heading toward a second ship that had been sailing with the *Eurylochus*. The German boarding party discovered their victim was carrying sixteen heavy bombers from Liverpool to the Gold Coast in Africa. The planes had no engines. Detmers later learned the aircraft motors were on the second ship.

The *Kormoran*'s officers and crew had been overjoyed by their earlier sinking of a ship loaded with food for Great Britain. Now they were thrilled to learn that they had made a direct contribution to the war by preventing sixteen heavy bombers from reaching the British forces battling Rommel's Afrika

Corps in North Africa. January 29, 1941, proved to be an extremely productive day for this raider.

Once again Detmers decided to use one of his torpedoes to sink a ship that was taking too long. The airwaves were quickly filling with messages flying in all directions as a result of the sinking of the *Afric Star* and the *Eurylochus*. This time, however, there were tragic consequences. Here is how Detmers described what happened next:

Just as the torpedo leapt out of its tube towards the *Eurylochus* something moved into the area of sea which was lit up by our searchlight. It was one of the ship's boats, which had been invisible up to now in the darkness, and it was obviously heading back to the *Eurylochus*. It was already quite close to the doomed ship and would reach her about the same time as my torpedo.

I immediately gave orders for our searchlight to be switched off, and for a signal to be morsed over by a blink lamp: "Torpedo away." At the same time a hand lamp was used to light up the course of the torpedo as it sped towards the *Eurylochus*. Unfortunately the time was too short for this to have any effect, and the boat arrived at the side of the *Eurylochus* at the same time as our torpedo.

Following the explosion resulting from the torpedo's impact against the ship's midsection, the *Kormoran* circled the rapidly sinking vessel, but failed to locate any survivors from the unfortunate lifeboat.

The airwaves remained alive with communications between British ships and several land stations. Among the information the *Kormoran*'s radio operator picked up was that a cruiser was rapidly approaching the area pinpointed by the *Eurylochus*'s distress call. Detmers needed no other warning to leave the area at top speed. Once again it was a fortunate decision. Two British cruisers, the *Norfolk* and the *Devonshire*, were steaming toward him at full speed. Either vessel was more than a match for the *Kormoran*.

The *Kormoran* made its escape, but soon after, one of its engines had to be shut down. Once again the fault lay with the bearings. The Chief Engineer reiterated to Detmers that the only metal they had on board that could be used to manufacture new bearings was too malleable to last long. They required a harder metal, and there was no way around that. Detmers considered the possibility of returning to Europe and putting into a French port for repairs. He knew that this would be a time-consuming process, and he did not want to waste what time was available to sink enemy ships. He radioed the navy for assistance in locating the metal his engineers needed. Meanwhile, the *Kormoran* would remain on station and in the war.

The following week was spent sailing south toward a planned rendezvous with a supply ship. Life aboard the raider settled down into a routine that permitted much time for recreation. The ship's large store of films always had something to offer, and the weather was mild and comfortable. A celebration of the crossing of the equator took place, and the absence of any ships for several days made life rather easy for a warship in the middle of the ocean. Twice each day the prisoners, whose number now exceeded 175, were allowed on deck for exercise. Watching the two women, both of whom were young and attractive, get their daily exercise became a hobby for several of the German sailors. The men kept their distance from the women, and neither woman ever reported an instance of a German sailor being disrespectful.

On February 7, the *Kormoran* came upon a ship flying the American flag with the name *Dixie* painted on her sides. It was the disguised German supply ship, *Nordmark*. The tanker was located exactly where she was supposed to be, at the latitude directly on line with Rio de Janeiro. The *Nordmark* served as a supply ship for German surface raiders and submarines operating in the Atlantic. Converted from the prewar identity of the tanker *Westerwald*, she was heavily armed with camouflaged 5.9-inch cannons and a selection of lighter-weight antiaircraft guns. Her present disguise as an American ship protected her from attack by either side in the war. Alongside the *Nordmark* was the British refrigerator ship *Duquesa* from which she drew a large amount of supplies for her cohorts. The *Duquesa* had been taken as a prize by the pocket battleship *Admiral Scheer*. When Detmers learned that the *Duquesa* could not be sent back to Europe as a prize because her coal bunkers were nearly empty and fuel could not be found for her, he regretted having sunk the *Antonis* with her load of 5,000 tons of high-quality South Wales coal.

In North Africa, Italian forces began surrendering to the British at Beda Fomm. Eventually ten Italian divisions were destroyed by two British Army divisions, and 130,000 Italian prisoners were taken in the campaign. Such Italian failures would bring Germany into the war in Africa.

Unable to obtain any of the hard metal his Chief Engineer needed so desperately, Detmers met briefly with the tanker's captain who did not often get visitors. Captain Grau, who explained that he saw few ships in the area and that most of them were flying the U.S. flag, invited Detmers to avail himself of the food supplies stored in the *Duquesa*. The big refrigerator ship had only enough coal to keep her cooling units operating, so raiders and U-boats could take all they wanted from her cargo. The *Kormoran*'s crew loaded up on 100 quarters of chilled beef and 216,000 eggs.

The *Nordmark* pumped 1,338 tons of fuel oil into the *Kormoran*'s tanks. In exchange, the *Kormoran* turned her prisoners over to the tanker for future shipment to a POW camp in Europe. Before their departure to an uncertain fate, the various ship captains were invited to join Detmers for "a friendly glass of beer." He thanked them for their cooperation in maintaining discipline among their crews. Detmers was impressed by the fact that the captains had opted to stay in the same quarters with their crews despite being given the opportunity to live in separate quarters. Records indicate that this was the only time Detmers, who restricted the use of alcoholic beverages on board his ship, drank a bottle of beer. The prisoners were later transferred to the *Portland*, a ship the Germans had taken as a prize. The *Portland* was sailing from Chile to France. The prisoners arrived in Bordeaux in the middle of March.

Later one of the officers from the *Afric Star* would recall that while aboard the *Kormoran* the prisoners "had been decently treated." He also pointed out that they were given "the same food as the Germans." George W. Povey, Third Officer aboard the *Eurylochus*, agreed that they had been "well treated" by their German captors. One reason for this, he said, was a "certain fraternity among seamen."

The *Kormoran* had a prearranged rendezvous with her sister raider, the *Pinguin*. The meeting was set for February 25, 1941, at 26° South by 2°, 30' West. The *Pinguin* was waiting when the *Kormoran* arrived, and both crews gave each other a cheering welcome. Although unable to supply Detmers with the metal his Chief Engineer required, the *Pinguin*'s Captain Kruder gladly exchanged films with Detmers. This gave each crew an new set of movies to while away the long hours at sea.

Detmers was increasingly concerned about his inability to locate the hardened metal needed to make new bearings for his engines. The engine room crew was busy almost daily changing worn bearings for the new ones they were making, knowing full well that the new bearings would last only a few days at best.

Detmers and Kruder made plans to meet at a location in the Indian Ocean on June 1. They would then divide the area into two operational zones to avoid accidentally coming in conflict with each other. Detmers decided to stay in the Atlantic in hopes of encountering a U-boat or supply ship carrying the metal the Naval War Department promised to send him. Meanwhile, the engineers continued their never ending task of making new bearings and replacing the old ones as they failed. This constant problem with the bearings forced the raider to reduce its speed as one engine was usually down for repairs.

For the next few weeks the *Kormoran* sailed throughout the area frequented by ships heading to and leaving Freetown. She had no luck at all. The only battling members of her crew did were the engine room crews who had to contend with increasing bearing breakdowns.

The United States continued to draw closer to participation in the war. On March 1, the U.S. Navy added a support force of three destroyer squadrons comprised of twenty-seven ships to the Atlantic Fleet.

A rendezvous had been arranged with a U-boat northeast of São Paulo so that the *Kormoran*, which was carrying a cargo of submarine torpedoes, could restock the underwater craft. The two vessels met on March 16. The precarious transfer took place in Force 5 seas, but was accomplished without the loss of one of the valuable weapons. The following day the *Kormoran* met at the same location with the pocket battleship *Admiral Scheer*. Then she was once more on her own, hunting the seaways for enemy ships sailing between South Africa and North America.

As was increasingly the case in areas of the world's oceans where raiders and submarines had previously been successful, this section of the Atlantic offered slim pickings for the hunter. Not until the morning of March 22 was a victim discovered. She was a small British tanker of 3,552 tons, and she was sailing from Freetown to Venezuela to pick up a load of oil. It wasn't a great prize after so many long days searching, but it was an enemy ship, and it was the best they could find.

During the night of March 16–17, the U-boat fleet suffered a severe blow to its morale with the sinking of two important boats, the U-99 and the U-100.

The *Agnita* was first spotted by the raider at 8:15 A.M., and earned someone a bottle of champagne. She was sailing out of the morning mist and heading directly for the *Kormoran* and her fate. Fifteen minutes later her details began to materialize as she left the haze behind. The most important of these details was the antisubmarine gun mounted so brazenly on her stern. Once again this obvious sign told Detmers that the approaching vessel was a target.

The raider signaled the oncoming ship, asking her name. Evidently the captain of the *Agnita* assumed that he was approaching another British vessel, and answered the question. In reply she was given the instructions the *Kormoran* typically gave her targets, "Heave to! No wireless!" The German crew quickly dropped all camouflage and exposed their vessel as a warship.

The little tanker's response surprised Detmers. Instead of following his orders, she turned hard away and picked up speed. Black smoke poured from her funnel and behind her she was "churning up the water furiously." At the same time, the tanker immediately began broadcasting the Admiralty's designated signal for a ship under attack by a surface raider, along with her identification and position.

The *Kormoran*'s radio operator quickly began jamming the *Agnita*'s distress call, and Detmers ordered his gunners to open fire. The second salvo convinced the British captain that escape was out of the question. The tanker slowed to a halt, and its radio fell silent. Evidently no one aboard the tanker seriously considered returning the raider's fire with the 4.7-inch stern gun or the two antiaircraft guns with which it was armed.

The tanker's crew of thirteen British and twenty-five Chinese sailors were taken aboard the *Kormoran*. An inspection found that the vessel was in poor repair, and the engines had been damaged in the shelling, so seeing it as a worthless vessel for his purposes, Detmers had charges set throughout the ship and watched it sink.

The *Agnita* turned out to be much more valuable than Detmers originally thought. As was the *Kormoran*'s habit, a boarding party had been sent to search the vessel before setting the charges. Among the items they returned with was a chart of the harbor around Freetown, an extremely busy British port in Sierra Leone. Carefully identified on the chart were the locations of defensive minefields around the harbor designed to keep enemy ships out. Also carefully marked were the routes a ship must take to enter the port safely. Detmers had copies made of the chart and gave one to every U-boat commander he came into contact with.

Three days later it was the *Canadolite*'s turn to defend herself. The tanker was also on her way to Venezuela to pick up oil. The 11,300-ton *Canadolite* was of Canadian registry, therefore clearly an enemy vessel. She was spotted in almost the same location as the *Agnita*. Uncharacteristically, Detmers had decided not to rush away from the place where he had sunk the little tanker in order to avoid the possibility of a British cruiser responding to the messages it had broadcast. Detmers questioned his radio operator concerning the speed and effectiveness with which he had jammed the *Agnita*'s call for help. They both concluded that it was highly unlikely the message had been received anywhere. The jamming had been effective, and there had been no response from anyone. So, instead of sailing away for safety, the *Kormoran* sailed south for a day and a half, then turned back north to return to the same location.

Shortly after 8:00 A.M. on March 25, a ship that turned out to be the *Canadolite* was seen off the starboard side of the raider. Through the heavy mist the ship appeared and disappeared from view. Finally the vessel's infamous stern gun could be seen clearly enough that the ship was considered an enemy. That having been accomplished, the raider fired a shot across the tanker's bow, and signaled her to "Heave to! No wireless!"

The Canadian tanker responded in the same way the British tanker had. The *Canadolite* turned and increased speed and began broadcasting an alert that she was under attack. Detmers thought the ship looked like she would make a good prize to send back to Germany, so he ordered his gunners to avoid hitting her where they might cause serious damage. A few shots convinced the tanker's captain that he could not outrun the raider, so he stopped broadcasting, shut down his engines, and began lowering his boats.

The captain, chief engineer, radio officer, and the gunnery petty officer of the *Canadolite* were taken aboard the *Kormoran* and replaced by a German prize crew with instructions to take the tanker to Bordeaux.

On March 28, the raider rendezvoused with two U-boats and the *Nordmark*. In return for replenishing its stock of torpedoes, one of the submarines transferred to the *Kormoran* a supply of the metal Detmers needed for his bearings problem. Unfortunately it was a small supply, which indicated to the raider's captain that the Navy did not really understand the difficulty he was having. On consideration, he decided that was just as well, for there was always the fear that he would be ordered to return to Europe for repairs if the naval staff had a clearer picture of the problem. That would have taken him out of the war for an extended period of time, something he did not want. So, it was "danka" for the metal and back to the war.

During the night of the twenty-eighth, Royal Navy forces struck a crippling blow at the Italian Navy in the Mediterranean. Three Italian cruisers and two destroyers were surprised by the British and sunk before they could even return the British ships' fire.

On April 9, the *Kormoran* encountered a slow moving British freighter with an unusual cargo. Five of the fifty-one crewmen aboard the 8,022-ton *Craftsman* were killed when the freighter at first tried to escape from the *Kormoran*, and Detmers was forced to fire into her to stop her radio from broadcasting an alarm. Once she had surrendered and the remaining crew taken aboard the raider, charges were detonated to sink her. To the surprise of everyone aboard the *Kormoran* who watched, the freighter sank only about three feet deep and appeared to come to rest there. It was as if she was sitting atop a sandbar. She was kept afloat by the thousands of floats attached to the huge antisubmarine net stored in her hold. She was hauling the net to Cape Town for use in protecting the harbor from U-boats. Finally, a torpedo ripped her hull open and she slowly began to settle down into the ocean. Behind her she left hundreds of floats, most as large or larger than a mine. For a long time after, these floats were mistaken for mines and caused more than one vessel to change course as they drifted on the ocean's currents.

The following day the *Kormoran* received two messages from the Naval War Department. Both contained good news. The first announced the safe arrival of the *Canadolite* and her German prize crew. The second announced the promotion of Theodor Detmers to full Commander. The news was received with general pleasure among the crew, and every man sought the opportunity to congratulate the new Commander.

On April 11, the United States continued its march toward war against Germany by declaring that the Red Sea was no longer a "combat zone." This allowed American cargo ships to bring supplies to British forces through Egyptian Red Sea ports.

The *Kormoran*'s next victim seemed even more determined not to sink than the *Craftsman*. The Greek freighter, *Nicholas de L.* was carrying a huge shipment of Oregon pine planks stacked high on her decks when she fell prey to the raider on April 12. The thirty-eight members of the freighter's crew were taken aboard the *Kormoran* and the usual charges spread throughout the ship. When these failed to sink her, Detmers fired several shells from his bigger guns into her. It appeared that the pine planks were keeping her afloat. Reluctant to use another valuable torpedo to sink another hulk, Detmers decided to leave the area and hope the freighter went under before her fate was discovered. It was not good policy to leave a vessel still afloat. There was always the possibility she might be discovered and towed into port for repairs, or as might be the case with the *Nicholas de L.*, though not in condition to be towed, her fate would be known and the location of her attacker determined. It was always best that a victim be sent to the bottom because it might be days or even weeks before her fate was guessed. And then it would be difficult or even impossible to determine where she was attacked. An overdue ship was normal during wartime, and did not draw much attention until she was so overdue that she would be presumed lost. Even then, no one would know if she had been sunk by an enemy or gone down on her own accord or as the result of a storm.

The time had come for the *Kormoran* to leave the Atlantic and sail for her original posting in the Indian Ocean. Before doing so, she paid one more visit to the *Nordmark* to top off her fuel supply and replenish her meat and egg lockers from the refrigerator ship that remained at her side. While there, Detmers spent a brief time visiting with Captain Rogge of the *Atlantis*, the most successful of the disguised raiders. Rogge told him of the relatively easy pickings in the Indian Ocean during the previous year, and how that had all changed now. Enemy merchant ships rarely ventured out into the ocean, instead they stuck close to the shore line where Allied planes and warships could quickly respond to calls for help. Detmers expected to rendezvous with the *Pinguin*, as he and Captain Kruder had planned. That was not to be, for before the date set for the meeting, June 1, the *Pinguin* would fall victim to a British warship. Kruder and most of his crew would go down with their ship.

During the first few weeks they saw only one other vessel, a brightly lighted ship flying the flag of the still neutral United States. The *Kormoran*'s appearance was altered and her identity changed from the original Soviet vessel to one of Japanese registry. They were now the *Kinka Maru*. Detmers soon realized that sailing the Indian Ocean was an unprofitable arrangement. It made him and his crew feel, as he later wrote, that "we seemed to be alone in the world."

On June 15 it looked as if the *Kormoran*'s luck was about to change. That afternoon the smoke of an approaching ship was spotted. As the two ships came within view of each other, Detmers watched her carefully through his glasses. He surmised that she was a passenger ship probably belonging to the British-India Company, and as such was likely to have a top speed much greater than his own. Under normal circumstances he would probably not attempt to give chase, but in this case he estimated that the two vessels would come to within 10,000 yards of each other. Although not an ideal distance, this was close enough so that the raider's gunners could accurately find the range and fire into her. Detmers had the alarm sounded when the ship was about 12,000 yards away, and then things went wrong. One of the routines followed by the crew when the alarm indicating that the camouflaging should be dropped and the guns manned was given was to put the smoke-generating equipment under air pressure. This would permit the almost immediate creation of a smoke screen against enemy fire should it be needed.

As the unknown ship came almost to within range, a valve on the equipment became stuck and the smoke generator immediately began pumping a large black cloud of smoke over the raider. Instead of protecting the *Kormoran* from enemy gunners, the smoke blinded the raider's gunners to their target. As a result, the ships passed each other without a shot being fired. Once the equipment was shut down and the smoke cleared, the target vessel was again out of range.

Frustrated, Detmers allowed the ship to sail out of sight. He then turned the raider around and gave pursuit, but the ship was never seen again. Needless to say, the routine of powering up the smoke generator when the alarm was sounded was changed. Henceforth the smoke-making apparatus would be put under pressure only if it appeared to be needed.

With so few ship targets available, Detmers decided to enter the Bay of Bengal and lay mines across the many shipping lanes there. That plan was upset when on June 24 the *Kormoran* sighted what appeared to be an Auxiliary Cruiser bearing down on it. Detmers feared a confrontation with any ship, but especially another Auxiliary Cruiser would bring every British cruiser and airplane in the area down on him. He knew that it would have been relatively easy for the enemy to seal him up in the Bay and sink him from the air or by long-distance shelling from a cruiser or other warship. With no other option available, the *Kormoran* ran at full speed back toward the open sea. Luck held out for the Germans, for the new metals used to construct bearings held out and the engines ran at full power.

About 23,000 yards behind the *Kormoran*, the British Auxiliary Cruiser *Canton* struggled to keep pace with the unidentified ship ahead of her. After about one hour, the *Canton*'s captain realized that the mystery ship's speed was too great for him to catch her, and he gave up the pursuit without ever learning the vessel's identity.

June 25 was spent like so many days had been since entering the Indian Ocean operational area, sailing alone without sighting another ship. At 2:00 the following morning, an officer awakened Detmers to report that he had seen what he thought was a light from a darkened ship. Detmers hurriedly dressed and ran to the bridge. It was an especially dark night with thick clouds blocking any possible light from the moon, and periods of rain showers adding to the lack of visibility. At first Detmers studied the area the officer pointed out to him without result. Then suddenly, as his eyes adjusted to the dark, he also saw a small sliver of light. It was a ship alright, and it had to be an enemy ship because she was running in total darkness except for that sliver of light. They surmised that the light, which was coming from above the ship's deck line, was probably the result of someone's carelessness in leaving a door, perhaps the one to the chart house, slightly ajar.

Detmers ordered his men to battle stations and turned the *Kormoran* around to bear down on the darkened vessel. Three times the raider signaled by lamp to the unknown ship asking its identity, but no response was made. She simply continued on her course without even changing speed. The ship was the 4,153-ton Yugoslav freighter *Velebit*. She was sailing empty from Bombay to Mombasa. The captain of the freighter was in the engine room at the time of the encounter, dealing with some engine problems. The officer in charge was unable to read the Morse code messages from the *Kormoran*, and so did nothing. His inaction proved to be the death knell for the ship.

With no response to his signals, Detmers resorted to gunfire to stop the ship, which by now he could clearly make out as a freighter riding high in the water, a clear indication that she was empty. Several salvos were fired at the ship, including three star shells to light up the target. These were followed by a second set of Morse code messages ordering the ship to stop and not send any radio messages. The freighter's radio remained silent, but she did not alter her speed. The German commander's frustration revealed itself when one message ordered, "Stop, damn you, stop!"

Finally, Detmers ordered his gunners to fire into the ship, which they did with great effect. The freighter almost immediately caught fire. Soon after, her screws ceased turning and she slowed to a stop. Detmers ordered his men to cease fire. By then the *Velebit* was blazing in several places. The *Kormoran* circled the burning ship and found only one lifeboat in the water. The nine men in the boat were brought aboard the raider. Not one of the men spoke enough German or English to fully answer Detmers' questions concerning why the ship did not respond to his requests for her identity or his order to stop.

Not wanting to expend any more shells or even a torpedo on the burning ship, the *Kormoran* sailed away, leaving the *Velebit* at the mercy of a strong wind that had come up. As it turned out, the flames eventually burned themselves out and the hulk beached itself on one of the nearby uninhabited Andaman Islands with several crew members who had stayed on board. Several weeks later the men were picked up by a passing ship they had signaled.

A few minutes before noon that same day, a ship was sighted leaving Ten Degree Channel and heading in the direction of Colombo. The vessel was the Australian freighter *Mareeba* of 3,472 tons. She was carrying 5,000 tons of sugar. The *Mareeba* was heading toward the *Kormoran*. Detmers decided to continue on his course, but to slow down to allow the ship to come closer. It was a clear day in which lookouts could see for quite a distance, but a sudden change in the weather worked to the raider's advantage. The *Kormoran* sailed into a rain squall, effectively hiding her from the *Mareeba*'s view. Inside the squall, the cruiser went to battle stations and changed course so that it emerged quite close to her target.

Seeing a German ship suddenly bolt out of the squall about 6,000 yards away shocked the freighter's bridge. Despite the usual warning to stop and not send a wireless alert, the *Mareeba* turned hard to port and began broadcasting the QQQ alert along with her position. The German opened fire immediately. The first few shells destroyed the radio room and set several fires. When they were 4,000 yards apart, the *Mareeba* stopped her engines. Because she was already beginning to sink, the crew quickly lowered her boats to get as far away from her as possible.

When the *Kormoran*'s radio operator could not assure Detmers that the signal sent by the *Mareeba* had successfully been jammed, he decided to leave the area as quickly as possible. After taking the forty-eight men from the freighter aboard, the raider raced off at high speed and kept going right through the night and into the next afternoon. Once again Detmers had made a fortunate decision, for the British finally concluded that two ships had vanished, and the QQQ message from the *Mareeba* helped them decide that an Auxiliary Cruiser must be in the area. On July 1 a naval task force that included the aircraft carrier *Hermes* and the cruiser *Enterprise* rushed out of Trincomalee to search for the unknown Auxiliary Cruiser.

The next three months passed slowly for the raider and her crew. They worked on the ship, scraping and painting. She was given a new identity, that of the Dutch freighter *Straat Malakka*. As part of her new disguise, the ships carpenter built a mock antiaircraft gun to mount on the stern. This enhanced the vessel's image as belonging to the Dutch allies of Great Britain. Detmers and his senior officers worked tirelessly inventing games and other diversions to keep the men occupied.

The lonely life of an Auxiliary Cruiser is emphasized by Commander Detmers' recording of the fact the *Kormoran* sailed in close enough to Engano Island for the crew to see it. It was the first time the men had actually seen land since leaving the Norwegian coast 258 days previously. No matter where they went, they failed to find any enemy ships. Once or twice they encountered, from a distance, fast moving vessels

On September 17, 1941, the work of raiders and U-boats was made more difficult and dangerous when the U.S. Navy announced that it was taking over responsibility for escorting most of the convoys on the Halifax to Britain run, and for traffic around Iceland.

they could not hope to catch, but potential targets where nowhere to be found.

Luck changed slightly on September 23 when the officer of the watch reported seeing a ship with its lights on. Although Detmers expected it to be a neutral, he approached anyway. The ship turned out to be the 3,941-ton Greek freighter *Stamatios G. Embiricos* bound for Colombo. The ship was taken without firing a shot. When Detmers asked the Greek captain why he sailed with his ship fully lighted, he explained that he thought any German cruisers or submarines in the area would be fooled into assuming he was a neutral vessel because of the lights, and therefore keep their distance. As it turned out, he was the one who was fooled. When the *Kormoran* first approached and asked his identity, he did not attempt to flee because he assumed that the ship requesting the information was a British warship. He was shocked when he learned that it was a German cruiser.

The Greek freighter was in unusually fine condition. Detmers would have liked to take her as a prize and send her back to Europe to be converted for war use, such as laying mines. The problem with this plan was that because of the oil shortage caused by the war, her owners had converted her from burning oil to using coal to power her engines. An inspection found that she had only enough coal to make it to her original destination, Colombo, where additional fuel would be loaded. If she were still reliant on oil, the *Kormoran* could have provided her with enough fuel to get her to Europe, but coal was out of the question. As a result, the vessel was sent to the bottom. Detmers observed that the situation "was very annoying."

The next two months passed without incident. The *Kormoran* arrived at a prearranged rendezvous with a German supply ship, and spotted at least one vessel flying the flag of the still neutral United States. Then on November 19, 1941, the *Kormoran*'s lookout reported sighting a ship approaching from the distance. It was the HMAS *Sydney*.

Following the battle with the Australian cruiser, lifeboats filled with German sailors were sighted and taken in tow by various vessels. Of the roughly 400 men aboard the raider when the battle began, 320 were made prisoners of war. Following reports of the first lifeboat rescued, a wide ranging search for the *Sydney* began. Not one member of her crew was ever discovered, nor was the ship herself found. The search continues to this day.

8

MICHEL _____

The Last Survivor

The raider *Michel*, also known as Ship 28, sank eighteen ships for a total of more than 127,000 tons. Most historians classify her as having engaged in two cruises, but because the second cruise was made from Japan, and she did not return home to Germany between the two, it could be considered an extension of the first.

Unlike her sister raiders, *Michel* had no previous life. She was still under construction in a Copenhagen shipyard when the German army occupied Denmark. She was originally intended to be the Polish freighter *Bielskoi*, but the Germans altered her design considerably to meet her new purpose. She was given six 5.9-inch guns, which were standard for the raiders, but to these was added one 4.1-inch gun. In addition, she received four 37-mm and four 20-mm guns, six torpedo tubes, and a large assortment of small arms. She was also given a small torpedo boat, named the *Esau*. Capable of reaching a top speed of forty knots, and armed with a heavy machine gun and two torpedoes, the small boat was to become a key element in the *Michel*'s success.

March 13, 1942, was late in the war for a raider to make it to sea unmolested. Gone were the days when they could slip through the English Channel or steam up the coast of Norway, losing themselves in the fog of the far north. One month earlier, on the night of February 11, two battlecruisers, the *Scharnhorst* and the *Gneisenau*, and the heavy cruiser *Prinz Eugen* fought their way up the Channel seeking the relative safety of German controlled waters. Their successful dash caused the British government a great deal of embarrass-

KMS *Michel*: First Cruise, March 9, 1942–March 1, 1943

1. *Patella*; 2. *Connecticut*; 3. *Menelaus*; 4. *Kattegat*; 5. *George Clymer*; 6. *Lylepark*; 7. *Gloucester Castle*; 8. *William F. Humphrey*; 9. *Aramis*; 10. *Arabistan*; 11. *American Leader*; 12. *Empire Dawn*; 13. *Sawokla*; 14. *Eugenie Livanos*; 15. *Empire March*. Courtesy of K. Rochford.

ment, and lead to strengthened patrols and increased vigilance in the Channel. Everyone concerned with getting the latest raider to sea knew that it was not going to be an easy situation, especially her commanding officer Captain Hellmuth von Ruckteschell. In spite of its dangers, the English Channel was the route of choice for the German Navy because it was the most fuel efficient. Because the navy was beginning to starve for fuel, the Channel was the quickest way to get a ship like the *Michel* into action.

It had taken ten months to complete the conversion of the *Bielskoi* into a commerce raider, and Ruckteschell had watched over and directed every detail. His experience serving as commander of the raider *Widder* had been invaluable in teaching him just what a raider needed to be successful. Now he, his ship, and crew were to undergo their first test together.

On the evening of March 13 she slipped out of Flushing and headed west. She was surrounded by five torpedo boats that kept as close as possible to their charge. Beyond the torpedo boats were nine minesweepers. The route had been swept of mines about four hours earlier, but the British were known to be quick in replacing them. Around midnight the minesweepers were doing their work as the explosions of British mines filled the night air. Soon the sound of British Motor Torpedo Boats could be heard approaching from the north, and the German torpedo boats tightened their net around the *Michel*. For the next few hours the British boats shadowed the miniconvoy. The British suspected that the large number of escorts meant that the boat trying to make its way toward the Atlantic was important, so additional Royal Navy vessels were summoned.

Once inside the Straits of Dover, the enemy fired several star shells to get a better look at the ship that was being escorted. The German torpedo boats opened fire on the sources of the shells and a brief gun battle ensued. At least three of the British boats were hit, one of which caught fire and was forced to withdraw.

This shadowing by the outgunned British boats continued with only an occasional brief encounter. It was obvious that they were not going to launch an attack directly on the convoy because they were waiting for additional firepower. In the midst of this, the raider ignored the enemy as best it could and maintained its course for the open sea.

As dawn broke a few minutes before 7:00, that additional firepower could be seen in the distance. Joining the shadowing Motor Torpedo Boats were several more MTBs and four destroyers, all racing toward the *Michel* and her escorts. When the opposing forces were less than 4,000 yards away, they all opened fire, including the *Michel*, which was the heaviest weaponed ship in the action. The two groups maintained a parallel course as the shooting continued. For some reason the destroyers had difficulty finding the range, and most of their shells passed harmlessly over the heads of the Germans. For their part, the Ger-

167

man torpedo boats experienced their own difficulty launching torpedoes and had to rely on their deck-mounted guns to keep the enemy and a distance. The *Michel*'s guns boomed above the rest and finally drove the outgunned destroyers off. Two of the destroyers were damaged when they came within range of German shore batteries that opened fire and sent them back to their bases.

Once they were beyond the reach of the Royal Navy and the danger was over, the escort returned to their bases and the *Michel* steamed on to Saint-Malo where her ammunition was replenished and her fuel tanks topped off. On March 20, she left European waters and headed out into the Atlantic to begin her cruise. About half the raider's crew had served on the *Widder*, but the remainder had no combat experience, so the *Michel*'s escape through the Channel served as a baptism of fire, preparing them for the job ahead.

Ruckteschell had been provided with a route that he was to follow precisely. There were some eighty German and Italian U-boats operating in the Atlantic at the time, and the last thing the German Navy wanted was for one of them to be fooled by the *Michel*'s disguise and sink her. The U-boats had been given the *Michel*'s route in order to avoid just such an occurrence.

The *Michel* arrived in her first operational area, which was just south of the Equator, on April 16 and rendezvoused with the tanker *Charlotte Schliemann* from whom she again topped off her fuel tanks. Captain Ruckteschell was anxious to get into action. Prior to sailing, he had made clear his intention to sink 200,000 tons of Allied shipping on this cruise. Had he succeeded, it would have been a spectacular feat, exceeding the total of the *Atlantis*, the most successful of the raiders.

On April 14, 1942, the American destroyer *Roper* attacked and sank U-85. This is the first time a ship of the U.S. Navy had sunk a German U-boat.

Three days later, the *Michel*, disguised as a Norwegian freighter, came on the British tanker *Patella*. She was carrying more than 9,000 tons of oil intended for use in Great Britain. Coming up from behind, the *Michel* swept down on the tanker and fired a warning shot that passed over her. The *Patella* responded by trying to increase her speed and sending out a radio alert that she was under attack by a surface vessel. A few shots into the bridge stopped the radio and brought the tanker to a halt. Sixty of her crew of sixty-three were taken as prisoners, and the tanker was sunk.

On the night of April 22, Ruckteschell launched the *Esau* to pursue another tanker. The American ship *Connecticut* was carrying a load of high octane gasoline, so when the *Esau*'s torpedo struck, the tanker's crew immediately began lowering the lifeboats to get as far away from her as possible. Her radio operator's insistence on sending an alert brought a second torpedo that struck the cargo and blew the ship apart in a large fireball. Unfortunately for most of the men in the boats, the fire swept across the surface of the water and consumed several of the boats. The *Michel* was able to rescue only nineteen of the fifty-four men in the *Connecticut*'s crew. She was the first American ship attacked and sunk by an Auxiliary Cruiser.

Nine days later, just as dawn was breaking on May 1, the *Michel*'s lookouts spotted a large ship sporting the telltale blue funnel of the British Blue Funnel Line. They were about 720 miles southwest of St. Helena, and the 10,306-ton liner *Menelaus* was heading for Norfolk, Virginia. Ruckteschell stopped and lowered the *Esau* into the water with instructions to speed out and around the liner, thus effectively surrounding her. He then resumed speed and soon began signaling her with his lamp to stop.

Aboard the *Menelaus*, First Officer Brind was among the first members of the crew to see the approaching stranger. Actually, the first thing he saw was the signal lamp ordering him to stop. He ordered the liner's signalman to respond with the current secret message. The code was two letters, to which the other vessel, if it were British, was supposed to respond with its own two letters. The approaching ship did not respond appropriately. Brind recognized that this was probably not an Allied ship, but decided to give it one more opportunity. He sent a signal asking her to identify herself.

Aboard the *Michel*, Ruckteschell and his officers struggled to get the meaning of the first two-letter signal sent by the liner. He knew it was a coded message that required a response, but he did not know what the response was supposed to be. In response to the second message, the German signalman tapped out the words, "New British Naval Pattrol." The word patrol was misspelled with a second T. The liner asked that the last word be repeated. It was, and the word patrol was once again misspelled. That did it for the First Officer. He could not imagine that a Royal Navy signalman would misspell patrol twice.

Brind immediately sent word to Captain Blyth, who was in his cabin, and ordered the engine room to go to full speed as quickly as possible. Captain Blyth arrived on the bridge and instructed the radio operator to begin sending an alarm over several frequencies giving the *Menelaus'* position and the signal that they were under attack by a surface vessel. He also ordered the liner's gun crews to their battle stations. The *Menelaus* was fairly well equipped for a confrontation with an enemy, having six guns aboard, one 4-inch, one 3-inch, and two 20-mm cannons.

In the raider's bridge the Germans watched in dismay as the liner's stern began to pull away from them. The radio operators tried frantically to jam the liner's distress signals, but the Britisher kept alternating wavelengths, making their job nearly impossible. In the twenty minutes that had passed since the liner was first caught sight of, she remained from five to six miles away. Out of desperation, Ruckteschell fired several volleys at her, but each shell fell far short of the escaping target.

The two ships sped across the surface, with the liner gradually pulling farther and farther away from the raider. Suddenly a lookout aboard the *Menelaus*
reported a small boat approaching at high speed. It was flying the Royal Navy
ensign and the international signal flag for the word "Stop." Brind and Blyth
examined the newcomer closely through their glasses. The men aboard were
wearing British duffle coats, which seemed to be too warm for this climate, and
they also noted that the men in the boat were all wearing the type of life vest
used by the British Merchant Marine, not the Royal Navy. Brind pleaded with
Blyth to open fire on the boat, but the Captain hesitated, deciding instead to
run his boilers far above their designed pressure to stretch his vessel beyond
her 14-knot design. It worked. The liner was soon doing 15½ knots.

The small boat swept passed the liner at high speed. She lowered the British
ensign and turned to face the large ship's side and fired a torpedo, which due to
excellent maneuvering by the liner's helmsman passed harmlessly astern. The
raider fired several more volleys, but to no use, because the target was still out
of range. Fearing that they would come under fire from the liner's cannons,
the *Esau* gave up the chase and headed back to the *Michel*, which was still
about 5 miles away.

A frustrated and embarrassed Ruckteschell brought the torpedo boat
aboard and headed south as fast as possible. He knew that at least several stations had picked up the liner's signal and expected that Royal Navy warships
would be converging on the area. He was correct. At least one cruiser and two
Armed Merchant Cruisers (AMCs) had been ordered after him.

Aboard the *Menelaus*, the officers and men congratulated themselves on a
fine job. The extra steam was released, and the ship resumed its voyage.

In the Battle of the Coral
Sea, ending on May 8, the
U.S. Navy succeeded in stopping for the first time the
Imperial Japanese Navy's
advance south. This was the
first battle in history between two fleets that never
made visual contact, and in
which naval artillery played
no role.

The *Michel* moved farther into the South
Atlantic and began searching for enemy ships in
the area previously worked by the raider *Thor*,
which had moved into the Indian Ocean. Ruckteschell's first task was to meet with the *Charlotte
Schliemann* once again to refuel. The two vessels
missed each other several times, and it was only
after the *Michel* sent her Arado seaplane out in
search of the tanker did they finally rendezvous.
On May 8 the tanker gave the raider fuel, and the
raider gave the tanker her prisoners. The two
parted company quickly to avoid detection.

For the next two weeks the *Michel* steamed back and forth across the usually
heavily traveled route between Cape Town and Montevideo with no result until the afternoon of May 20. Ruckteschell had devised a strategy that he would
use with some regularity for attacking ships during the remainder of the

Michel's cruise. Once a target was discovered, the *Esau* would be lowered and sent in a great arc around the ship so that she would neither be heard nor seen, and then attack the target from the opposite direction of the raider. This would make the captain of the targeted vessel believe that he was under attack by two raiders working in coordination and improve the chances he would surrender his vessel more quickly.

The tactic wasn't necessary on this day with the empty Norwegian freighter *Kattegat*, which was heading for La Plata to pick up a cargo. Despite the fact that the freighter had three lookouts on duty, the raider wasn't seen until a volley of shells exploded around the *Kattegat*'s bridge and radio room. The Norwegians immediately signaled that they were abandoning the ship, and the *Michel* ceased firing. The crew was taken aboard the raider and the freighter sunk. Not one member of the *Kattegat*'s crew was injured or killed in the attack. Then things quieted down again, and the raider continued crisscrossing the area.

The American Liberty ship *George Clymer* was launched from the Oregon Ship Building Company's Portland yard on February 19, 1942. She was one of 330 Liberty ships built at the yard during the war, and was delivered for service on April 8, 1942. Soon after, she sailed from Portland with a mixed cargo, which included two dozen airplanes, intended for Cape Town. She passed through the Panama Canal without incident and sailed into the Atlantic heading south. On May 30, when she was about 400 miles from the Ascensions, and just beyond the air cover offered by the air base there, the freighter's main shaft and thrust block bearings split, leaving her without the ability to move under power. She immediately sent out an SOS, giving her present position. The distress signal was responded to by Cape Town, but the freighter heard little else.

Unable to maneuver under her own power, the *George Clymer* was under the control of the ocean currents and during the next few days drifted more than 200 miles from her original position. On June 2 another SOS was broadcast in the hope there was a ship nearby that could lend a hand. This time the signal was picked up by the *Michel*. The freighter was about 900 miles to the north. Ruckteschell considered the possibility that it was a trap, but decided to investigate. En route to the *George Clymer*'s location, the *Esau* was lowered into the water and sent ahead of the raider.

The torpedo boat arrived near the freighter on June 6, and found just what had been reported, a loaded Liberty ship adrift. The *Esau* fired her two torpedoes into the freighter and

In the Pacific Ocean, Germany's Japanese ally suffered a stunning defeat at the hands of the U.S. Navy at the Battle of Midway. Japan's losses included four aircraft carriers and 250 aircraft and an equal number of experienced pilots.

then withdrew just beyond the horizon to await events. In a sorry case of everyman for himself, several members of the crew quickly lowered boats and abandoned ship without waiting for orders. Left behind were the remaining merchant crew and the Naval Armed Guard manning the *George Clymer*'s single gun.

The following morning, with the freighter still afloat, the crewmen returned to her, and the attempt to make repairs continued. Later that morning a British reconnaissance plane flew over and reported that help was on the way. Early that evening the British Armed Merchant Cruiser *Alcantara* arrived to remove the crew. Because the Liberty ship was too damaged to be able to be towed into port, she was sunk by the AMC. Believing the torpedoes had been fired from a U-boat that might still be in the area, the *Alcantara* left the scene hastily, which was good judgment because minutes later the *Michel* approached the position just in time to see the twin masts of the AMC rushing off. The *Alcantara* had the misfortune to engage another disguised raider, the *Thor*, in a gun battle in the Atlantic in July 1940 following a prolonged chase, and had been severely damaged in the encounter. Taken by surprise by the *Michel*, she would probably have suffered a worse fate.

The *Esau* was taken aboard the raider, and her crew and commander, Lieutenant Malte von Schack, were congratulated on a job well done. The search for more targets was resumed.

At dusk on June 11, the lookouts found what they had been anxiously searching for, a British cargo ship. The 5,186-ton *Lylepark* was en route to Cape Town from New York, where she had been loaded with 8,000 tons of military supplies. Ruckteschell steered directly toward her and ran up his speed. When he was confident of the range, the raider opened fire without warning. The first salvo struck the bridge area, and the second set the boat deck aflame. The order to abandon the ship was quickly given and the boats lowered. The *Lylepark*'s Captain C. S. Low and her First Officer decided to try to avoid capture and attempted to escape in a damaged lifeboat, which quickly sank under their combined weight. The two were separated and eventually each man found refuge on a life raft.

Two days later, an aircraft passed overhead. Low fired a signal rocket, but the craft appeared to pay no heed. The captain could make out a ship's smoke on the horizon, and correctly surmised that it was an aircraft carrier judging by the way the airplane dropped low on approaching it. A short time later he heard the sound of a small boat's engine and was thrilled to see a boat approaching flying the Royal Navy ensign. The aircraft had seen the rocket and reported it as soon as it had landed on the escort carrier HMS *Archer*.

The *Archer* eventually dropped Low off at Freetown, where he was soon joined by the First Officer, who had been rescued by the 14,500-ton British freighter

Avila Star. Their adventure did not end there however. Low arranged passage back to England for himself and his First Officer on the *Avila Star.*

On July 6, the highly decorated U-boat commander Adalbert Schnee lined up the large freighter in the sights of his U-201 and fired several torpedoes at the *Avila Star.* Captain Low first attempted to enter a boat that was too badly damaged to float. He then spent some time in the water, finally finding safety in another lifeboat full of survivors from the freighter. Eventually they were rescued by a Portugese destroyer. Twenty-two surviving crew members of the *Lylepark* were taken aboard the *Michel.* The prisoners were transferred to the disguised blockade runner and minelayer, *Doggerbank.*

The Allied ship convoy PQ-17 left Iceland for Archangel on June 27 with thirty-five merchant vessels. In a series of air and U-boat attacks on July 5 and 7, German forces sank twenty-four of the cargo ships. Losses included 200 aircraft, 400 tanks, and 3,300 vehicles intended for the Soviet Army.

The following weeks were quiet for the raider. Ruckteschell tried to anticipate what routes Allied ships attempting to avoid the U-boats might use, but had no luck. In the middle of July the *Michel* hit the jackpot, three ships in three days.

The first victim was the old 8,006-ton British passenger liner *Gloucester Castle.* Built in 1911, she was the oldest and smallest passenger vessel belonging to the Union Castle Line, and had actually been retired before the war. The need for ships of all sizes and configurations brought her back into service. The *Gloucester Castle* sailed from Birkenhead on June 21. Her destination was Cape Town, South Africa. In addition to her crew of 142, she carried twelve passengers, all women and children planning to join relatives in South Africa. Her cargo consisted of predominantly military supplies, including aircraft parts and gasoline.

During the first leg of the *Gloucester Castle*'s voyage, she sailed as part of a convoy, but by the night of July 12, off the coast of Portugese Angola, she was alone. Despite the ship's movement, everyone on board suffered from the heat and humidity. All lights were out so as not to attract attention, and the only noise that could be heard, other than the engines and the rushing waters, were the cabin fans, which succeeded in only moving the hot humid air around.

The night was so black that it was only a miracle that allowed the raider's lookouts to find the liner. It was several miles away, steaming in a southerly direction. The *Michel* increased speed, kept all her lights off, and raced down on the unsuspecting *Gloucester Castle.* At 7:00 the liner was just over a mile away, and Ruckteschell opened fire without warning.

Aboard the passenger liner, the first anyone knew of the presence of an enemy ship were the explosions that rocked the vessel and the rattle of machine-gun fire from the raider. The first volley killed or wounded everyone in the radio room and blew away the radio aerial. Drums of gasoline stored on the forward deck were hit by shells and exploded, spreading flames throughout the superstructure of the old ship. The liner first rolled to starboard and then to port and sank in less than five minutes before the startled eyes of the German gunners who had caused the disaster.

Ruckteschell had a motorboat quickly lowered into the water and a search for survivors begun. In the end, only fifty-seven members of the crew and four passengers were rescued. Those who perished included eighty-five crewmen, six women passengers, and two children. The *Gloucester Castle* disappeared so quickly and completely that her fate, and the fate of those aboard her, were not known by the Allies until after the war had ended.

The 7,983-ton American tanker *William F. Humphrey* was sailing in ballast from Cape Town to Trinidad. On the evening of July 16, 1942, about 800 miles off the west coast of Africa, the Tidewater Oil Company tanker met her fate in a rain of some sixty shells and hundreds of rounds of automatic weapons' fire. A second tanker, the 7,984-ton *Aramis*, sailing a nearby parallel course, was struck by two torpedoes, but managed to race away from the scene.

The two tankers had been spotted by lookouts on the *Michel*. Ruckteschell decided to attack both at once, so he had the *Esau* brought on deck and lowered into the water. As usual, she was armed with two small torpedoes similar to those used by aircraft against ships, and her machine gun.

Von Shack fired both torpedoes at the *Aramis*. Both exploded on impact against the vessel's hull, but the explosions caused no serious damage. The tanker rocked back and forth several times then righted herself and raced away from the scene as quickly as she could, heading in a westerly direction.

As for the *William F. Humphrey*, she continued to take a pounding from one salvo after another of the *Michel*'s 5.9-inch guns. Within seconds of the attack, the tanker's Naval Armed Guard manned their 5-inch gun and began returning fire. Then the *Michel* let loose with three torpedoes, one of which set the vessel ablaze. The Naval Armed Guard did the best they could, but they were so badly outgunned that it was futile.

In less than ten minutes, the tanker was slipping beneath the churning water. Of the forty-eight men aboard the *William F. Humphrey*, forty-one were merchant marine crewmen, and seven were members of the Naval Armed Guard; the *Michel*'s boats rescued twenty-nine. Of these, one member of the Naval Armed Guard died of his wounds while aboard the raider, and three crewmen died while in Japanese prison camps. A fourth member of the crew, Fireman Philip McKeever, had the misfortune to be aboard another torpedoed ship later in the war. This time it was a Japanese freighter, the *Junyo Maru*, and it was transporting prisoners of war when it was struck and sank by a torpedo from an Allied submarine off the coast of Sumatra.

Ten men from the doomed tanker, including the captain, floated around on rafts and managed to elude capture as the *Michel* searched for survivors. They had made the decision to trust their fate to the sea. The following day, with the raider long gone, they recovered two lifeboats that had been left behind, and set their sails for the African coast. Five days and 450 miles later they were picked up by the Norwegian freighter *Triton*, which took them to Freetown.

The *Michel* had sped away toward the west, in search of the *Aramis*, still wondering why the tanker had not radioed for help. What they did not know was that her radio had been damaged in the attack, and she could not transmit. The next morning they caught sight of the tanker as she zigzagged her way across the ocean. Keeping her distance at the horizon, the *Michel* trailed the *Aramis* all day, and attacked her after nightfall. Of the forty-three crewmen on the *Aramis*, twenty-three were taken aboard the raider as prisoners. The rest went down with the ship.

Ruckteschell decided three ships in as many days was enough good luck, so he decided to leave the area and head for a planned rendezvous with the raider *Stier* near Trinadade Island off the Brazilian coast. The *Michel* also rendezvoused with the *Charlotte Schliemann* once again to refuel and transfer her prisoners. When completed, the only prisoners left aboard the raider were three men from the *William F. Humphrey* who were in the ship's hospital and were too badly wounded to be transferred. For those prisoners who were moved to the tanker, life took a decidedly bad turn. The food and living conditions aboard the *Charlotte Schliemann* were terrible in contrast to those aboard the *Michel*. Things got even worse when the tanker sailed to Japan and they were turned over to Germany's allies for keeping. Many did not survive the next three years. Abuse and torture were the fate of most prisoners of war in Japanese hands.

On August 14 one of those incidents occurred that disturbed many of the men aboard the raiders, especially those who had been merchant seamen before the war and remained bonded to their "brothers of the sea." At about 9:00 the night before, the crew was sent to battle stations as a ship had been spotted by the lookouts. The *Michel*, evidently unseen by its victim, rushed up on her in the dark and opened fire with several salvos. The 5,874-ton British freighter *Arabistan* didn't know what hit her. She sank in minutes. The raider searched all that night without finding a single survivor. The follow-

On August 19, Canadian and British forces made a disastrous landing near Dieppe as a dress rehearsal for a major invasion of the continent. Of 6,000 men who took part in the operation, 3,600 were lost, along with 103 airplanes and 30 tanks. Bitter lessons were learned for the future.

ing morning one man was lifted from the sea. The *Arabistan*'s chief engineer was the only survivor from among the freighter's sixty member crew.

Following another refueling from the *Charlotte Schliemann*, *Michel* headed for the Indian Ocean. On the way there she encountered the 6,778-ton motor vessel *American Leader*. Launched in mid-1941, the freighter had been present in Manila Harbor when Japanese planes attacked U.S. forces there on December 8, 1941. In preparation for her wartime duty, she had been armed with an old 4-inch gun and four machine guns. According to her Third Officer, George Duffy, two of those machine guns jammed whenever they were used. The guns were manned by a Reserve Ensign and eight enlisted men of the Naval Armed Guard. She was crewed by fifty-eight men, including the gun crews.

Sailing from Indian Ocean ports with a variety of raw materials intended for the United States, many members of the crew had been hoping that when they reached Cape Town, the British authorities would put their ship into a northbound convoy. Unfortunately no convoy was being formed, so the Admiralty instructed the *American Leader* to head west for the Straits of Magellan and enter the Pacific Ocean. This was probably done so that she would avoid contact with the many U-boats and surface raiders operating in the Atlantic. She left Cape Town on September 7, 1942. Three nights later, when she was about 850 miles west of Cape Town, the *American Leader* became the *Michel*'s tenth victim.

Without warning, as was Ruckteschell's increasing habit, the raider fired several salvos into the freighter and then finished her off with several torpedoes. Most, if not all the lifeboats were destroyed in the attack, and as the ship sank by her stern, those who survived found themselves in the churning water clinging to rafts and floating debris. The *Michel* picked forty-seven men from the water that night. Eleven men were never heard from again.

The next night another freighter was found. This time it was the British 7,241-ton *Empire Dawn*. She was sailing in ballast from Durban for Trinidad, where she was to pick up a cargo intended for New York. Again the attack was conducted without warning. Severely wounded when the bridge was hit by automatic weapons fire, Captain W. A. Scott quickly realized that his vessel was doomed and signaled the raider that he was stopping and abandoning ship. The firing continued for some time. Half the forty-four man crew was killed in the attack. The rest were rescued from the water by the *Michel*'s boats.

Later that month, the raider received some supplies, including fresh produce, from a passing blockade runner, the *Tannenfels*, and rendezvoused with the raider *Stier*. Soon after, most of the prisoners were put aboard the *Uckermark*, from which the *Michel* received a resupply of ammunition, fuel, and her mail. The *Uckermark* passed over into the Pacific Ocean and dropped her prisoners at the Japanese-occupied island of Java. The men from the *American Leader* and the *Empire Dawn* spent the rest of the war as prisoners of the Japanese, an experience that cost nearly half of them their lives.

The *Michel* was ordered into the Indian Ocean, and passed the Cape of Africa without incident. Naval Command wanted the raider out of the Atlantic prior to the start of a hugely successful U-boat campaign against Allied shipping in the South Atlantic. What Ruckteschell did not know was that the *Michel* was now the last surface raider Germany had in operation. His radio room had picked up what he suspected was some kind of distress signal originating from the *Stier*, but then he heard nothing more. What he would later learn was that the *Stier* had met her doom in a battle with the American Liberty Ship *Stephen Hopkins* on September 24, and those surviving members of the crew had been rescued by the *Tannenfels*. The *Thor* meanwhile was headed for Japan, where she would meet her end in a fiery ball along with the *Uckermark*.

Over the next five weeks the *Michel* found and sank three Allied freighters. On November 2, it was the *British Reynolds* of 5,113 tons. At 8:30 on the night of November 29, it was the turn of the American freighter *Sawokla*, which had left Colombo ten days earlier and was heading for Cape Town. Thirty-nine of *Sawokla*'s fifty-nine crew, Naval Armed Guard, and passengers were rescued after the ship was sunk by a torpedo. Ten days later the crew of the 4,816-ton Greek freighter *Eugenie Livanos* were busy celebrating the feast of St. Nicholas when their ship was struck by shell fire and a torpedo. Nineteen prisoners were added to those already in the *Michel*.

On November 8, the Allied invasion of French North Africa began under the code name Operation Torch.

On December 20, Ruckteschell received orders to head for home. The news was greeted with cheers by the crew, and the raider turned back for the South Atlantic. Re-entering what had been its original operational area off the west coast of Africa, the raider sent her aircraft aloft to search the area ahead of them on January 2, 1943. The plane, which had no luck during the entire cruise, returned with news that a British freighter was nearby sailing in a north-westerly direction.

Aboard the 7,040-ton *Empire March*, lookouts had seen the aircraft, but because it had flown away on an easterly heading, they had assumed it was British from a base on the African coast. The *Empire March* was on its way from Durban to Trinidad with her holds full of iron, peanuts, tea, and jute when at about 9:45 that night a salvo of 5.9-inch shells shattered her bridge and radio room. The firing continued for about eight minutes and was capped off by several torpedoes. Twenty-six of the twenty-nine men aboard the freighter were taken aboard the *Michel*.

Six days later the crew was informed that the *Michel* was instructed not to attempt to break through the Allied blockade of Europe, which by then would have been a nearly impossible feat, but instead to turn back around toward the Indian Ocean and head for Japan. No one was happy about this new turn of events. The members of the crew were looking forward to going home, and the prisoners did not want to even think what life as a prisoner of the Japanese was going to be like.

The disastrous ending of the invasion of the Soviet Union was foretold on January 31, when Field Marshall Paulus surrendered what was left of his army to the surrounding Soviets in Stalingrad. Ninety thousand German soldiers became prisoners of war out of a force originally numbering 280,000.

The raider made brief stopovers at the Japanese controlled ports of Batavia and Singapore. At the latter, according to instructions, the prisoners were deposited with the Japanese Army where they would suffer the same abuse as all prisoners of war did. On March 2, the German raider was tied up to a buoy in the harbor of Kobe, Japan, where the captain and his crew were met by the German Naval Attaché, Admiral Paul Wenneker, and Gunther Gumprich, formerly commander of the raider *Thor*, which was now nothing more than a pile of scrap in Yokohama Harbor.

And so ended the first, and longest, phase of the *Michel*'s career as a German surface raider. In 358 days at sea, she had sunk fifteen ships for a total of 99,386 tons. The ship was taken in hand by Japanese tugs and deposited in the shipyard operated by Mitsubishi, which had been contracted to perform her refitting for future service. Ruckteschell, who had long suffered from painful migraine headaches soon added stomach and heart problems to his medical condition. As a result, he requested that he be replaced as commander of the *Michel*, and the job was given to Gumprich.

On May 1, 1943, with all work completed, the *Michel* left Japan and headed for the Indian Ocean. She was now the only warship the German Navy had operating on the high seas. The war was closing in on Germany, and the oceans were now mostly under control of the Allied navies. The crew was now a mixture of men from the *Thor* and the original crew of the *Michel*. Captain Gumprich, who was ten years younger than Ruckteschell and a much more open personality, drilled his crew daily in order that they get used to working together.

It was a short cruise, lasting only 170 days. In that time she sank three vessels, all Norwegian. The first was a 7,715-ton freighter named *Hoegh Silverdawn*, sailing from Freemantle. On the afternoon of June 14, the *Michel*'s aircraft reported sighting a freighter sailing west. Late in the evening, the raider's lookouts spotted the freighter, and she bore down on her with her guns roaring away. In less than forty-five minutes the freighter was gone. Twenty-seven of the fifty-eight passengers and crew died in the attack. Three men slipped away in a raft and were rescued by an American ship a week later, but the most spectacular escape was made in a lifeboat under command of Captain E. Waaler.

KMS *Michel*: Second Cruise, May 3, 1943–October 10, 1943

1. *Hoegh Silverdawn*; 2. *Ferncastle*; 3. *India*; X. Sunk by USS *Tarpon*. Courtesy of K. Rochford.

Nineteen people survived for thirty-one days a trip of 2,860 miles, finally landing in India. Two had been lost along the way.

Two days later it was the turn of the *Ferncastle*, a 9,940-ton tanker that sank quickly from the impacts of four torpedoes. Thirteen prisoners were lifted from the water from among her crew of thirty-seven. A handful of men managed to escape and were later picked up by another ship.

Except for a near encounter with an American cruiser, the next three months passed uneventfully. Gumprich took his raider into the Pacific for fear that the Allies would have learned of his presence from the escaped survivors. He knew his days at sea were limited to what fuel he had. There were no German supply tankers left, and the Japanese were already too hard pressed to bother helping him. He would soon have to give up the cruise and head back to Japan.

The *Michel* was near Easter Island when on September 10 a tanker was spotted in the afternoon. The raider kept her distance to avoid detection and after nightfall attacked her without warning. Within seconds the ship burst into flames so hot that the raider's boats could not approach her to search for survivors. There were none. All thirty-eight members of the crew died with their ship. The vessel had been the *India*, of 9,977 tons, and she was sailing from Peru to Australia.

Later that month, the *Michel* had one of the strangest encounters of any raider. During the night of September 29, she suddenly found herself completely surrounded by the dark shapes of ships, many of them. Unable to turn away, Gumprich moved along with what he assumed was a convoy until he could gradually extricate himself from the group. He might have considered attacking some of them, but was deterred by the silhouettes of several nearby destroyers. Although we cannot be sure, it is possible that the raider found herself in the middle of a U.S. Navy Task Force, of which the destroyers were the smallest of the warships that would have responded to any attack.

The beginning of the end for the *Michel* came on the night of October 16, 1943. It was a bright moonlit night with a calm sea when the raider fell into the sights of the U.S. submarine *Tarpon*. The Germans were heading for Tokyo Bay, and hoping they could get there safely. The sub tracked her target, which Commander Thomas L. Wogan assumed was a Japanese freighter, for some time, and then just after midnight he fired four torpedoes at her, two of which struck the target.

The explosions rocked the *Michel*. Hundreds of men, including all the Norwegian prisoners, died in the first minutes as the gapping holes in the hull allowed the ocean to rush in. Watertight compartments were closed, battle stations were manned, and the raider began firing wildly around her, not quite sure where the enemy was. Commander Wogan realized by the amount of firing coming from his target that this was no ordinary freighter, but he wasn't sure what it was. One thing was obvious though, this was a heavily armed vessel. Several more torpedoes found their mark, and the *Michel*, listing to port, began to gradually slip down by her stern. Gumprich responded with the abandon ship alarm.

The captain could be seen on the bridge directing rescue operations for the wounded as the ship slipped from sight. Some men eventually made it to shore. A few were picked up by passing Japanese civilian boats, but it appears that the Japanese Navy did very little in the way of rescue operations despite constant complaints and urging by German officials in Tokyo. The final death count was 15 officers and 248 crewmen. It was several months before the Allies realized that the ship the *Tarpon* sank off the Japanese coast was the last of Germany's disguised commerce raiders.

KMS *Stier*: May 9, 1942–September 17, 1942

1. *Gemstone*; 2. *Stanvac Calcutta*; 3. *Dalhousie*; 4. *Stephen Hopkins*; X. Sunk by *Stephen Hopkins*. Courtesy of K. Rochford.

9

STIER

Sunk by a Liberty Ship

From September 1941 through the end of World War II, the United States constructed approximately 2,750 cargo vessels known as Liberty Ships. Later in the war a speedier version, known as Victory Ships, was added to the American Merchant Marine fleet. The mass production of so many Liberty and Victory Ships in such a short period of time remains one of the greatest feats of naval construction in history. Based on the design used for an 1879 British "tramp" steamer, the Liberties carried every imaginable form of cargo, from fresh water to mules to enemy prisoners transported from Europe to the United States.

The SS *Patrick Henry* was the first Liberty Ship launched. It slipped into Chesapeake Bay on September 27, 1941. Built at the Bethlehem-Fairfield Shipyard in Baltimore, the *Patrick Henry* made thirteen wartime voyages for a total of 175,000 miles. Like all that followed, she was 441½ feet long, carried almost 11,000 tons of cargo, including an assortment of planes, trucks, and tanks on her deck, and was powered by a 2,500 horsepower reciprocating steam engine that could make 11 knots. That speed, slow even by standards of the time, was quickly reduced by the wear and tear and barnacle buildup on the hull resulting from long sea duty.

In addition to a crew of merchant sailors numbering between forty and forty-five, most Liberties were also assigned a handful of U.S. Navy sailors from the U.S. Naval Armed Guard. Their duties included maintaining and operating the small amount of defensive weapons placed aboard most civilian cargo ships, including Liberties. Nearly 145,000 Americans served in the Naval Armed Guard. Many fought gallantly to protect the ships to which they were assigned.

Six months after the *Patrick Henry* slipped into the water, one of her most famous sisters was launched from a Richmond, California shipyard operated by famed industrialist Henry J. Kaiser. One of only eleven merchant ships designated a "Gallant Ship" by the U.S. Maritime Commission, the SS *Stephen Hopkins* was launched on April 14, 1942, and delivered to the Maritime Administration four weeks later. Operated by the Luckenbach Steamship Company, she was commanded by Captain Paul Buck. Buck wasted little time telling his crew that should they encounter a German raider while at sea, they would fight with every weapon aboard. Also on board was U.S. Navy Lieutenant (jg) Kenneth Martin Willet and Merchant Marine Cadet/Midshipman Edwin O'Hara.

Built in Kiel for the Atlas Levante Line, the *Cairo* was launched in 1936. She was a 4,778-ton cargo ship some five feet shorter than the *Stephen Hopkins*, with a maximum speed of 14.5 knots. Although slow for the use the German navy put her to, she was still faster than most merchantmen, especially Liberty ships.

With the outbreak of war, the German Naval Operations Staff (SKL), took control of the *Cairo* in November 1939. She was put under the command of Naval Captain Pahl and placed on picket duty in the Baltic. In May 1940, the *Cairo* was given a new captain, Commander Horst Gerlach, a slender good-natured man who quickly became popular with his crew. Gerlach, who was born in 1900, served aboard the battle cruiser *Seidlitz* while still a teenager. Between the wars, he was posted to naval headquarters in Berlin, and commanded an antisubmarine vessel. Early in 1941 Gerlach took the *Cairo* to Holland where the work of converting her to a commerce raider was begun. The final alterations were completed in Germany, and on November 11, 1941, she was formally rechristened as a German Naval war vessel. Gerlach named her *Stier*, German for bull. It was a reference to his wife, Hildegard's astrological sign, Taurus.

It was now 1942, and the former *Cairo*, now the *Stier*, was ready to battle Germany's enemies. Hidden behind an ingenious curtain of camouflage and false structures were six 5.9-inch cannons, two 37-mm antiaircraft guns, and four 20-mm antiaircraft guns. In addition, two 21-inch torpedo tubes were installed below her water line. She also carried two Arado AR-231 floatplanes concealed in her holds.

The *Stier*'s crew was for the most part young and lacked experience. Although the Captain appeared satisfied with them, First Officer Lt. Ludolf Peterson, who had the most wartime experience, especially on a raider, was not. Peterson, who had served on two famous surface raiders—the *Admiral*

Scheer and the *Lutzow*—and the disguised auxiliary raider *Pinguin*, thought the crew too inexperienced in the ways of a commerce raider. He had little faith in the ability of *Stier*'s gunners, something that was borne out in their first encounter with a British merchantman.

Everyone associated with the auxiliary raider program realized that it was approaching the end of its life. America's entry into the war made the open seas an even more dangerous place in which to operate. Just getting out to sea had grown increasingly precarious. The latter was a major concern of both Gerlach and Peterson. Ever since the successful channel dash of the *Scharnhorst, Gneisenau,* and *Prinz Eugen* embarrassed the Royal Navy in February, the English Channel had become infested with British destroyers and Motor Torpedo Boats (MTB). This force had given the *Michel* a difficult time in her escape to sea on March 13. Now it was the *Stier*'s turn to run the gauntlet.

Late on the afternoon of May 12, 1942, *Stier* began her journey into naval history from the Dutch port at Rotterdam. She hid behind a simple disguise as the minesweeper *Sperrbrecher 171*, and sailed in the company of sixteen armed minesweepers and four torpedo boats, *Falke, Iltis, Kondor,* and *Seeadler*. All had been sent to escort the raider through the Channel. The minesweepers formed a vanguard that reached out as far as 1 mile from *Stier*. The size of the escort may actually have backfired, for it was obvious to any enemy observer that so many escorts could only mean that the escorted vessel was of unusual value. Such an escort had to attract British attention and result in a call for an all out attempt to intercept the convoy at any cost.

> The previous day, Luftwaffe aircraft flying off of Crete scored a victory in the Mediterranean when they attacked and sank three British destroyers, the *Jackal*, the *Kipling*, and the *Lively*.

Two hours after midnight, German radar began picking up British MTBs ahead and to the north of the convoy. Several of the escorts fired starshells, but the MTBs could not be seen even though several German vessels reported hearing their engine noise. The British forces appeared to be running parallel with the convoy, probably waiting for additional support from destroyers before attacking. As the Germans approached the Straits of Dover, British shore batteries opened up on them, but they remained just out of range.

Finally, about 3:30 on the morning of the thirteenth, the British forces attacked. Starburst shells revealed that the MTBs had almost fully encircled the convoy. Every vessel on both sides with a clear shot opened fire, and the sky was lit up even though the night had been shrouded in mist. A few minutes before 4:00 A.M., a torpedo fired by one of the British MTBs found its target amidship the *Iltis*, which was just off the *Stier*'s starboard. She broke in two and quickly sank out of sight. Less than fifteen minutes later, as the battle raged around the convoy, the *Seeadler*, which was directly in front of the *Stier*, was also hit amidship by a torpedo. In seconds she rolled over, split in two and sank, taking most of her crew with her. Antiaircraft shells from the German gunners found a target in MTB-220, the only British vessel lost in the melee.

As the convoy began its approach to Boulogne and the protection of German shore batteries, the British MTBs withdrew. The *Stier* remained unscathed from the attack. A handful of German and British survivors were picked up by German boats following the battle. Nearly 200 German sailors lost their lives escorting the raider.

Over the next few days the *Stier* gradually made her way down the French coast in preparation for breaking out of the Allied blockade. On May 20 she eased out of the port of Royan and made for the open sea. Her assigned position was midway between the coasts of Africa and South America where she was to sink enemy merchant ships and decoy Allied war vessels. Both Gerlach and Peterson agreed that their mission was less important than those of the earlier raiders. It also offered a limited chance of success although more risk was involved. But, it was their mission, and they would carry it out to the best of their abilities. On May 26, the raider reached her station in the South Atlantic. As the *Stier* settled down in midocean to await her first victim, little did her crew know that their raider's maiden cruise would last barely four months.

On the same day, the Japanese First Carrier Fleet left the Inland Sea. It was headed to Midway with four aircraft carriers, two battleships, and numerous cruisers and destroyers. Admiral Nagumo did not realize that his fleet was destined for destruction in the pivotal sea battle of the war.

Also on her maiden cruise was the Liberty Ship SS *Stephen Hopkins*. Captain Paul Buck took his ship out of the San Francisco Bay area and headed south, arriving first in New Zealand, then in Australia. It was in Australia that fate played a terrible trick on Captain Buck and the *Stephen Hopkins*. Another Liberty, the SS *Robert P. Harper*, was supposed to carry a load of grain to Capetown, South Africa, but due to an accident at sea was unable to make the trip. The *Hopkins* was ordered to replace the *Harper*, and deliver the grain instead. The voyage proved to be an extremely rough one, with the Hopkins encountering two severe storms, one with Force 9 winds, the other with winds reaching a Force 11. The *Hopkins* was badly battered and blown far off her assigned course. The ship was far behind schedule when she finally limped into port. Buck allowed that his ship would remain in the South African port for several weeks while repairs were made. The delay caused by the weather and repairs would eventually force her to encounter the *Stier*.

Cape Town was also the port of call of the British merchant ship *Gemstone*, several months before the *Stephen Hopkins'* arrival. Under the command of Captain E. J. Griffiths, the 4,986-ton steamer left Cape Town about June 1 with a load of iron ore destined for Baltimore. Before sailing, Griffiths visited the offices of the Royal Naval Control Officer, Cape Town, to pick up his routing instructions. These were orders from the Royal Navy concerning the route each ship should take to its destination. It took into consideration weather factors and reports of U-boat and surface raider activities. Although not all merchant captains followed the Royal Navy's recommendations, most did, feeling perhaps a sense of security that someone at least knew the course they were taking. Others sailed their own routes, not trusting the security in South Africa.

The first few days out of Cape Town passed uneventfully for the *Gemstone* and her crew. Then, on the morning of June 4, about 175 miles east of Brazil's St. Paul Rocks, as Captain Griffiths was enjoying his breakfast, a shot was fired across his ship's bow. Griffiths dropped his utensils and rushed to the bridge to see what had happened. He was unable to make out the vessel that had fired on him because it had maneuvered itself into a position placing it squarely in the glare of the morning sun. This made it virtually invisible to the *Gemstone*'s lookouts, and to the captain. Griffiths later explained that he assumed he was under attack by a U-boat. He quickly ordered his ship about so his stern faced the enemy. This reduced the size target he made, and allowed the possible use of his stern mounted 4-inch gun. He then ordered the radio operator to broadcast a distress signal that they were under attack, giving their location.

The raider closed on the *Gemstone* while continuing to fire. Griffiths wondered why not a single shot had struck his ship. He, of course, was not aware of the poor quality of the *Stier*'s gun crews. The British captain strained to see the enemy through the sun's glare. Finally, when she was about 8,300 yards off, he realized that he was being attacked by a heavily armed Auxiliary Cruiser. With only the single antiquated 4-inch cannon to defend his ship, Griffiths thought it prudent to surrender her and allow the crew to be taken off her alive. Besides, he had sent out a distress signal, and hopefully a Royal Navy warship was in the vicinity. Records show that another vessel had

Meanwhile on the other side of the world, the U.S. Navy was inflicting the first decisive defeat of modern times on the Imperial Japanese Navy at Midway. In four days of fighting, the Japanese lost four aircraft carriers, one heavy cruiser, and at least 250 carrier-based aircraft. American losses included the carrier *Yorktown*, one destroyer, and 147 aircraft. The Americans chased the Japanese across the Pacific until fuel shortages stopped the pursuit.

picked up the distress signal, but it was not a Royal Navy ship. The still unidentified ship waited for several hours before repeating the *Gemstone*'s call for help. Later, German naval officials surmised that the mysterious vessel had probably been close enough to observe the raider firing on the cargo ship and had waited until the former had sailed away before taking the chance of exposing herself to possible attack. Those same records indicate that the call was responded to by a land-based radio.

Two days later the *Stier* came upon the 10,170-ton tanker SS *Stanvac Calcutta*. The one-year-old ship was owned by the Socony Vacuum Company (now Mobil), and sailed under a Panamanian flag. She left Montevideo, Uruguay, on May 29, 1942, in ballast. Her destination was Caripito, Venezuela, where she was to take on a cargo of oil. It would be almost a year before her owners or the U.S. Navy had any clue as to her fate.

It was about 10:00 A.M. June 6, and Captain Gustaf O. Karlsson was in the mess having coffee with First Mate Aage Knudsen. Rain squalls periodically drummed against the steel ship, occasionally reducing the otherwise good visibility across the nearly calm sea. While Karlsson and Knudsen discussed the work details for the day ahead, the ship's lookouts, reinforced in number due to reports of German U-boats in the area, kept their eyes peeled for potential enemies. As an extra precaution, the *Calcutta*'s two guns, a 4-inch 50-caliber naval rifle mounted on the stern, and an extremely old 3-inch 23-caliber antiaircraft gun mounted on the bow, were maintained in a state of readiness for almost instantaneous use. Both guns were old and not really suited for modern warfare.

The stern gun was manned by nine members of the Naval Armed Guard under the command of Ensign Edward L. Anderson of Beaufort, South Carolina. The bow gun was manned by five volunteers from the ship's crew of forty-two merchant sailors. Anderson had placed Hartswohl E. Sarrazin of La Place, Louisiana, in charge of the weapon. Sarrazin had once served in the Navy and came as close as any of the crew to being experienced, although his only actual gunnery experience was the training Anderson gave him and the four other members of his volunteer gun crew.

Not only were the guns and crews kept on the alert, but Anderson had extra ammunition secured near the naval rifle. As events transpired, those additional rounds were needed.

At about ten minutes after the hour, one of the lookouts called to the bridge that he saw a ship approaching "off the starboard bow." The watch officer, the ship's Third Mate, put his binoculars to his eyes and watched what appeared to be a merchant ship about one mile away. As he sought some sign of identification, a white puff of smoke that rose above the forward section of the mystery ship suddenly appeared. Within seconds this was followed by the unmistakable boom caused by the firing of a large caliber gun. This was followed by the sight and sound of a shell dropping into the ocean about 100 yards ahead of the *Calcutta*. It was the traditional shot across the bow of a warship. It was soon followed by another, as the *Stier* ran up her signal flags ordering the tanker to stop and shut down her engines.

Within moments of the first shot, Captain Karlsson and First Mate Knudsen arrived on the bridge to take command of the ship. Karlsson immediately ordered the alarm sounded. This sent every man aboard into general quarters to prepare for an attack, and the members of the two gun crews to their weapons. Seconds later Ensign Anderson arrived on the bridge and made radio contact with his gun crews. At the forward gun, the merchant seamen rammed a shell into their 3-inch antiaircraft gun and aimed it at the ship in the distance. Gun Captain Sarrazin reported "Bow gun ready, sir" to the bridge. The sailors on the stern gun loaded their weapon and reported their readiness also, but they could not point the rifle at the enemy unless the ship swung around.

Aboard the *Stier*, Gerlach ordered that another warning shot be fired and the German naval ensign bearing the swastika be unfurled. He hoped the tanker's captain would realize that he was under attack from a German warship and heed his instructions to stop.

Gerlach did not know that Captain Karlsson and Ensign Anderson had an agreement that they would not surrender the ship without a fight.

As he watched the German flag whip in the wind, Captain Karlsson spoke to everyone on the bridge, "She's a German raider all right. But if he thinks we're going to lie down and give up he's mistaken." He then ordered the helmsman to take a sharp turn to starboard so that they could bring the stern gun to bear. He called to the engine room, "Give us everything you can." Karlsson hoped that his empty ship might be able to outrun the raider while his gun crews kept her at bay.

Anderson ordered both guns to commence firing once the raider was in range. Both guns opened fire, but the raider remained unscathed, although the shells did come close. The *Stier* returned fire. One of her shells hit the *Calcutta* at the waterline. The firing continued for at least ten minutes as Captain Karlsson maneuvered his ship in a zigzag that gave each of his two guns equal opportunity to fire at the raider. The *Stier* returned fire, putting holes in the tanker's hull in at least a dozen places.

When the *Calcutta*'s stern gun scored a direct hit on one of the *Stier*'s guns, killing its entire crew, Gerlach ordered a concentration of fire on the tanker's stern. The Naval Armed Guard sailors of the stern gun stayed at their post, firing their rifle at the enemy even when their own magazine exploded beneath them. The merchant seamen at the bow demonstrated the same degree of determination and courage, as they too continued firing even when all around them was burning or smoking rubble. The bow gun had the added problem that its ammunition was so old that many shells failed to fire at all.

As the *Calcutta* listed heavily from the amount of seawater pouring in through the numerous holes in her hull, First Mate Knudsen attempted to shift ballast to right the ship. Failing this, and returning to find that the bridge had taken a direct hit and the captain had died, along with the radio operator and the helmsman, Knudsen blasted the abandon ship signal. After taking one final shot, two members of the forward gun crew were killed and the remaining three wounded by a well-placed German shell.

The *Stanvac Calcutta* was quickly abandoned as the surviving members of the crew scrambled into lifeboats. Eleven of her crew did not live long enough to escape the sinking tanker.

The *Stier* pulled alongside the lifeboats and lifted the exhausted seamen aboard. Of the thirty-seven men plucked from the water by the *Stier*'s crew, fourteen were wounded, several seriously. They joined the crew of the *Gemstone* as prisoners of war. One of the most seriously wounded died shortly after and was buried at sea with full honors. The remaining wounded were treated by the *Stier*'s doctor. First Mate Knudsen and Ensign Anderson survived, the latter with a broken leg as well as several shrapnel wounds. Captain Gerlach and most of his crew were impressed by the valiant struggle the men of the *Stanvac Calcutta* had engaged in to save their ship. It had taken 123 shells from the *Stier*'s guns, and two torpedoes from her small boat to put the tanker under.

When the *Stanvac Calcutta* failed to arrive in Caripito, she was listed as missing, and eventually as lost. It was almost a year before her actual fate was learned. One of the badly wounded sailors aboard the tanker ended up in a French hospital. Seaman Saedi Hassan wrote the ship's owners in New York City requesting a pair of shoes, cigarettes, and "any comforts" that could be sent through the Red Cross. It took officials at Socony Vacuum a while to identify Hassan and establish his relationship to the lost vessel. The company later received reports from former prisoners of a German supply ship who said they had met crewmen from the *Stanvac Calcutta* after they were transferred to it from the *Stier*. From these reports they pieced together the story of the tanker's demise.

Life on board the *Stier* was not harsh or cruel for the prisoners, given the circumstances. For the most part, the prisoners ate the same food as the German crew, and in the same quantities.

The *Stier* now entered a period of inaction that lasted nearly two months. Day after day she steamed off the coast of South America without finding any prey. Twice she met with her supply ship, the tanker *Charlotte Schliemann*, to refuel. With the exception of the most severely wounded of the *Stanvac Calcutta*'s crew, the prisoners were transferred to the tanker. This proved a radical change for them, as the tanker was a rat-infested vessel whose holds were littered with timber, wire, and a wide assortment of other rubbish. The men lived in fear of being turned over to Germany's ally, Japan, where they all knew an even worse fate awaited them. Their worse fears came true when some five months later they were handed off to the Japanese authorities at Singapore.

Those who survived tell a harrowing tale of abuse and neglect at the hands of the Japanese.

In one of those strange turns of events that can only happen during war, Captain Griffiths of the British cargo ship *Gemstone* was saved from this fate by Captain Gerlach. When the German learned that the prisoners aboard the *Charlotte Schliemann* were to be turned over to the Japanese, he had Griffiths transferred back to the *Stier*.

Generally bad weather since their arrival in the South Atlantic had prevented Gerlach from making use of the *Stier*'s two seaplanes. They were tiny models produced by the Arado Aircraft Company, and designated AR 231. Originally built to be housed on U-boats, only a limited number had been constructed due to their being underpowered. The planes had great difficulty getting airborne in any kind of wind condition. This was especially true when the planes tried to lift off while at sea.

July proved to be an important month for the Allies in the Atlantic. Convoy escort vessels began to be fitted with High Frequency Direction Finding sets to help locate U-boats and surface raiders. Eleven U-boats were sunk during the month.

During July, the *Stier*'s pilot, Sergeant Karl Heinz Decker, made several attempts to take advantage of the nice weather they were experiencing and take his craft aloft and search for potential victims. Several attempts proved fruitless, and the planes were unable to be used to extend the *Stier*'s range of vision. Gerlach wrote in his log that the AR 231 was "totally unsuited for the Atlantic, even under the most favorable circumstances."

In late July, the *Stier* had a prearranged rendezvous with another raider, the *Michel*. They met north of St. Helena. Following a brief meeting between Gerlach and Captain Ruckteschell, at which they decided to work in tandem for a while, the officers and men of both raiders enjoyed some leisure time together at which many swapped war stories.

The joint action did not last long, for the two raiders soon lost contact with each other and resumed their individual patrols. Perhaps some of the *Michel*'s luck had rubbed off on the *Stier*, for a few days later she encountered her first potential victim since sinking the *Stanvac Calcutta* on June 6. It was 8:15 A.M. on August 9, 1942, when she came upon the British merchantman *Dalhousie*, a cargo ship of 7,072 tons, sailing in ballast from Cape Town to Trinidad. The raider's lookout first spotted the single funnel and three masts off in the far distance. Both ships were on a parallel course. At first Gerlach kept the *Stier* on the same course, staying out of sight of the *Dalhousie*'s bridge. Then he gradually drew closer to his target, attempting to avoid discovery until he was close enough to force the vessel to stop.

As the two ships drew closer, Gerlach signaled the merchantman to stop and fired a warning shot. The *Dalhousie* was out of range of the raider's guns, so the vessel's captain decided to make a run for it. Pouring on the steam and sending emergency radio signals that she was under attack by a surface raider, the *Dalhousie* bravely responded to the *Stier* with her own 5-inch gun. The ships were about 16,000 yards apart, too far for the merchantman's gun to reach her target. Her efforts were focused on escape. The *Stier* gave chase, closing gradually on the *Dalhousie* for nearly thirty minutes as the German gunners got the range and began pounding the cargo ship. Finally, the futility of attempting to outrun his attacker convinced the British captain to obey the German's order to abandon his ship. All thirty-seven men aboard the cargo vessel left her in lifeboats and were picked by the *Stier*. Their ship was then sunk by a final torpedo from the *Stier*.

The *Michel* arrived just as the *Dalhousie* was slipping below the surface. Both raider skippers decided to abandon the area and go their own way in case any Allied war ships in the area had picked up the *Dalhousie*'s call for help. The *Stier* headed south. Gerlach sought permission from Naval headquarters to sail around the Horn and patrol the west coast of South America. Despite reports that an American cruiser had sailed south in search of German raiders in the South Atlantic, permission was not given.

U-boat wolf packs returned in force to the North Atlantic. Among the first hit was convoy SC-94. Of thirty-six ships that left Canadian ports, thirteen were sunk by U-boats between August 5 and 10, at a cost to the German navy of two submarines.

Gerlach, and probably most of his officers and crew, was frustrated by the lack of action. They had been on patrol for nearly three months and had sighted only three targets, all of which were sunk. Gerlach felt that he had been sent to a station with few targets, and that his ship's performance had been all but ignored when it came time for SKL to distribute awards.

Instead of being sent to the Pacific, as he wanted, Gerlach was ordered to reconnoiter one of the Tristan da Cunha Islands as a possible base for raider use. A small group of volcanic islands discovered by the Portugese in 1506 and now belonging to Britain, they were mostly uninhabited. The German Navy was especially interested in Gough Island, which Gerlach reported could be used as a safe haven for raiders in need of repairs. In fact, he stayed there long enough to perform some badly needed repairs and maintenance to the *Stier*, and as a place to rendezvous with the tanker *Charlotte Schliemann*. The tanker gave the raider oil and other supplies and received the raider's prisoners in return. The exchange proved disastrous for the prisoners, for they were later handed over to Germany's ally, the Japanese, where their treatment was dramatically worse. Like many of the raider captains, Gerlach was not happy to learn later that his prisoners had been given to the Japanese, whose cruelty to prisoners was known to the Germans.

September 1942, the *Stier*'s final month of existence, began in the most frustrating way for a raider. Early in the morning of the fourth, the *Stier*'s lookout sighted what appeared to be a ship partially hidden in the morning sun's glare. Unable to identify it, he did manage to report that it had one funnel and two masts, and she appeared to be moving fast. Gerlach turned east and headed toward her. The ship, which turned out to be the 29,000-ton French passenger vessel *Pasteur*, was under Allied control. She was steaming along at more than twenty knots, far exceeding the *Stier*'s maximum speed of 14 knots under the best circumstances. When Gerlach realized that any pursuit was useless, he turned away and hoped no one aboard the *Pasteur* had seen his ship. Evidently none had, because the vessel gave no alarm and never reported a sighting.

On September 17, all atomic research being conducted in the United States was put under military control. Its sole objective was now weapons development.

On September 19, the lookout again reported sighting a ship. The unknown vessel was moving fast, but not as fast as the *Pasteur*. The *Stier* pursued this one for nearly twenty-four hours, but was unable to get close enough to attack. Frustration aboard the raider increased. On the same day, the SS *Stephen Hopkins* left Cape Town after a prolonged delay while the storm-caused damage was repaired. She sailed in ballast, heading to Dutch Guinea where she was to pick up a load of bauxite bound for the United States.

Over the next few days the *Stier* rendezvoused with the *Michel* and a supply ship, the *Tannenfels*. The meeting took pace about 650 miles north-northwest of the Tristan da Cunha Islands. The *Tannenfels* was a blockade runner sailing from Japan to France. Her cargo included a Japanese seaplane, which she transferred to the *Stier*. The gift might have been welcomed until Pilot Decker noticed that in addition to lacking a bomb rack, the craft had no radio for communications between the plane and the ship, and was in need of extensive repairs before it could even be launched. Meanwhile, the *Stephen Hopkins* received a radio message warning that a German raider was in the area. Captain Paul Buck ordered his lookouts to stay on alert. After two days, the *Michel* departed, leaving the *Stier* and the *Tannenfels* together.

Rain squalls swept across the area on September 24, reducing visibility to virtually zero. The sea itself was relatively calm, but the three ships were essentially blind until suddenly the rain and haze broke and the *Stier* and the *Hopkins* were practically alongside each other. It was 8:52 A.M., and they had each effectively materialized out of the gloom to each other's surprise.

On board the *Stier*, Captain Gerlach was just leaving the bridge. He was stopped dead in his tracks by the shouted alarm. "Ship in sight to starboard!"

Within minutes, signal flags flew to their positions ordering the ship to "Stop at once." Men rushed to their battle stations and readied their weapons. Gerlach gave the order, and at 8:56 the raider commenced firing.

On board the *Hopkins*, Captain Buck rushed to the bridge from his cabin as soon as word reached him that a ship had been sighted. He took one look at the oncoming vessel and ordered his Third Mate, Walter Nyberg, to sound the alarm. Almost instantly bells began clanging, and the shouted command rang throughout the Liberty Ship, "Battle stations, battle stations, man your guns." As his ship sprung into action, Captain Buck watched as the *Tannenfels* came into view. They were both bristling with weapons. Then his worst nightmare happened, both ships ran up the German naval ensign and began firing. The first shell, fired by the smaller of the two enemy vessels, the *Stier*, fell into the sea about 100 yards off the *Hopkins'* bow. Buck recognized it as the traditional shot across the bow, warning the target ship to stop. Just as suddenly the signal to stop appeared above the smaller craft.

Gerlach expected the ship before him to follow his instructions, especially since most of his armaments were now visible to the enemy captain, and the man must realize he was greatly outgunned.

There was no mistaking that the *Hopkins* was outgunned, but Captain Buck wasn't about to give up his ship to a Nazi without a fight. He ordered the *Hopkins* swung around hard to port so as to give his greatest weapon, the World War I era 4-inch cannon on his stern, a chance to fire back. The cannon was supplemented by two 37-millimeter antiaircraft guns. For closer ranges there were also four 50-caliber and two 30-caliber machine guns. The machine guns served no purpose at the distance that separated the *Stier* and the *Hopkins*. The *Tannenfels* kept her distance and focused on jamming the emergency signal the *Hopkins'* radio operator, Hudson Hewey, was frantically transmitting.

On board the *Stier*, Captain Gerlach watched the *Hopkins* swing around in what he mistook for an attempt to turn and run. He quickly ordered his helmsman to turn hard to starboard so that he could prepare to give chase. After losing two targets earlier in the month, Gerlach was not about to lose another. He ordered additional shells fired into the ship itself, warning shots were over.

The *Stier's* second shot hit the *Hopkins* amidships, instantly killing two men. More shells followed. Among those injured by the first few shells was Ensign Kenneth Willet, the commander of the Naval Armed Guard. Willet was responsible for defending the *Stephen Hopkins*. He was hit by pieces of steel shrapnel that ripped open his stomach as he rushed toward the stern cannon. Stunned by the impact and staggering, he scooped his entrails up in his arms and attempted to push them back into the open cavity in his body as he continued rushing toward his gun. Once there, he took command of his gun crew.

Pending his arrival, eighteen-year-old Merchant Marine Cadet Midshipman Edwin O'Hara, who had become friends with Willet and practiced with the 4-inch gun under the Ensign's tutelage, had assumed temporary command.

O'Hara then climbed down into what was possibly the most dangerous place on the ship, the ammunition magazine just below the gun. It was considered a "death trap" by the sailors assigned to the weapon and the last place any of them wanted to be during a battle. From there O'Hara passed up shells to the men at the gun. One of them, seventeen-year-old Moses Barker of Fort Worth, Texas, recalled the speed with which the gun crew worked, "I concentrated on getting shells into the gun's breech. I didn't look up much at the German ships because every time I did, it looked like they were firing right at me." He was right. The *Stephen Hopkins'* gun crew was a primary target of the raider's gunners.

Aboard the *Stier*, the gunners increased their firing. The return fire surprised them all, but not as much as the accuracy, or luck, of the first shells fired from the *Hopkins'* stern gun. One struck the steering control, jamming the helm and causing the raider to begin circling. A second entered the *Stier's* engine room and severed an oil supply line, cutting off oil to the engines, forcing them to stop. Also damaged was the ship's electrical system. This prevented Gerlach from firing a torpedo, because the firing system was electrically controlled.

Both ships were now less than a 1,000 yards apart as they pumped shells into each other at a maddening rate. Explosions filled the air with their deafening roar and flames leaped about throughout both vessels. And still, that stern gun aboard the Liberty Ship continued firing. Ensign Willet, fading fast and still clutching his intestines in an attempt to persevere and carry out his duties, had also to cope with the increasing number of gun crew members who were being disabled or killed by the shelling, especially once the *Stier* came close enough for the effective use of her lighter caliber weapons. The shells from these guns were striking with such frequency that the roar of the gun was periodically silenced by the chattering of bullets against the steel tub protecting the gun and against the gun itself. Adding to the murderous hail of shells aimed at the *Hopkins'* stern gun by the *Stier's* gunners, the *Tannenfels* now approached the Liberty Ship close enough so that her machine guns raked the gun crew and the *Hopkins'* entire deck with devastating results. Second Mate Joseph Layman directed the firing of the *Hopkins'* 37-mm guns. They produced a withering hail of fire that cut down several of the *Stier's* gun crew members and shattered several of the German ship's guns, until Layman and his crews were all killed and at least one of the 37-mm antiaircraft guns was blown off its mount.

On board the *Stier*, the situation was getting worse. The cutoff of electrical power meant that the ammunition hoists that brought the shells up from the ammo bunker to the guns were out of action. Crew members quickly formed a bucket brigade of sorts, passing shells from hand to hand. Another bucket brigade, this one a true fire-fighting bucket brigade, was formed to fight the blazes that were breaking out all over, because the ship's fire hoses had been made useless by a direct hit on the *Stier*'s water main. Several fires raged completely out of control, as burning oil from the engine room seeped into other compartments setting additional fires. Captain Gerlach continued to direct his guns, with special emphasis on the *Hopkins*' stern cannon that was doing so much damage to his ship.

At the stern gun, most of the teenaged gun crew members had by now either been killed or so badly wounded that they could not function. In a startling show of bravery, the members of the *Hopkins*' merchant marine crew stepped into the breach and replaced fallen gun crew members. They kept up the firing for as long as they remained alive, which for some was only a few minutes. Ensign Willet, his intercom phone pressed against his ears, his hands literally holding his body together, directed the firing of anyone who helped man the gun, and called encouragingly to the crew members below who were, like their German counterparts, passing shells up to the deck from the ammunition magazine by hand.

The engine room crew aboard the *Hopkins* struggled to keep track of what was happening. Enemy bullets periodically rained down on them through the large funnel over the log desk. They must have had difficulty controlling the steam pressure and keeping the engine running, as each large shell from the *Stier* rocked the *Hopkins* mercilessly and the vibrations following the impacts caused leaks in the water and steam systems. Working in near darkness, because the light bulbs had by now been shattered by the vibrations and only the dim red emergency lights were lit, Fireman Mike Fitzpatrick, Third Assistant Kenneth Vaughan, and Oiler Andy Tsigonis fought gallantly to keep the engine going. Suddenly a salvo of shells from the *Stier*'s 5.9-inch guns pierced the *Hopkins*' thin steel hull and smashed into the boiler with a roar. The resulting explosion destroyed the engine room, killing all three men instantly, and filled every space with scorching steam. Steam poured out of the engine room and rose into the sky above the *Hopkins*.

By now the *Stier* and the *Stephen Hopkins*, unable to move under their own power, drifted close enough to each other that men on each ship raked the other with machine-gun fire. No one was ready to surrender, and everyone appeared to be ready to go down with their ship while still fighting. On the stern of the *Hopkins*, Moses Barker continued loading the gun as shells exploded around him. Suddenly he found himself yelling "Fire, fire," but without a response. Looking around him he realized that everyone was dead, including Ensign Willet, "so I tripped the trigger." Unable to load the last five shells because they had been rusted into their containers, and thinking that he was the last man alive, Barker left the blood soaked gun and went forward to find a lifeboat. Seconds later the magazine was hit and exploded. What happened then is not known exactly, but Cadet O'Hara miraculously survived the explosion, for he reappeared on the deck. The explosion must have loosened the last five shells, for somehow the obviously mortally wounded O'Hara, weakened by his injuries and massive blood loss, managed to fire the last of the shells before he died and the *Stephen Hopkins*' stern gun finally fell silent. The shells slammed into the *Stier*, which by now was burning in a dozen places. The bark of the gun startled the rest of the crew as they were abandoning the *Hopkins*. It also startled the Germans. Except for an occasional machine-gun blast, the fighting had all but ceased as the surviving crew members of the *Stephen Hopkins* scrambled to the relative safety of the lifeboats.

Captain Gerlach received damage reports from throughout his ship. The *Stier* had paid a heavy price, especially that exacted by the *Hopkins*' stern gun. She had been hit below the waterline several times and was taking on water in at least three locations. Both ship's hospitals had been hit as well as the bridge, and the fuel bunker was set ablaze. Fires raged out of control with no fire-fighting equipment operating. The power plant was down, and the helm remained locked. The biggest danger by far was the fire reaching toward the hold where the torpedoes were stored. Several men attempted to flood the hold, but the flooding valves could not be reached because of the fire. Should the fire reach that hold, the torpedoes would explode and send the raider down quickly. Gerlach knew that there was no hope of stopping the spread of fire; his crew had been reduced to lowering buckets over the side and collecting seawater to splash on the flames. It was a brave but futile effort. He called a quick meeting of officers on the damaged bridge. It was a broken man who told his officers the time had come to abandon their ship. Gerlach ordered that all lifeboats and rafts be lowered or dropped into the water and the wounded be helped by those men still not seriously injured. A few "Sieg Heils" were shouted and cheers rang out for the Fatherland and the Fuhrer, and then the officers went about their duty of safely abandoning the burning ship.

A signal was sent to the *Tannenfels* that the *Stier* was to be abandoned. The blockade runner moved as close as she dare to the burning raider.

Another well-placed shell ripped into the *Hopkins*' radio room, blowing it completely away and killing Hudson Hewey as he continued his efforts to find help for his ship.

The *Stephen Hopkins* was like a burning death house waiting for its complete destruction. Her decks were littered with the bodies of dead crewmen and awash in blood. Bulkheads were pierced like sections of Swiss cheese, and her plating was ripped open with jagged edges testifying to the power that had torn her apart. Smoke poured from the freighter from bow to stern as the lucky few who had survived the battle jumped overboard and swam to lifeboats that had been lowered or merely dropped into the sea. The last anyone saw of Captain Paul Buck was a report from Assistant Engineer George S. Cronk. He said he watched as the captain threw the ship's code book over the side. Buck then walked around the other side of the bridge, out of Cronk's view, and vanished.

Crewmen aboard the *Tannenfels* watched in disbelief as smoke filled the sky over the battle scene. Many could not believe that the powerful raider had been sunk by what appeared to be a lightly-armed merchant ship. From their distance they could see how many guns the enemy vessel had been firing, unlike many aboard the *Stier*, who thought they had been fighting a warship of some kind, possibly an armed cruiser.

The crew of the *Stier* quickly gathered up their wounded as well as several prisoners who had been too seriously wounded to transfer earlier, including Saedi Hassan of the *Stanvac Calcutta*, and made for the lifeboats. Few looked back at the enemy ship, but those who did could see little, for she was engulfed in flames and slowly sinking by her stern into the sea. It was 10:00 A.M. The fiercely contested battle had lasted just more than one hour. The *Tannenfels* recovered the crew and prisoners from the *Stier* and hauled them onto her deck. The *Stier*'s crew watched in silence as their own ship, also engulfed by flames, suddenly exploded as the fire reached the torpedo hold. She sank quickly after the explosion. The *Stier* had been hit by at least fifteen shells from the *Hopkins*' stern gun. Three crew members had been killed in the battle, including the ship's doctor, and thirty-three were wounded.

The crew of the *Stephen Hopkins* fared much worse. The *Tannenfels* searched the area for survivors, but found none. A rain squall hindered the search when it reduced visibility dramatically. Thirty-one days later the fifteen surviving members of the crew and armed guard of the *Stephen Hopkins* dragged themselves and their single lifeboat ashore near a remote fishing village on the Brazilian coast. Captain Buck, Ensign Willet, and Cadet O'Hara were not among them. Forty-two men had perished either during the battle or as a result of their wounds and the prolonged exposure during their efforts to reach land.

When the *Tannenfels* reached Bordeaux, Captain Gerlach reported that his ship had encountered an unidentified American warship. When told that his battle had been with a lightly–armed Liberty Ship, he at first refused to believe it. No cargo ship with a single 4-inch gun could have inflicted the damage that had caused his vessel to sink. Lieutenant Peterson expressed the feelings of many of the *Stier*'s crew when he said, "We could not but feel that we had gone down at the hands of a gallant foe."

Both the *Stephen Hopkins* and the *Stanvac Calcutta* were honored as "Gallant Ships" by the U.S. Maritime Commission. Captain Buck and Cadet O'Hara were posthumously awarded the Merchant Marine Distinguished Service Medal. Ensign Willet was awarded the Navy Cross, also posthumously. Moses Barker, who went on to serve in the gun crews of several other merchant ships until he was discharged at war's end, received a commendation from the Secretary of the Navy for his valor aboard the *Stephen Hopkins*.

Forty years after the end of the war, the Merchant Marine demonstrated that it never forgets its own. A 30,000-ton tanker built by the American Ship Building Company was delivered to the U.S. Military Sea Lift Command in 1985. It was named the *Paul Buck*.

Appendix A

Identities of the Raiders

Each of the disguised Auxiliary Cruisers had at least four identities. First was the name given each vessel after it was converted for wartime use. Second was the official identity number assigned by the German Navy. Next, was the identity letter assigned each cruiser as its presence in the war became known to the British Admiralty. Finally, there was each ship's name before it was taken over by the navy. Each of these identities is listed here.

New Name	Ship Number	Admiralty Id	Original Name
Atlantis	16	C	*Goldenfels*
Komet	45	B	*Ems*
Kormoran	41	G	*Steiermark*
Michel	28	H	*Bielskoi*
Orion	36	A	*Kurmark*
Pinguin	33	F	*Kandelfels*
Stier	23	J	*Cairo*
Thor	10	E	*Santa Cruz*
Widder	21	D	*Neumark*

APPENDIX B _____

TECHNICAL DATA

Name	Length	Beam	Tonnage	Draught	Speed
Atlantis	488.1 ft.	61.3 ft.	7,862	31.1 ft.	16 knots
Komet	358.5 ft.	50.2 ft.	3,287	19.9 ft.	16 knots
Kormoran	515.1 ft.	66.3 ft.	8,736	30.5 ft.	18 knots
Michel	436 ft.	55 ft.	4,740	24.6 ft.	16 knots
Orion	463.5 ft.	61.1 ft.	7,021	27 ft.	14 knots
Pinguin	485.6 ft.	61.3 ft.	7,766	31.1 ft.	17 knots
Stier	408.5 ft.	56.6 ft.	4,778	21.4 ft.	14 knots
Thor	379.7 ft.	54.8 ft.	3,862	26.5 ft.	17 knots
Widder	477 ft.	63.1 ft.	7,851	28.3 ft.	14 knots

APPENDIX C

ARMAMENT DATA

Name	Aircraft*	5.9-inch Cannons	Antiaircraft Guns**	Torpedo Tubes	Mines
Atlantis	2	6	7	4	92
Komet	2	6	6	6	30
Kormoran	2	6	7	6	360
Michel	2	6+	8	6	0
Orion	1	6	7	6	228
Pinguin	2	6	7	4	300
Stier	2	6	6	2	?
Thor	1	6	7	4	?
Widder	2	6	5	4	?

Notes:
*Although there were some variations, the usual aircraft carried by a raider was the Arado AR 196A. In addition to the aircraft, three raiders, *Komet*, *Kormoran*, and *Michel*, carried a motorboat capable of launching torpedo attacks on enemy ships.

**The usual complement of these weapons were 37-mm and 20-mm guns. In addition, *Atlantis*, *Orion*, *Pinguin*, and *Widder* each had one 75-mm; and *Thor* one 60-mm.

+The *Michel* was also equipped with a 4.1-inch canon.

APPENDIX D

WAR RECORDS OF THE RAIDERS

Name	Number of Ships Sunk	Number of Ships Taken as Prizes	Tonnage Sunk or Taken	Length of Cruise	Fate of Raider
Atlantis	16	6	145,968	622 days	sunk
Komet	7*	1	52,130	524 days+	sunk
Kormoran	9	2	68,274	352 days	sunk
Michel	18	0	127,018	528 days+	sunk
Orion	13*	1	96,785^	510 days	survived
Pinguin	16	16	154,710^	328 days	sunk
Stier	4	0	30,728	142 days	sunk
Thor	18	4	152,134	653 days+	sunk
Widder	9	1	58,644	180 days	survived

Notes:
*Includes ships sunk by *Komet* and *Orion* working together.
+Total of two independent cruises.
^Includes ships sunk by mines.

APPENDIX E _____

THE *SYDNEY* CONTROVERSY

The total disappearance of the Australian Light Cruiser HMAS *Sydney* following its battle with the raider *Kormoran* on November 19, 1941, was that nation's greatest wartime naval disaster. Not a single member of the ship's crew of 645 men survived. The result of that loss has been a debate and controversy in Australia that continues to this day. In much the same way that the assassination of President John F. Kennedy has produced a set of theories around a government conspiracy that feeds on some people's need to blame hidden forces, the *Sydney* sinking has tormented Australia since the event. Instead of books with titles like "Who Killed Kennedy?," we have "Who Sank the *Sydney?*"

As recently as November 1997 the Australian government issued a 191-page document titled "The Sinking of HMAS *Sydney.*" It attempts to put to rest unfounded rumors that the government has managed to keep secret the fact the *Sydney* was actually sunk by a Japanese submarine working with the *Kormoran.* There has never been any evidence of this or any other conspiracy theory produced.

The only witnesses to the sinking were the crew of the German raider. Many of them were busy attempting to save their own lives as their ship was also burning and sinking. Although some people in Australia find it difficult to understand how the *Kormoran* managed to come so close to the *Sydney,* and then managed to sink her, and the *Sydney*'s radio silent all this time, until someone somewhere produces real evidence to the contrary, and not just unfounded rumors and theories, we must accept the accounts given by the German sailors as true.

BIBLIOGRAPHIC ESSAY _____

I have included here books that were either originally published in English, or in the case of translations, I refer only to those translated into English. The vast majority are long out of print, but a determined searcher will be able to find most of them.

Several books about Germany's disguised commerce raiders have been written since the end of World War II. Chief among these are *German Raiders of World War II* by August Karl Muggenthaler (Prentice-Hall, Englewood Cliffs, NJ, 1971) and *The Secret Raiders* by David Woodward (W.W. Norton, New York, 1955). A third, which also includes information on raiders of earlier wars, is *German Raiders* by Paul Schmalenbach (Naval Institute Press, Annapolis, MD, 1979). The last was originally published in Germany in 1977. Another book that discusses the careers of all types of German surface raiders in both World Wars is *The Sea Raiders* by Captain Kenneth Langmaid (Jarrolds Publishers, London, 1956).

The records of individual disguised commerce raiders have been the subject of a number of books, including some by officers who served on them. The *Atlantis* was the subject of three volumes. That raider's captain cowrote his own book, which was first published in Germany, then England, and finally in the United States: *The German Raider* Atlantis by Wolfgang Frank and Captain Bernhard Rogge (Ballantine Books, New York, 1956). Also from the crew of the *Atlantis* is *Atlantis: The Story of a German Surface Raider* by Ulrich Mohr as told to A. V. Sellwood (T. Werner Laurie Ltd., London, 1955). The third book on this raider is *Raider 16* by Edwin Hoyt (World Publishing Company, New York, 1970). The story of the sinking of the *Zimzam* and the adventures encountered by her survivors is told in Zimzam: *The Story of a Strange Missionary Odyssey* edited by S. Hjalmar Swanson (The Board of Foreign Missions of the Augustana Synod, Rock Island, IL, 1941). The *Speybank*, a prize taken by the *Atlantis* and sent to Europe, was turned into a disguised minelayer by the Germans and had an exciting career under the name *Doggerbank*, which ended tragically when a U-boat believed the vessel's disguise and torpedoed her. The *Speybank/Doggerbank* story is told in *The Ship with Five Names* by Charles Gibson (Abelard-Schuman Ltd., London, 1965).

The commander of the *Kormoran* wrote an account of his ship's adventures and her sinking: *The Raider* Kormoran by Captain Theodor Detmers (William Kimber and Co., London, 1959). Another perspective on that raider is offered in *Prisoner of the "Kormoran"* by W. A. Jones as told to James Taylor (Australasian Publishing Co. Ltd., Sydney, 1944). The battle to the death between the *Kormoran* and the *Sydney* continues to be a source of controversy in Australia. Among the publications that have fueled this controversy are: *H.M.A.S. Sydney* by Geoffrey Scott (Horwitz Publications Ltd., Melbourne, 1962), *Who Sank the* Sydney by Michael Montgomery (Cassell Australia Ltd., Auckland, 1981), and *HMAS* Sydney: *Loss and Controversy* by Tom Frame (Hodder and Stoughton, New South Wales, 1993). In 1997 Richard Summerrell compiled a volume for the Australian Archives: *The Sinking of HMAS* Sydney. It is a guide to Australian government records concerning the sinking of the cruiser.

The commanding officer of the *Orion* published his memoir of her cruise: *The Black Raider* by Kurt Weyher and Hans Jurgen Ehrlich (Elek Books Ltd., London, 1955). The experience of having your ship taken by a raider was written about by an officer who was serving aboard the *Rangitane*, which was captured and sunk by the *Orion* and the *Komet* working together: *Caught by a Nazi Raider* by Geoffrey Alan Barley (The New Zealand Shipping Company, London, 1941). Robert Eyssen, former commander of the *Komet* published a book in German in 1960 about his ship, but to the best of my knowledge it has never been translated into English. *Komet 1940–1941* by Charles H. Noack (Naval Historical Society of Australia, Sydney, 1997) provides a description of what it was like to serve aboard the *Komet*.

The story of the American Merchant Marine is told in *Heroes in Dungarees* by John Bunker (Naval Institute Press, Annapolis, MD, 1995). The history of the sailors of the Naval Armed Guard that served aboard U.S. flag merchant ships is related in *Unsung Sailors* by Justin F. Gleichauf (Naval Institute Press, Annapolis, MD, 1990).

Several hundred books have been published dealing with World War II at sea. Most make at least a passing mention of the German disguised commerce raiders, and it would be of no real value to include them here. On the other hand, the World Wide Web has made it available for many people to publicize and archive their passions. Several sites I found especially helpful and/or interesting while researching and writing this book are:

Arsenal of Dictatorship: http://home.inreach.com/rickylaw

German Armed Forces of World War II: http://www.uwm.edu/~jpipes/start.html

American Merchant Marine at War: http://www.usmm.org/

U.S. Naval Armed Guard and WW II Merchant Marine: http://www.armed-guard.com/

Index

About the Author

JAMES P. DUFFY is a writer specializing in military history. He is the author of 12 books, including *Hitler Slept Late and Other Blunders That Cost Him the War* (Praeger, 1991), *The Assassination of John F. Kennedy: A Complete Book of Facts* with Vincent L. Ricci (1992), *Target Hitler: The Plots to Kill Adolf Hitler* with Vincent L. Ricci (Praeger, 1992), *Czars: Russia's Rulers for Over One Thousand Years* with Vincent L. Ricci (1995), and *Lincoln's Admiral: The Civil War Campaigns of David Farragut* (1997).